PLANET OF THE APES

CHILDREN OF FIRE

PLAN∃

ROSS RICHIE Chief Executive Officer • **MATT GAGNON** Editor-in-Chief • **WES HARRIS** VP-Publishing • **LANCE KREITER** VP-Licensing & Merchandising • **PHIL BARBARO** Director of Finance
BRYCE CARLSON Managing Editor • **DAFNA PLEBAN** Editor • **SHANNON WATTERS** Editor • **ERIC HARBURN** Assistant Editor • **ADAM STAFFARONI** Assistant Editor • **CHRIS ROSA** Assistant Editor
STEPHANIE GONZAGA Graphic Designer • **CAROL THOMPSON** Production Designer • **JASMINE AMIRI** Operations Coordinator • **DEVIN FUNCHES** Marketing & Sales Assistant

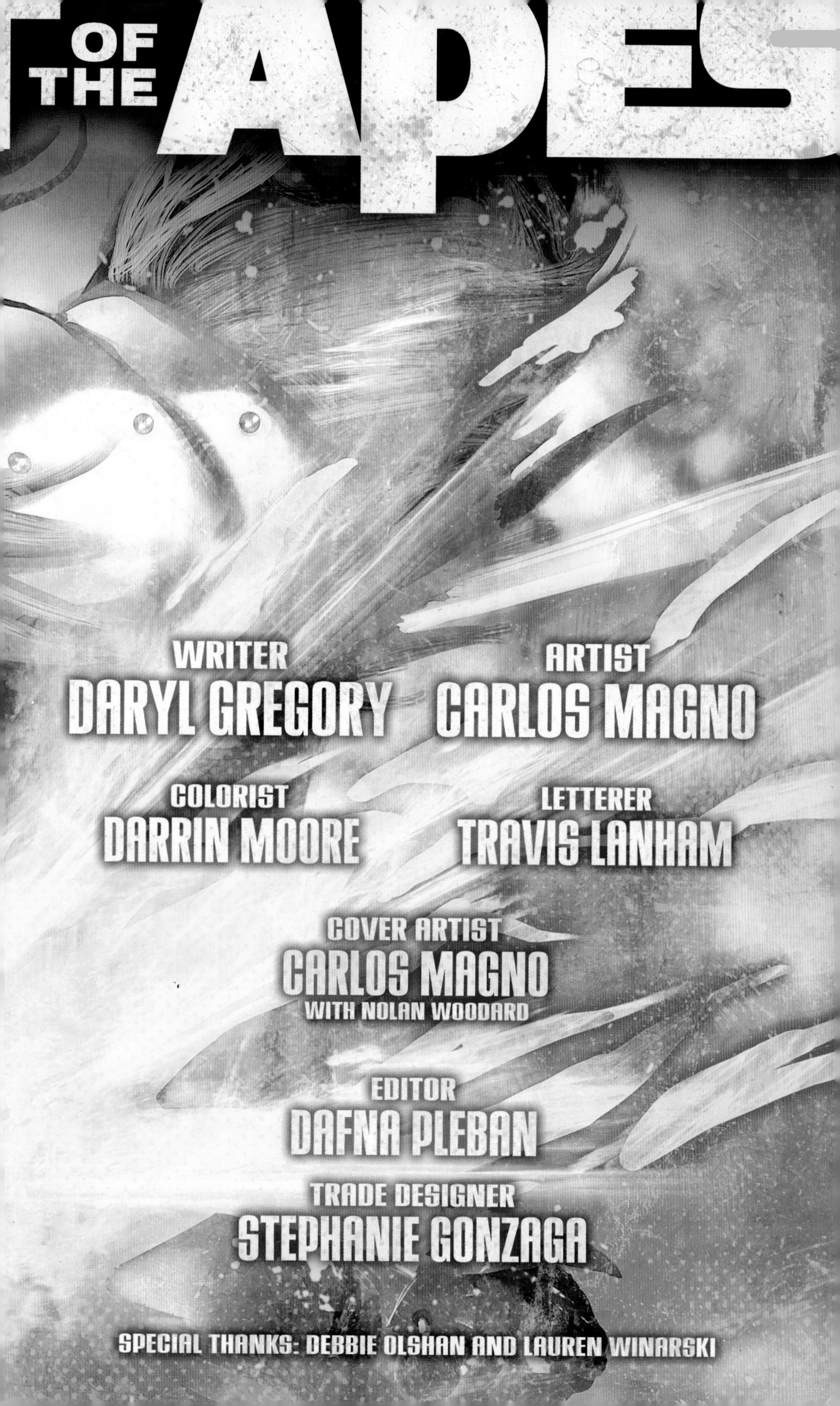

OF THE APES

WRITER
DARYL GREGORY

ARTIST
CARLOS MAGNO

COLORIST
DARRIN MOORE

LETTERER
TRAVIS LANHAM

COVER ARTIST
CARLOS MAGNO
WITH NOLAN WOODARD

EDITOR
DAFNA PLEBAN

TRADE DESIGNER
STEPHANIE GONZAGA

SPECIAL THANKS: DEBBIE OLSHAN AND LAUREN WINARSKI

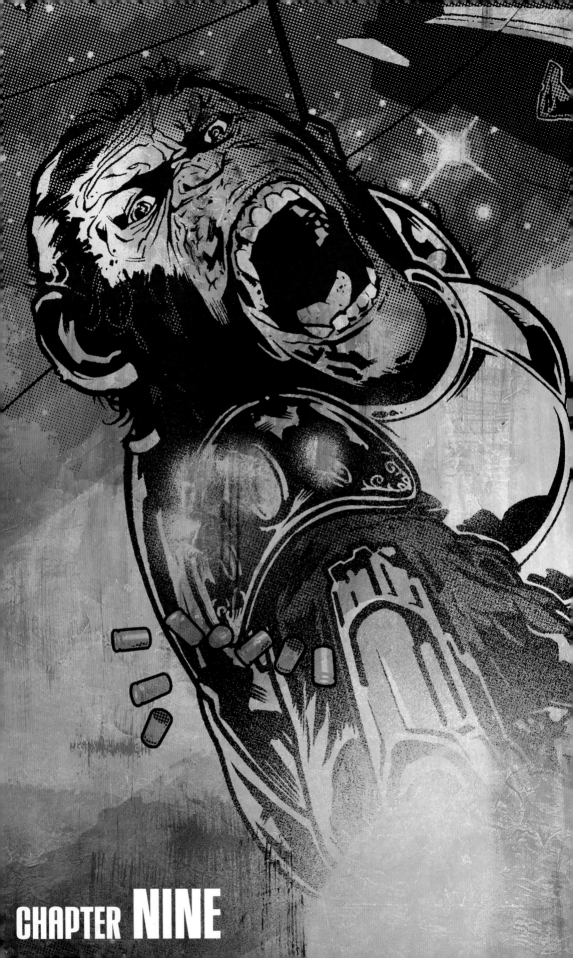

CHAPTER **NINE**

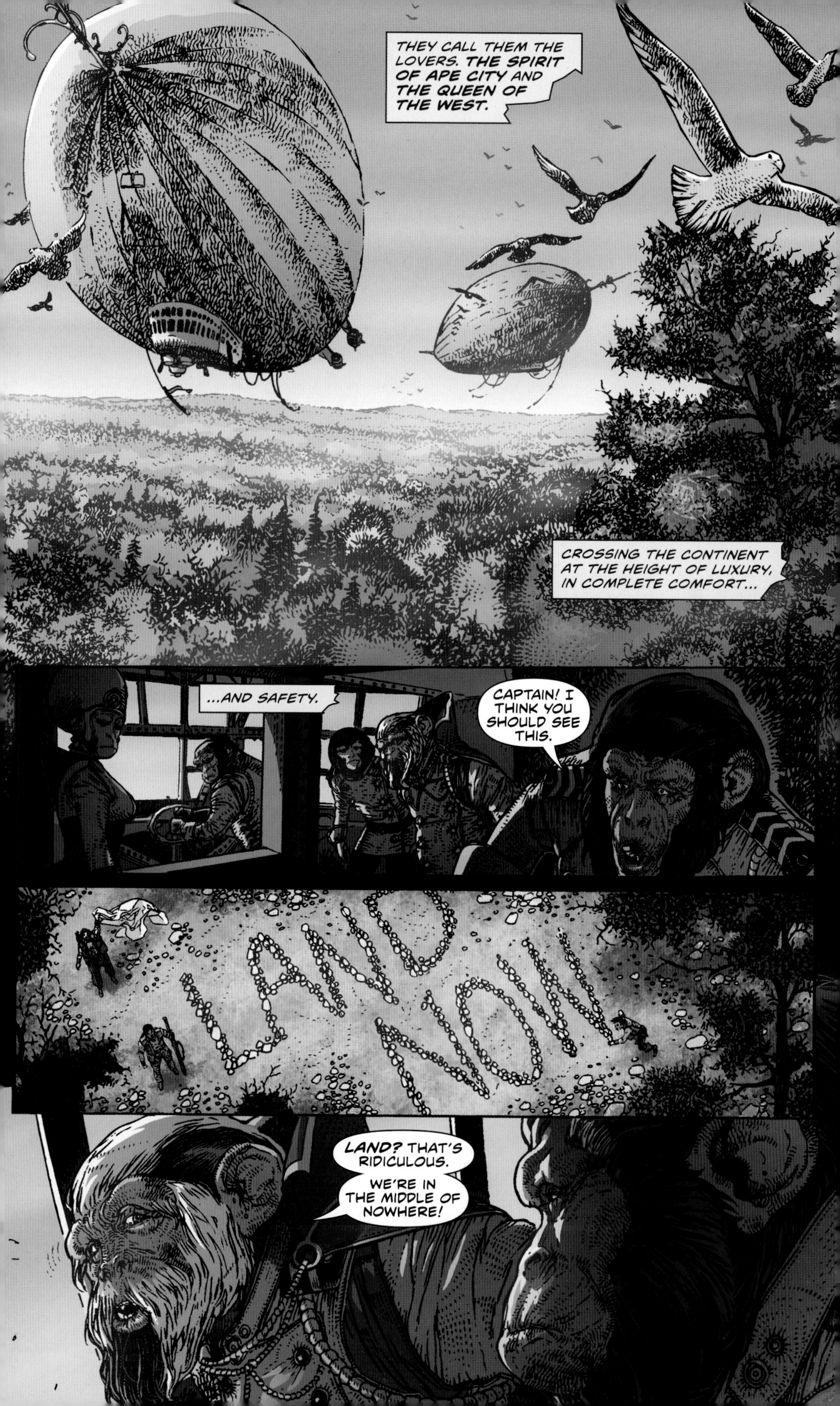
THEY CALL THEM THE LOVERS. THE SPIRIT OF APE CITY AND THE QUEEN OF THE WEST.
CROSSING THE CONTINENT AT THE HEIGHT OF LUXURY, IN COMPLETE COMFORT...
...AND SAFETY.
CAPTAIN! I THINK YOU SHOULD SEE THIS.
LAND NOW
LAND? THAT'S RIDICULOUS.
WE'RE IN THE MIDDLE OF NOWHERE!

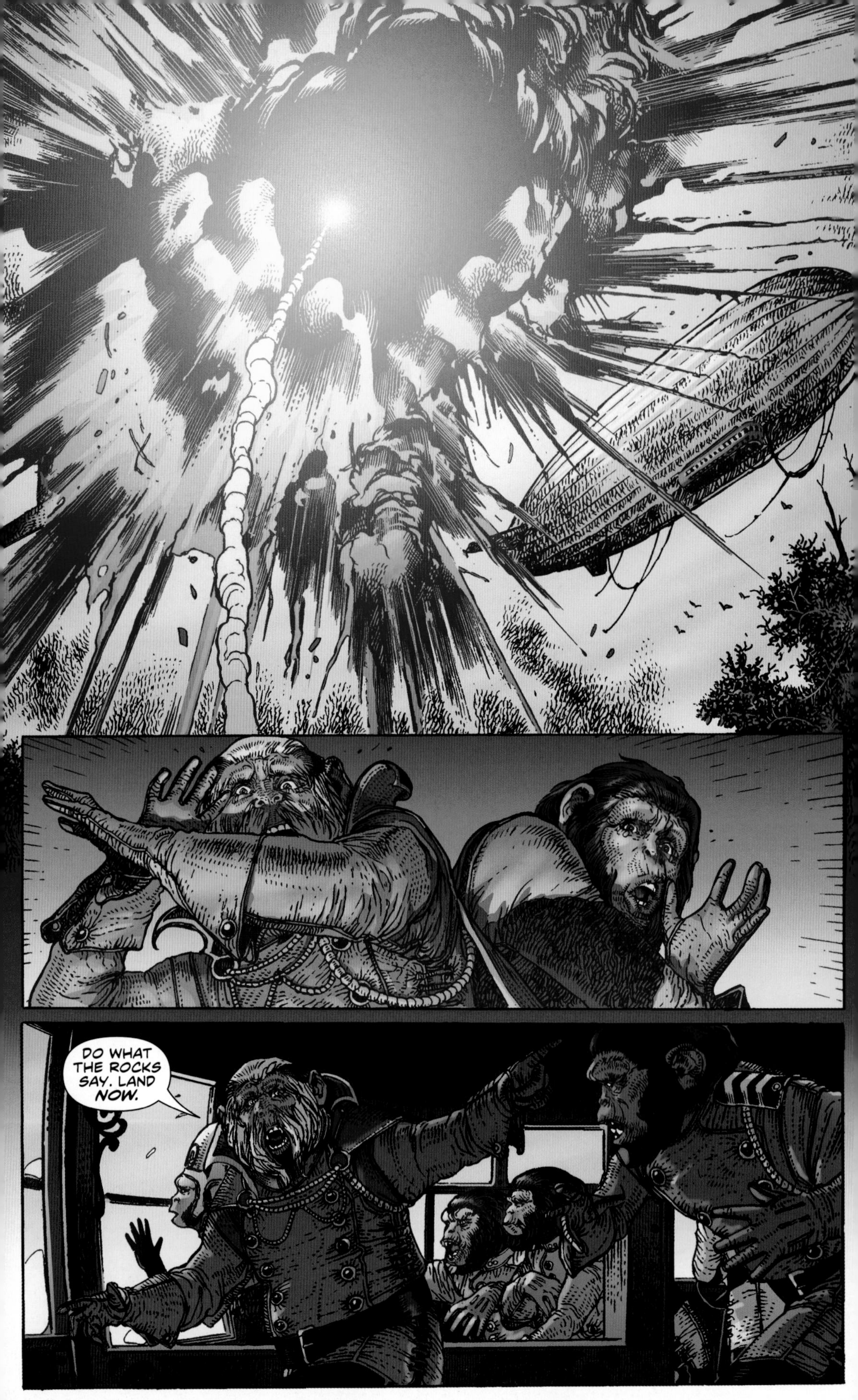
DO WHAT THE ROCKS SAY. LAND NOW.

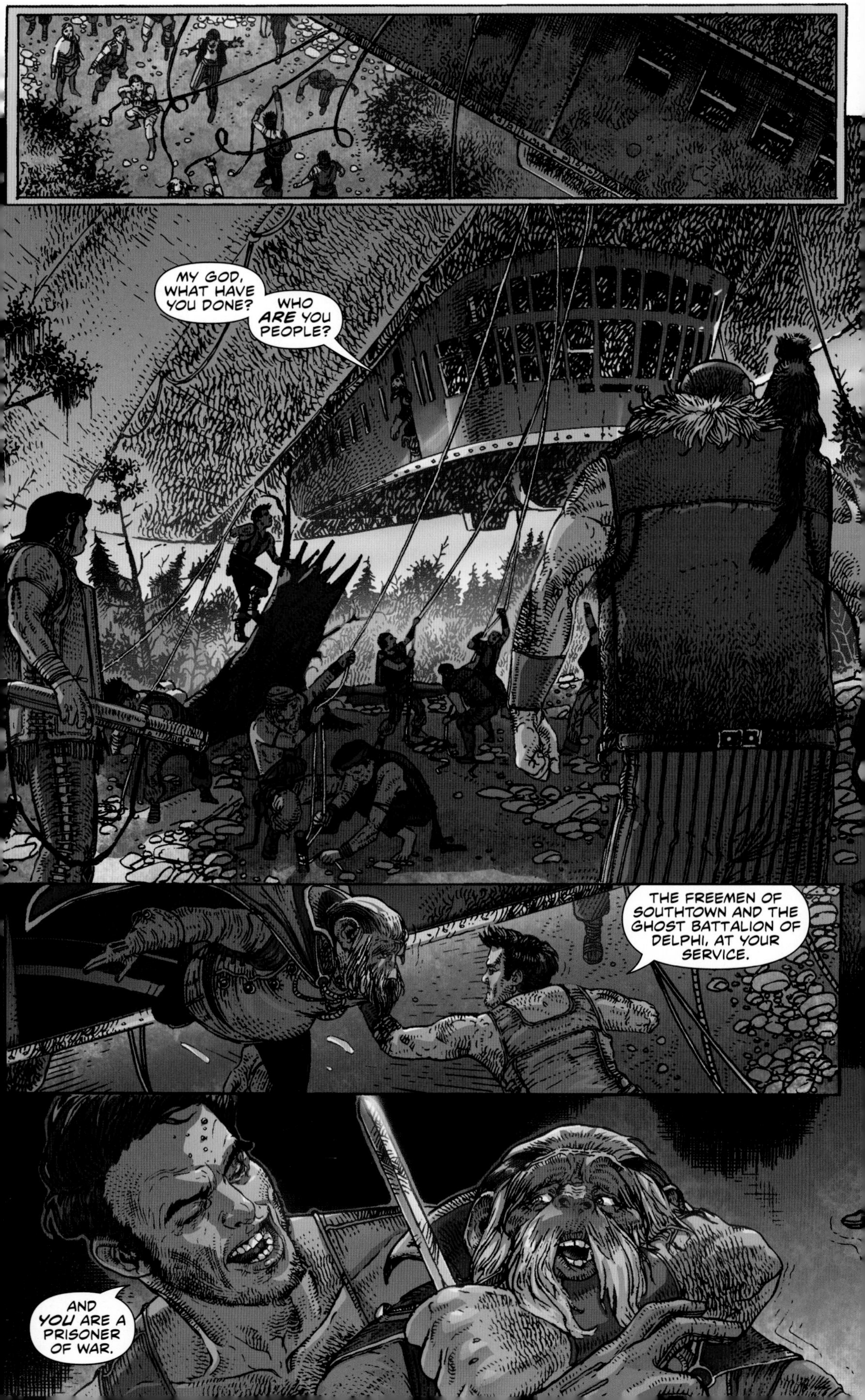
MY GOD, WHAT HAVE YOU DONE?
WHO ARE YOU PEOPLE?
THE FREEMEN OF SOUTHTOWN AND THE GHOST BATTALION OF DELPHI, AT YOUR SERVICE.
AND YOU ARE A PRISONER OF WAR.

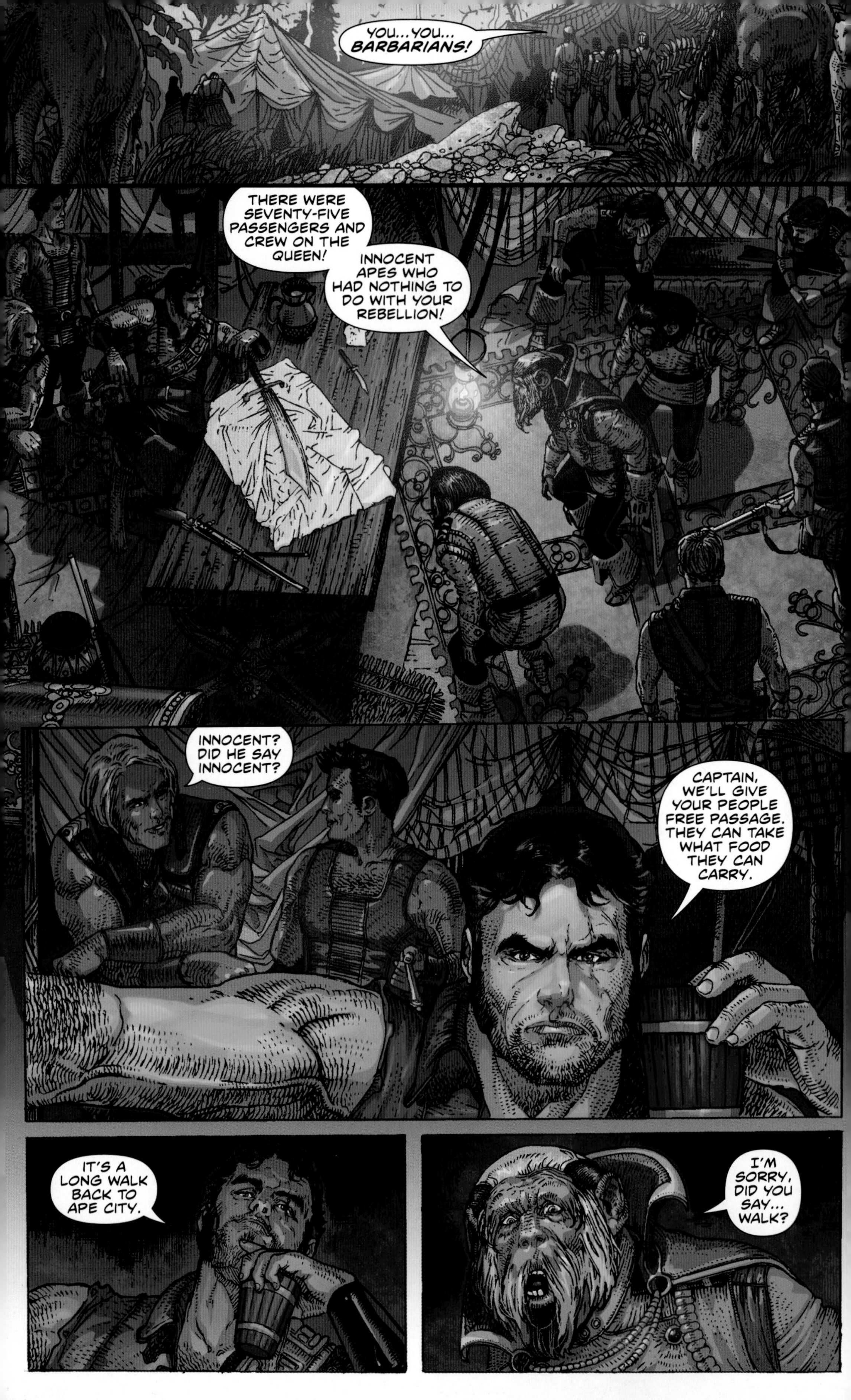
YOU...YOU... BARBARIANS!
THERE WERE SEVENTY-FIVE PASSENGERS AND CREW ON THE QUEEN!
INNOCENT APES WHO HAD NOTHING TO DO WITH YOUR REBELLION!
INNOCENT? DID HE SAY INNOCENT?
CAPTAIN, WE'LL GIVE YOUR PEOPLE FREE PASSAGE. THEY CAN TAKE WHAT FOOD THEY CAN CARRY.
IT'S A LONG WALK BACK TO APE CITY.
I'M SORRY, DID YOU SAY... WALK?

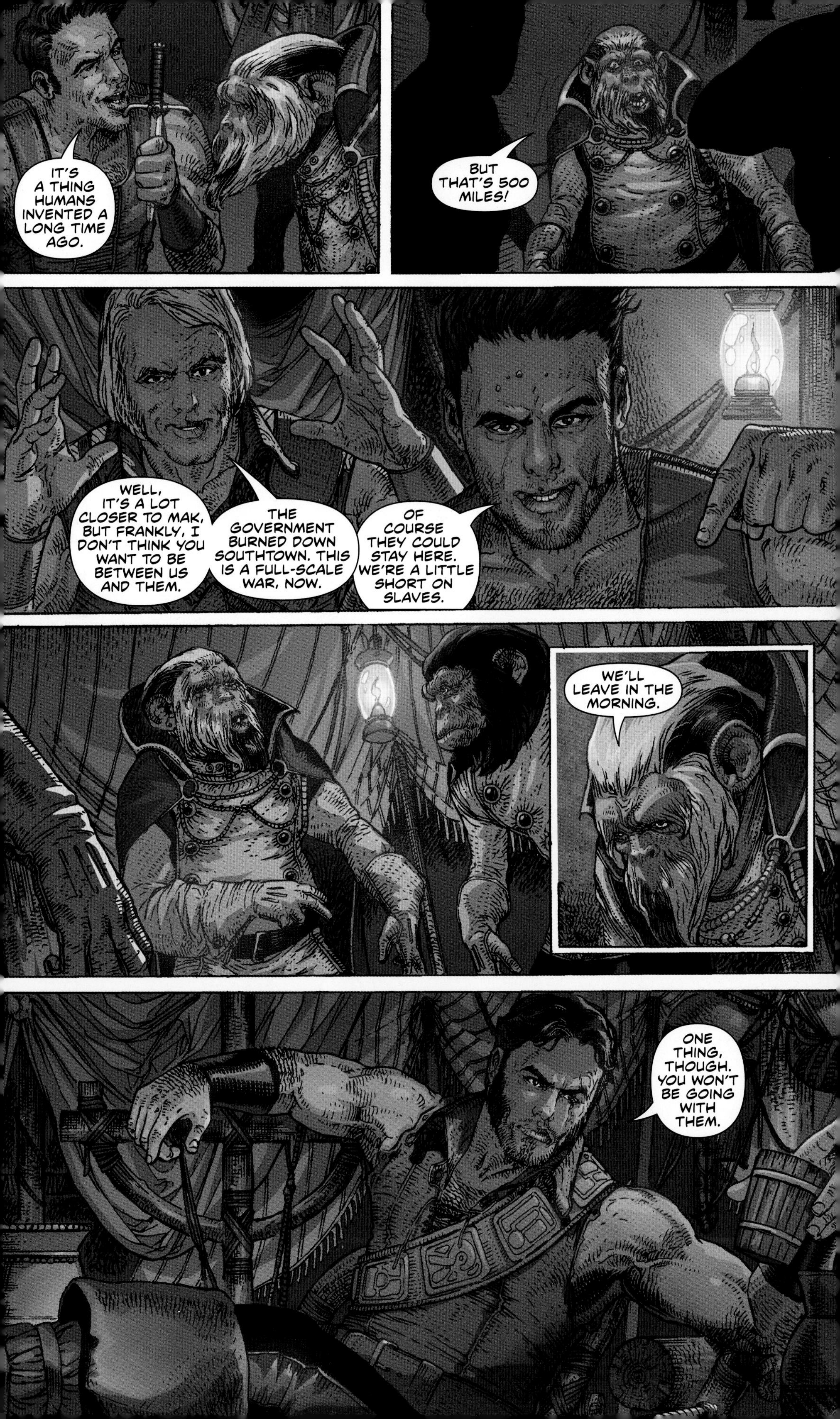
IT'S A THING HUMANS INVENTED A LONG TIME AGO.
BUT THAT'S 500 MILES!
WELL, IT'S A LOT CLOSER TO MAK, BUT FRANKLY, I DON'T THINK YOU WANT TO BE BETWEEN US AND THEM.
THE GOVERNMENT BURNED DOWN SOUTHTOWN. THIS IS A FULL-SCALE WAR, NOW.
OF COURSE THEY COULD STAY HERE. WE'RE A LITTLE SHORT ON SLAVES.
WE'LL LEAVE IN THE MORNING.
ONE THING, THOUGH. YOU WON'T BE GOING WITH THEM.

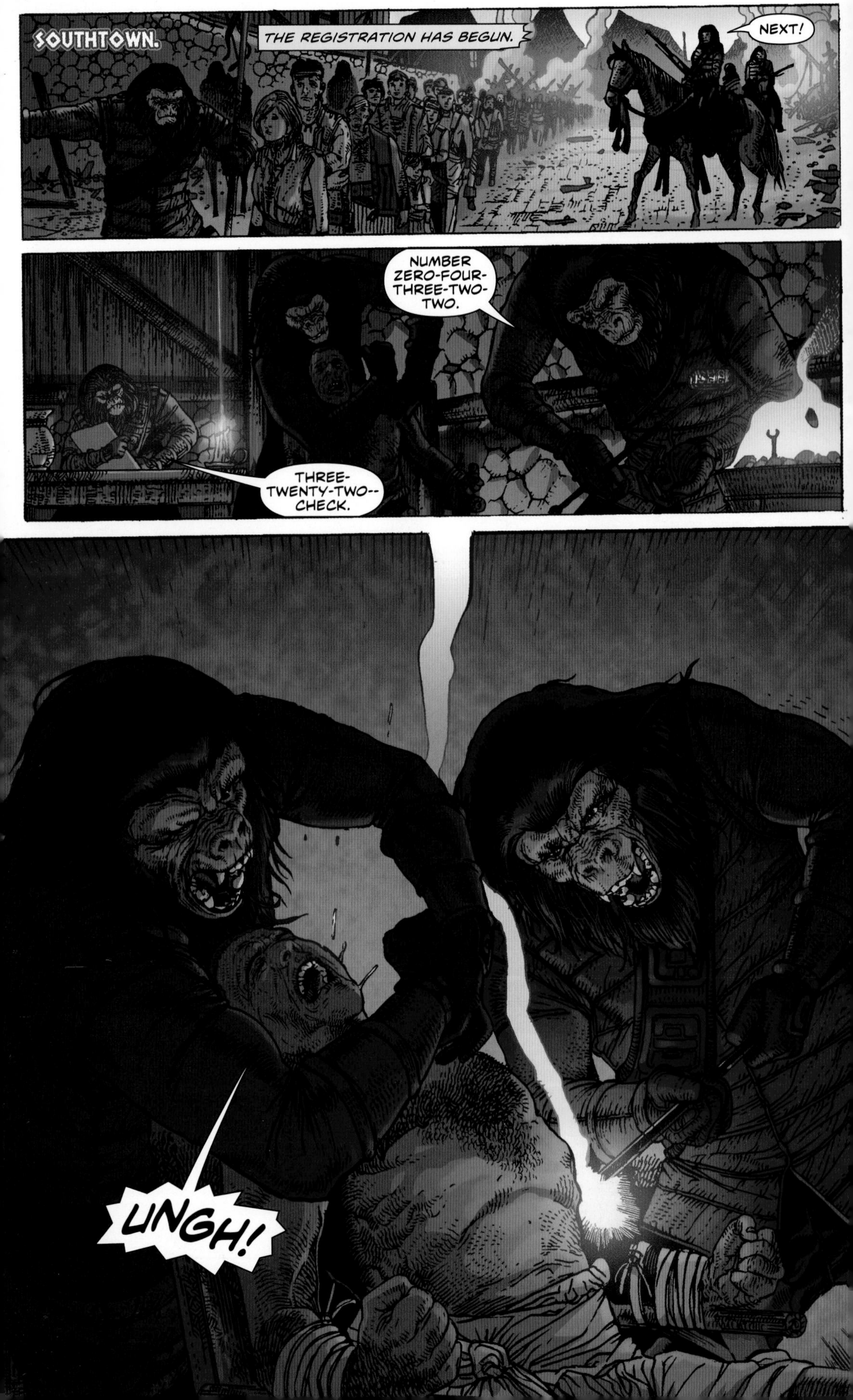
SOUTHTOWN.
THE REGISTRATION HAS BEGUN.
NEXT!
NUMBER ZERO-FOUR-THREE-TWO-TWO.
THREE-TWENTY-TWO--CHECK.
UNGH!

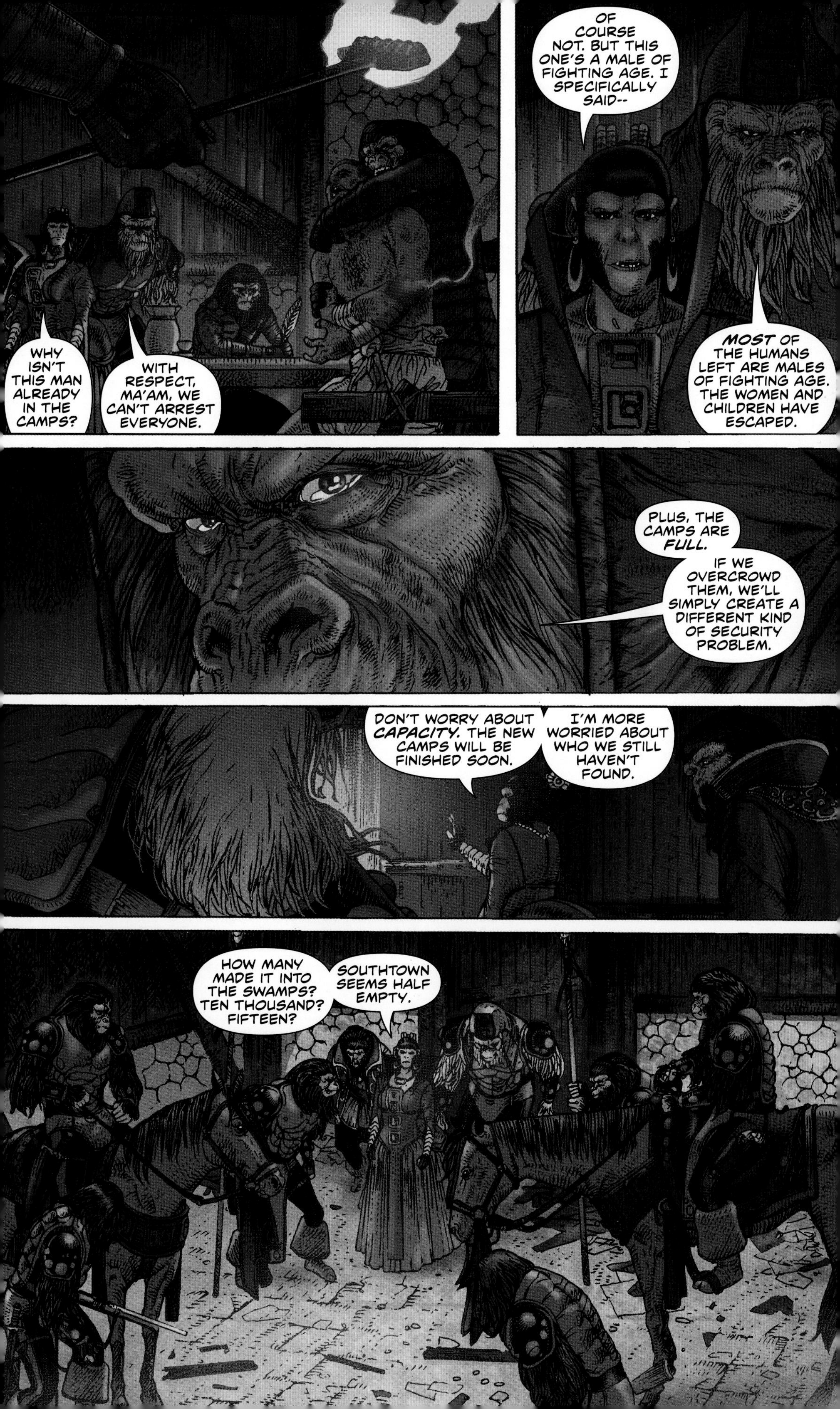
WHY ISN'T THIS MAN ALREADY IN THE CAMPS?
WITH RESPECT, MA'AM, WE CAN'T ARREST EVERYONE.
OF COURSE NOT. BUT THIS ONE'S A MALE OF FIGHTING AGE. I SPECIFICALLY SAID--
MOST OF THE HUMANS LEFT ARE MALES OF FIGHTING AGE. THE WOMEN AND CHILDREN HAVE ESCAPED.
PLUS, THE CAMPS ARE *FULL*.
IF WE OVERCROWD THEM, WE'LL SIMPLY CREATE A DIFFERENT KIND OF SECURITY PROBLEM.
DON'T WORRY ABOUT *CAPACITY*. THE NEW CAMPS WILL BE FINISHED SOON.
I'M MORE WORRIED ABOUT WHO WE STILL HAVEN'T FOUND.
HOW MANY MADE IT INTO THE SWAMPS? TEN THOUSAND? FIFTEEN?
SOUTHTOWN SEEMS HALF EMPTY.

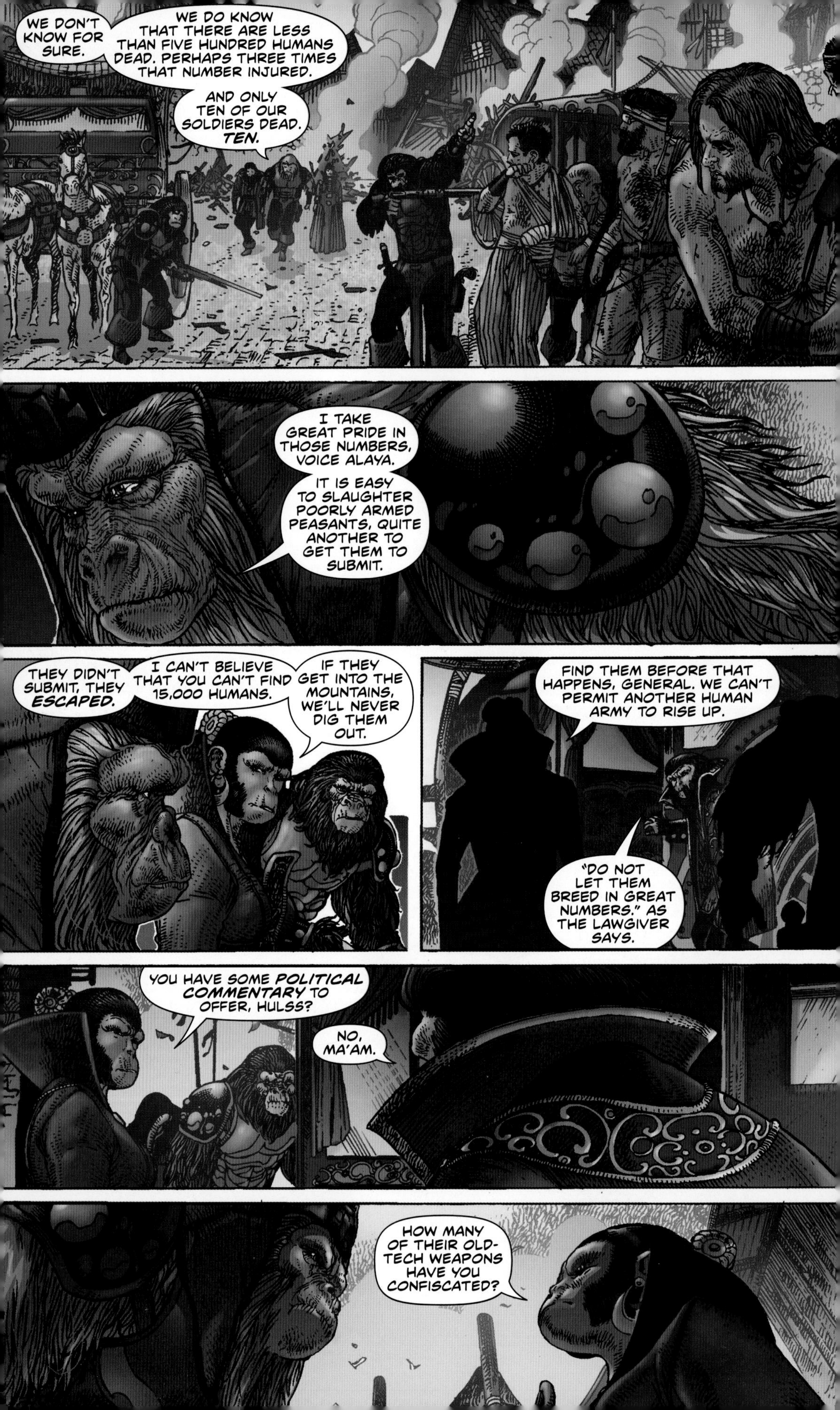

WE DON'T KNOW FOR SURE.
WE DO KNOW THAT THERE ARE LESS THAN FIVE HUNDRED HUMANS DEAD. PERHAPS THREE TIMES THAT NUMBER INJURED.
AND ONLY TEN OF OUR SOLDIERS DEAD. *TEN.*
I TAKE GREAT PRIDE IN THOSE NUMBERS, VOICE ALAYA.
IT IS EASY TO SLAUGHTER POORLY ARMED PEASANTS, QUITE ANOTHER TO GET THEM TO SUBMIT.
THEY DIDN'T SUBMIT, THEY *ESCAPED.*
I CAN'T BELIEVE THAT YOU CAN'T FIND 15,000 HUMANS.
IF THEY GET INTO THE MOUNTAINS, WE'LL NEVER DIG THEM OUT.
FIND THEM BEFORE THAT HAPPENS, GENERAL. WE CAN'T PERMIT ANOTHER HUMAN ARMY TO RISE UP.
"DO NOT LET THEM BREED IN GREAT NUMBERS." AS THE LAWGIVER SAYS.
YOU HAVE SOME *POLITICAL COMMENTARY* TO OFFER, HULSS?
NO, MA'AM.
HOW MANY OF THEIR OLD-TECH WEAPONS HAVE YOU CONFISCATED?

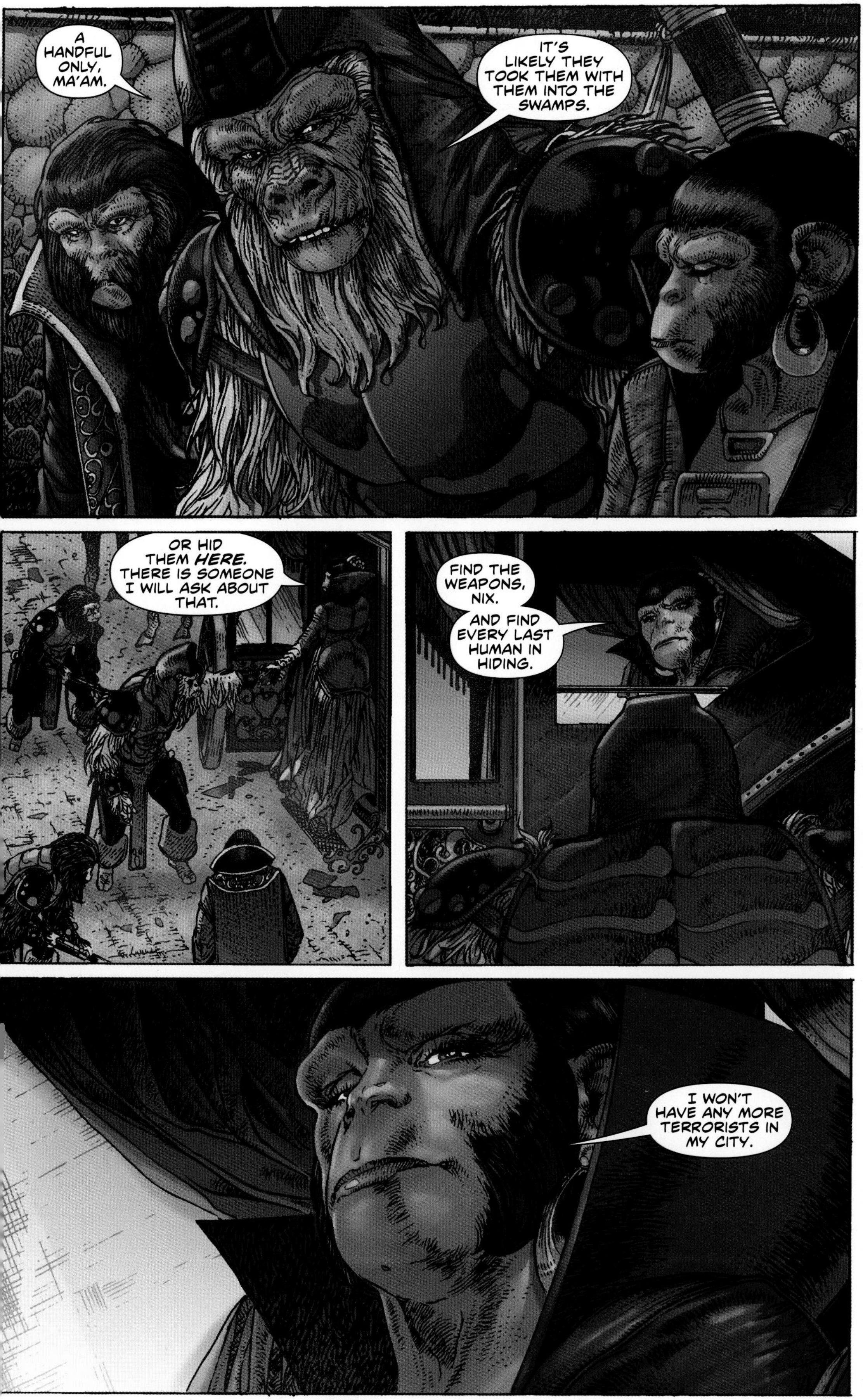
A HANDFUL ONLY, MA'AM.
IT'S LIKELY THEY TOOK THEM WITH THEM INTO THE SWAMPS.
OR HID THEM *HERE*. THERE IS SOMEONE I WILL ASK ABOUT THAT.
FIND THE WEAPONS, NIX.
AND FIND EVERY LAST HUMAN IN HIDING.
I WON'T HAVE ANY MORE TERRORISTS IN MY CITY.

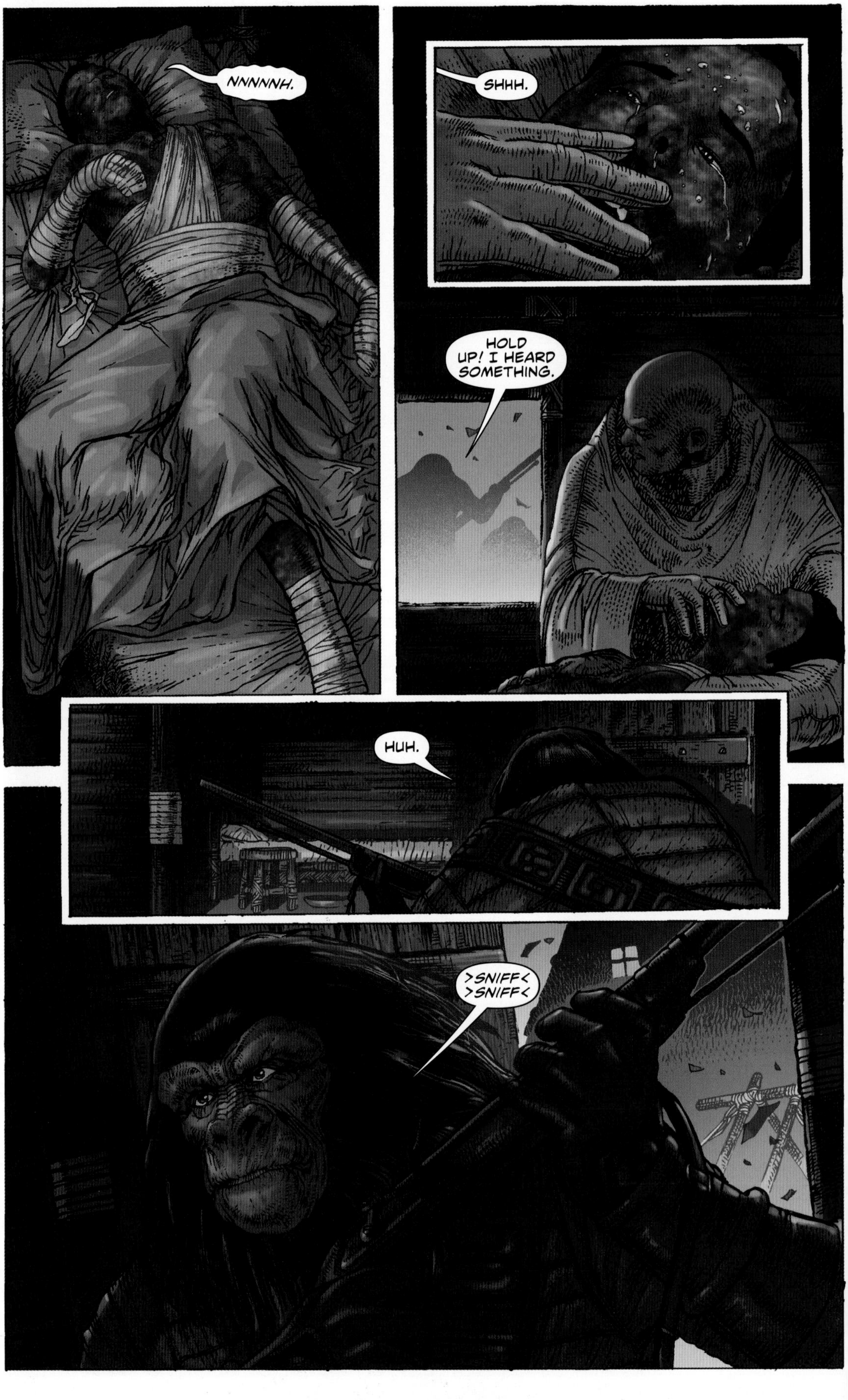
NNNNNH.
SHHH.
HOLD UP! I HEARD SOMETHING.
HUH.
>SNIFF<
>SNIFF<

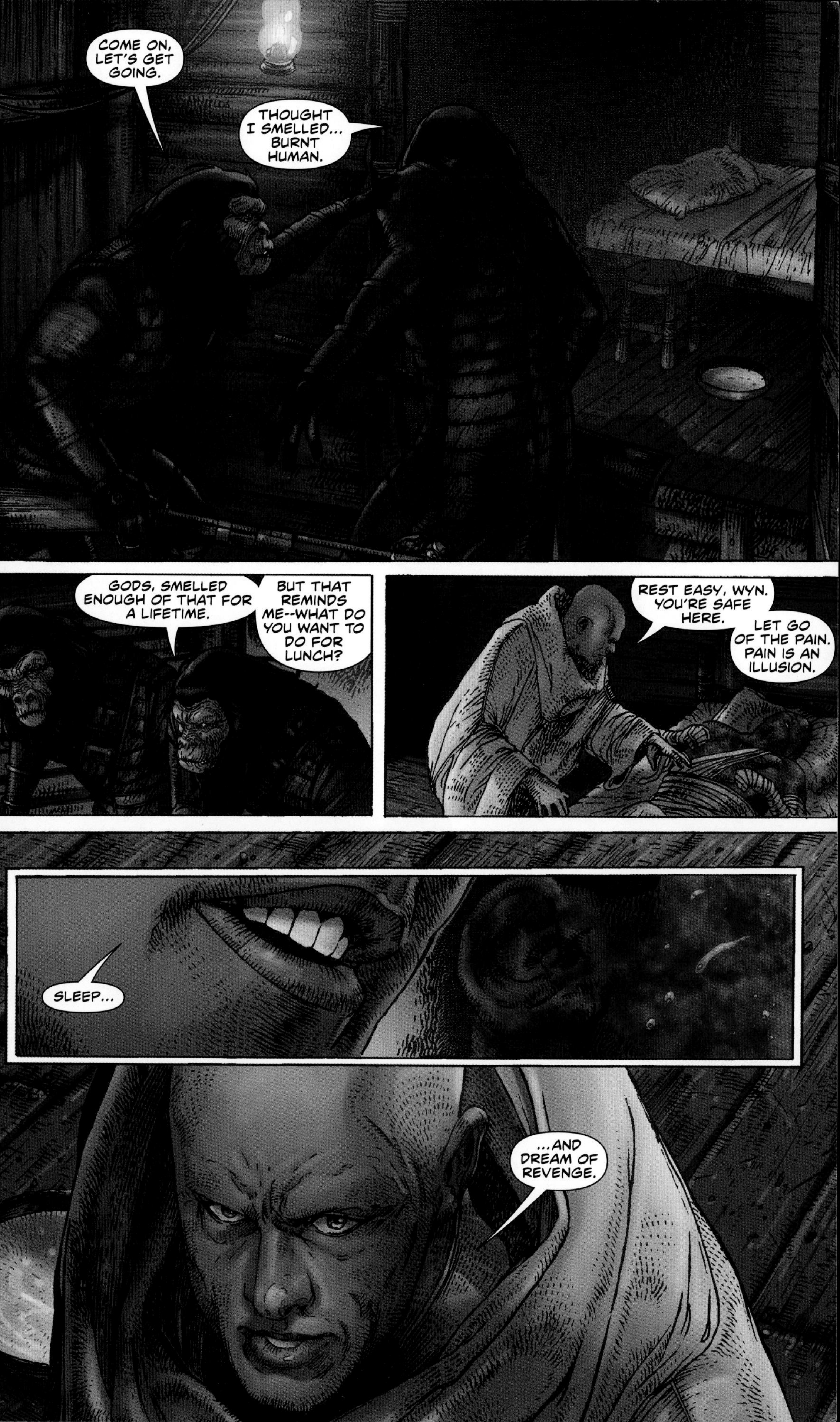
COME ON, LET'S GET GOING.
THOUGHT I SMELLED... BURNT HUMAN.
GODS, SMELLED ENOUGH OF THAT FOR A LIFETIME.
BUT THAT REMINDS ME--WHAT DO YOU WANT TO DO FOR LUNCH?
REST EASY, WYN. YOU'RE SAFE HERE.
LET GO OF THE PAIN. PAIN IS AN ILLUSION.
SLEEP...
...AND DREAM OF REVENGE.

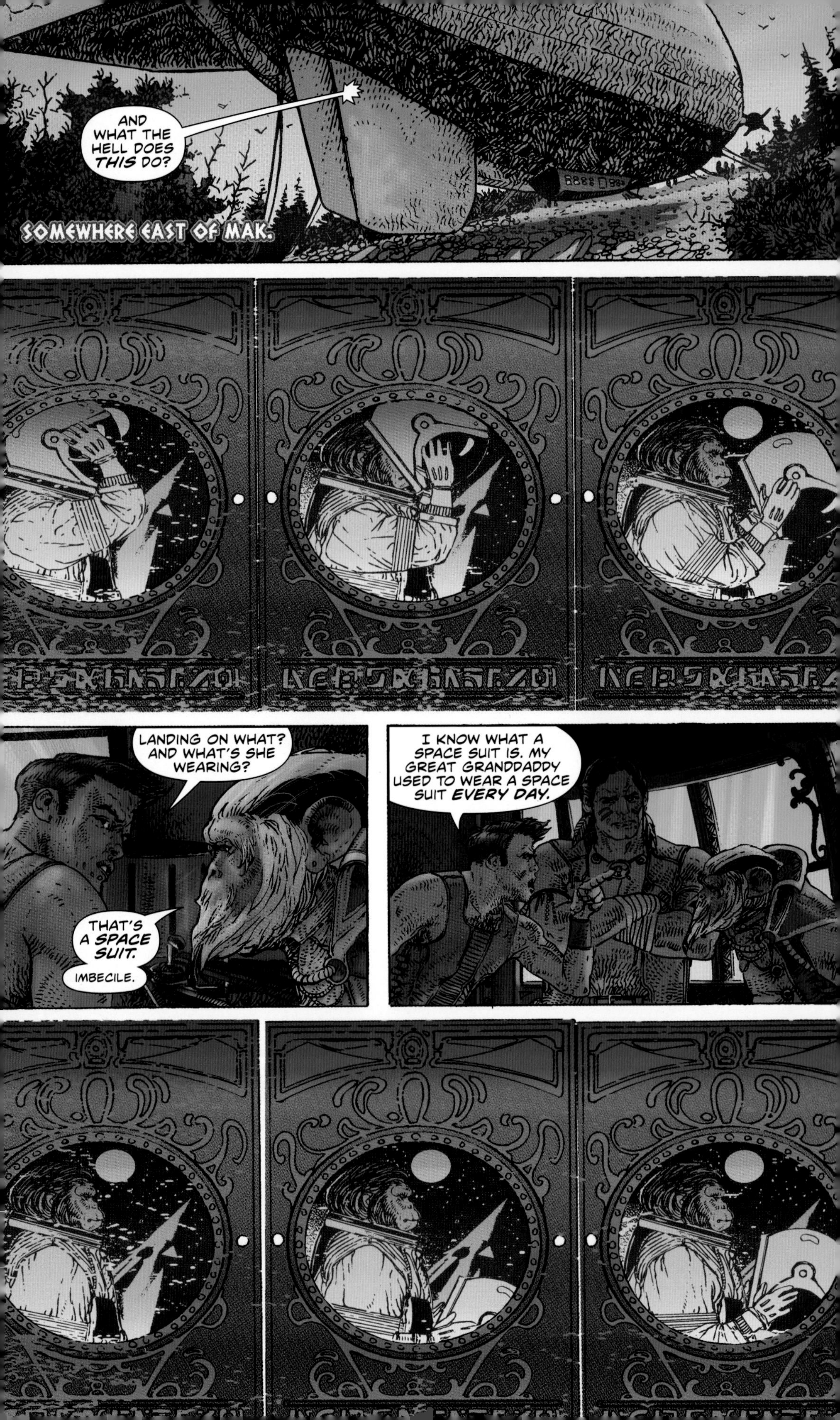
AND WHAT THE HELL DOES THIS DO?
SOMEWHERE EAST OF MAK.
LANDING ON WHAT? AND WHAT'S SHE WEARING?
THAT'S A SPACE SUIT.
IMBECILE.
I KNOW WHAT A SPACE SUIT IS. MY GREAT GRANDDADDY USED TO WEAR A SPACE SUIT EVERY DAY.

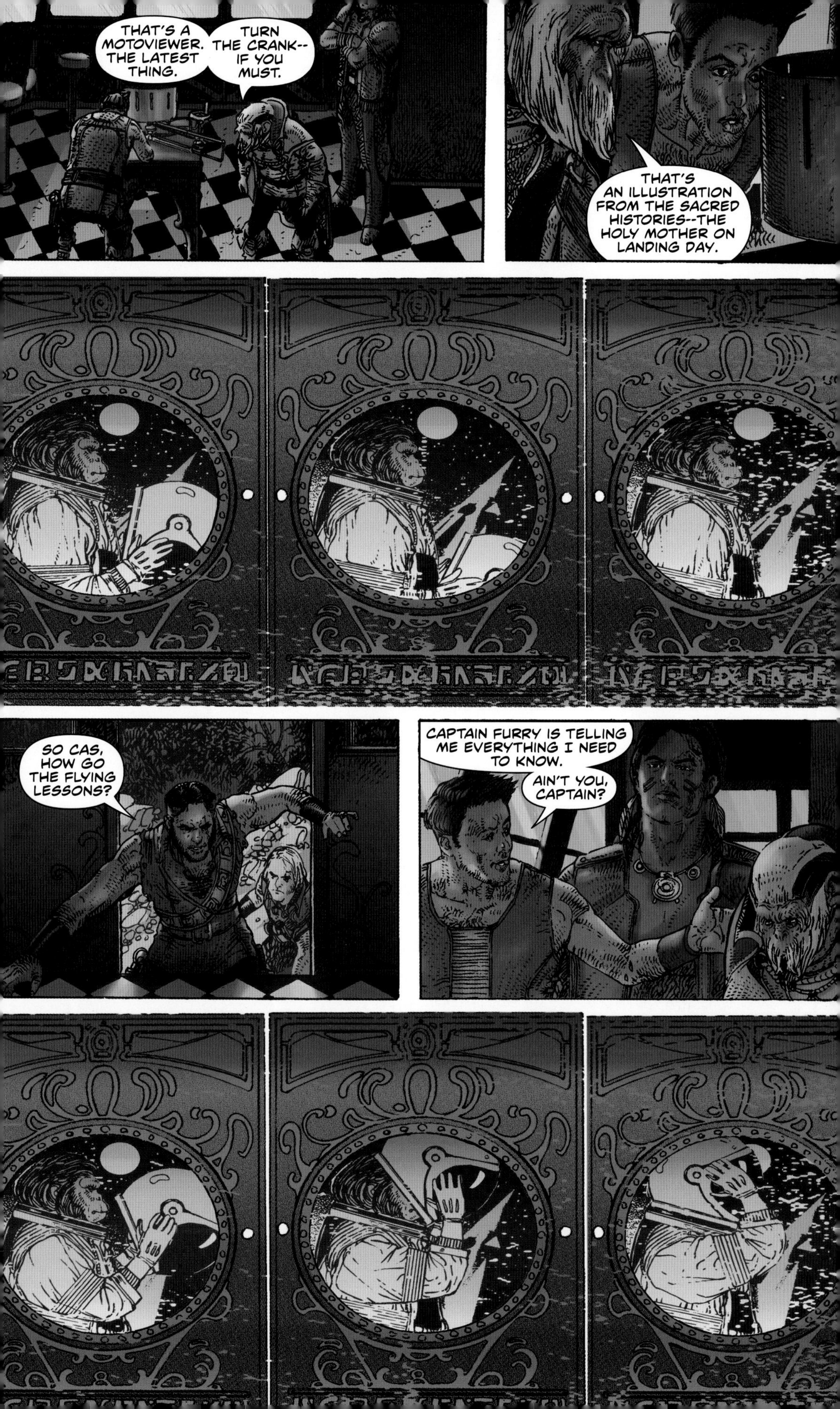

THAT'S A MOTOVIEWER. THE LATEST THING.
TURN THE CRANK-- IF YOU MUST.
THAT'S AN ILLUSTRATION FROM THE SACRED HISTORIES--THE HOLY MOTHER ON LANDING DAY.
SO CAS, HOW GO THE FLYING LESSONS?
CAPTAIN FURRY IS TELLING ME EVERYTHING I NEED TO KNOW.
AIN'T YOU, CAPTAIN?

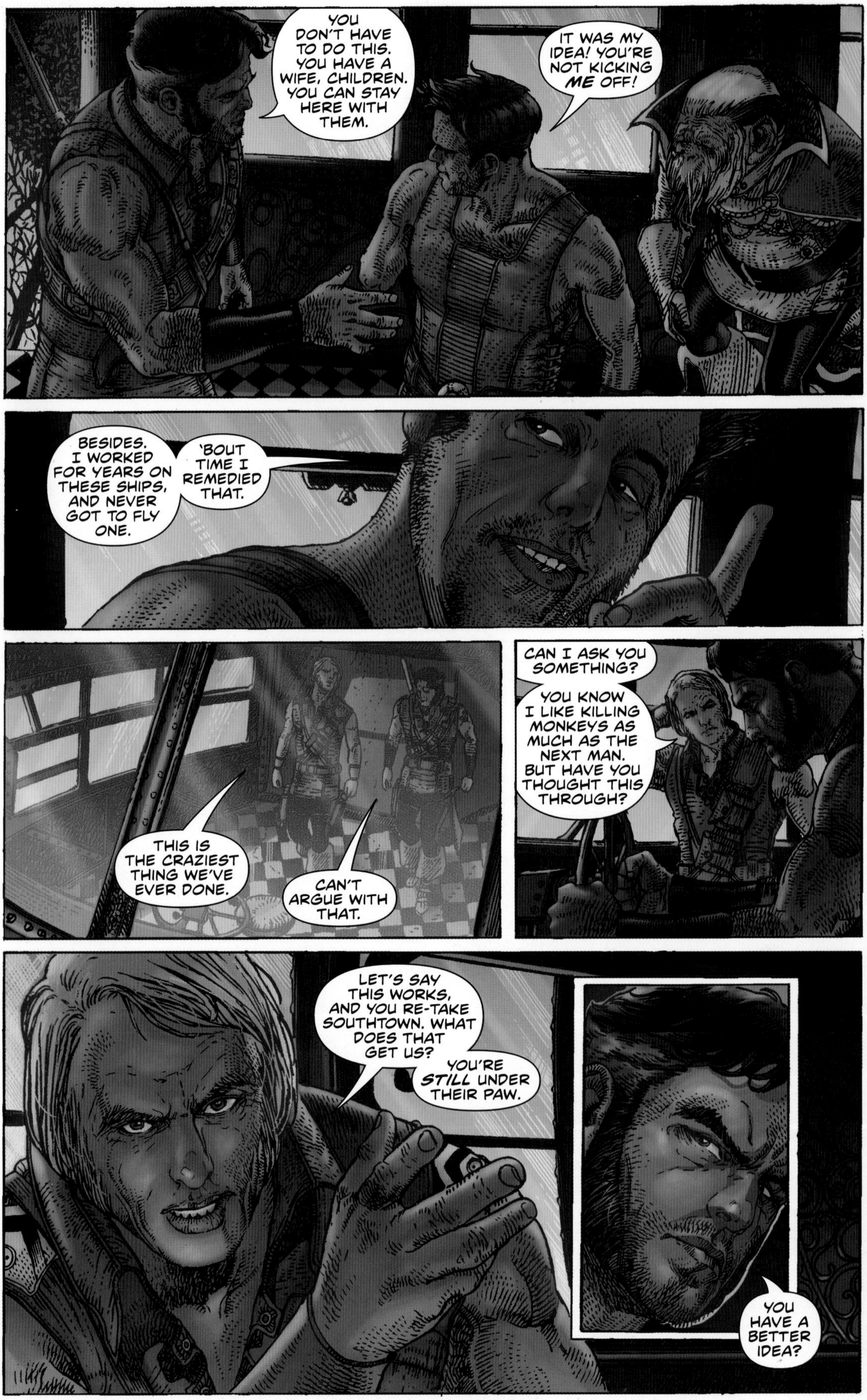
YOU DON'T HAVE TO DO THIS. YOU HAVE A WIFE, CHILDREN. YOU CAN STAY HERE WITH THEM.
IT WAS MY IDEA! YOU'RE NOT KICKING *ME* OFF!
BESIDES. I WORKED FOR YEARS ON THESE SHIPS, AND NEVER GOT TO FLY ONE.
'BOUT TIME I REMEDIED THAT.
THIS IS THE CRAZIEST THING WE'VE EVER DONE.
CAN'T ARGUE WITH THAT.
CAN I ASK YOU SOMETHING?
YOU KNOW I LIKE KILLING MONKEYS AS MUCH AS THE NEXT MAN. BUT HAVE YOU THOUGHT THIS THROUGH?
LET'S SAY THIS WORKS, AND YOU RE-TAKE SOUTHTOWN. WHAT DOES THAT GET US?
YOU'RE *STILL* UNDER THEIR PAW.
YOU HAVE A BETTER IDEA?

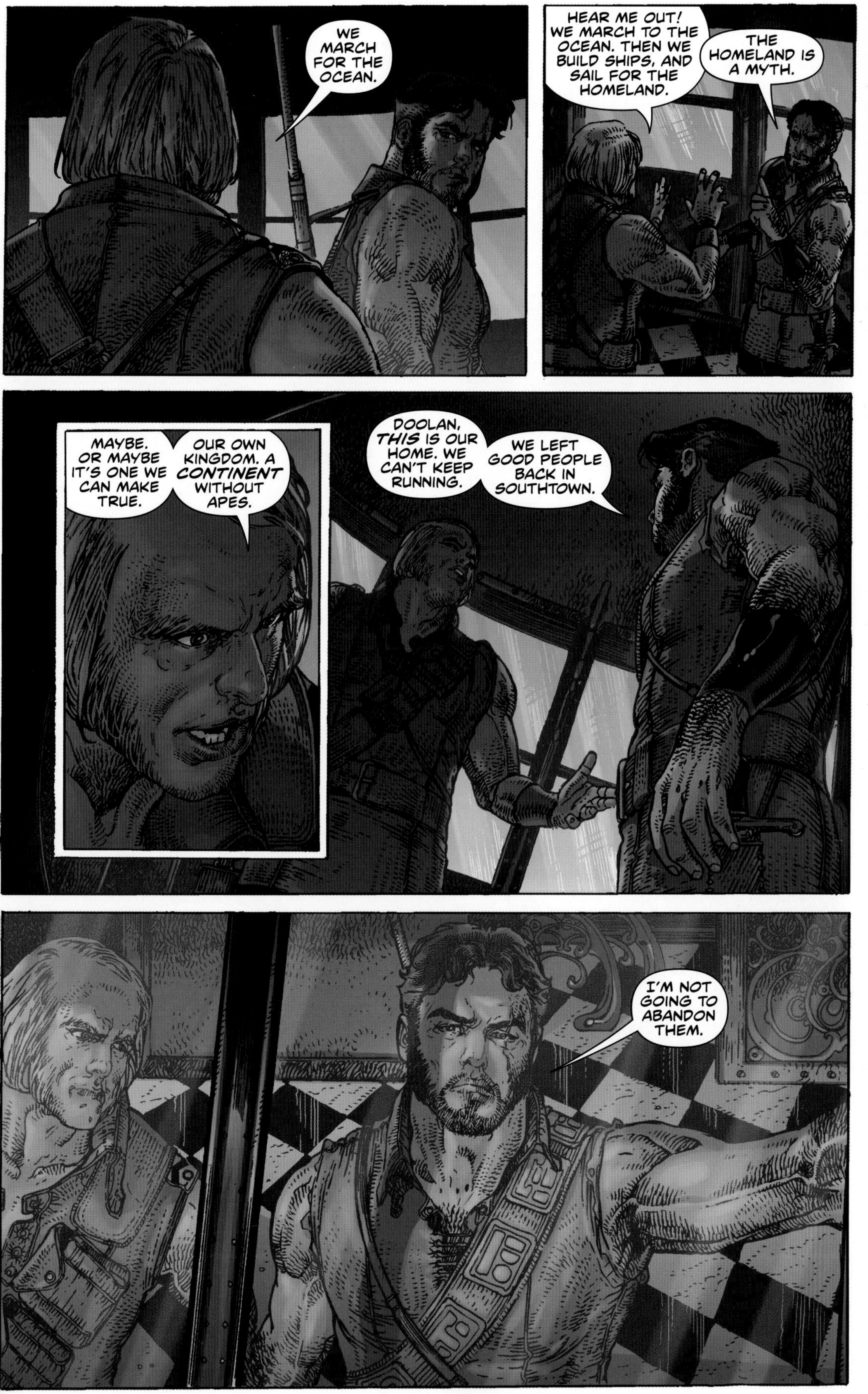
WE MARCH FOR THE OCEAN.
HEAR ME OUT! WE MARCH TO THE OCEAN. THEN WE BUILD SHIPS, AND SAIL FOR THE HOMELAND.
THE HOMELAND IS A MYTH.
MAYBE. OR MAYBE IT'S ONE WE CAN MAKE TRUE.
OUR OWN KINGDOM. A *CONTINENT* WITHOUT APES.
DOOLAN, *THIS* IS OUR HOME. WE CAN'T KEEP RUNNING.
WE LEFT GOOD PEOPLE BACK IN SOUTHTOWN.
I'M NOT GOING TO ABANDON THEM.

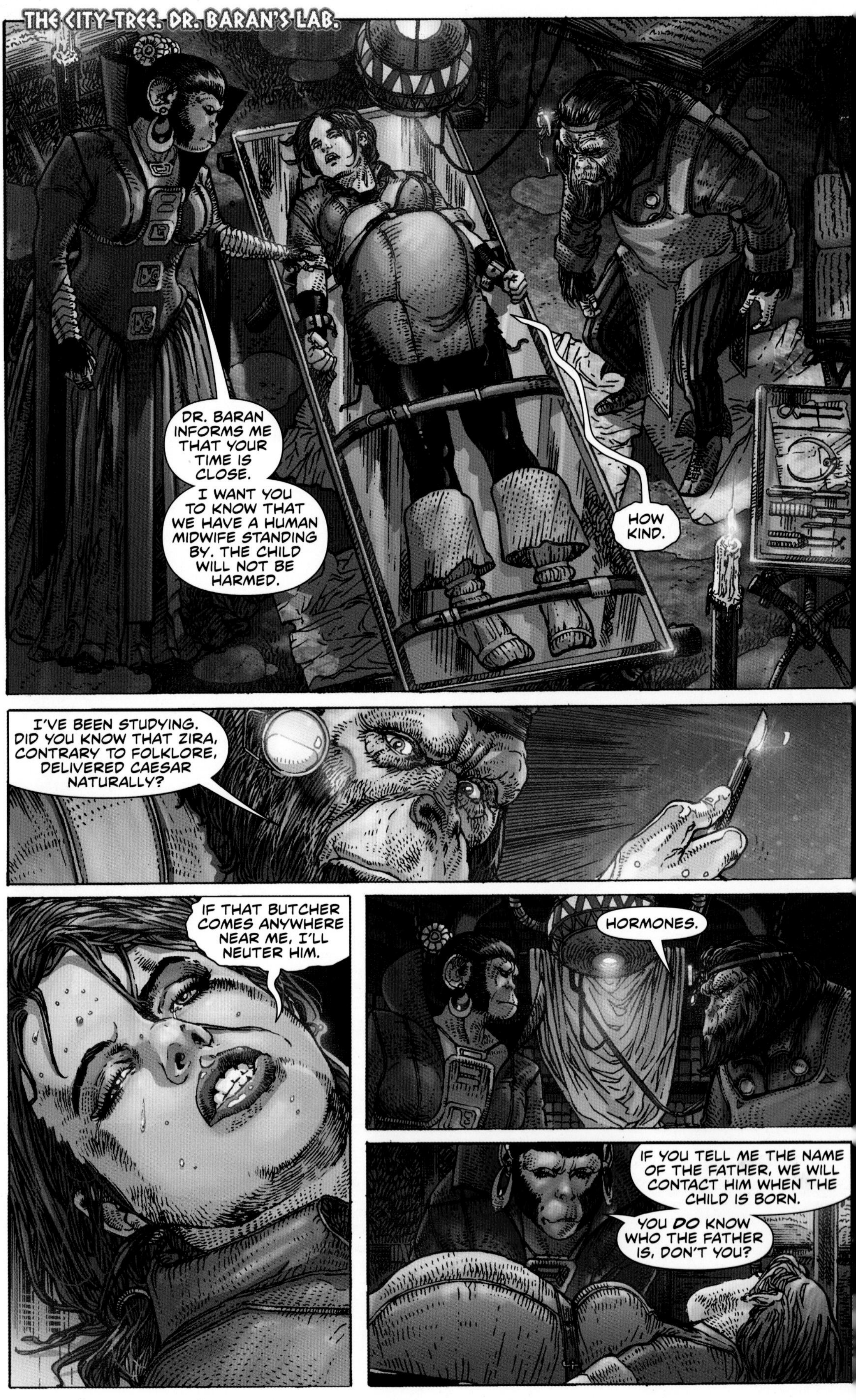
THE CITY TREE. DR. BARAN'S LAB.
DR. BARAN INFORMS ME THAT YOUR TIME IS CLOSE.
I WANT YOU TO KNOW THAT WE HAVE A HUMAN MIDWIFE STANDING BY. THE CHILD WILL NOT BE HARMED.
HOW KIND.
I'VE BEEN STUDYING. DID YOU KNOW THAT ZIRA, CONTRARY TO FOLKLORE, DELIVERED CAESAR NATURALLY?
IF THAT BUTCHER COMES ANYWHERE NEAR ME, I'LL NEUTER HIM.
HORMONES.
IF YOU TELL ME THE NAME OF THE FATHER, WE WILL CONTACT HIM WHEN THE CHILD IS BORN.
YOU *DO* KNOW WHO THE FATHER IS, DON'T YOU?

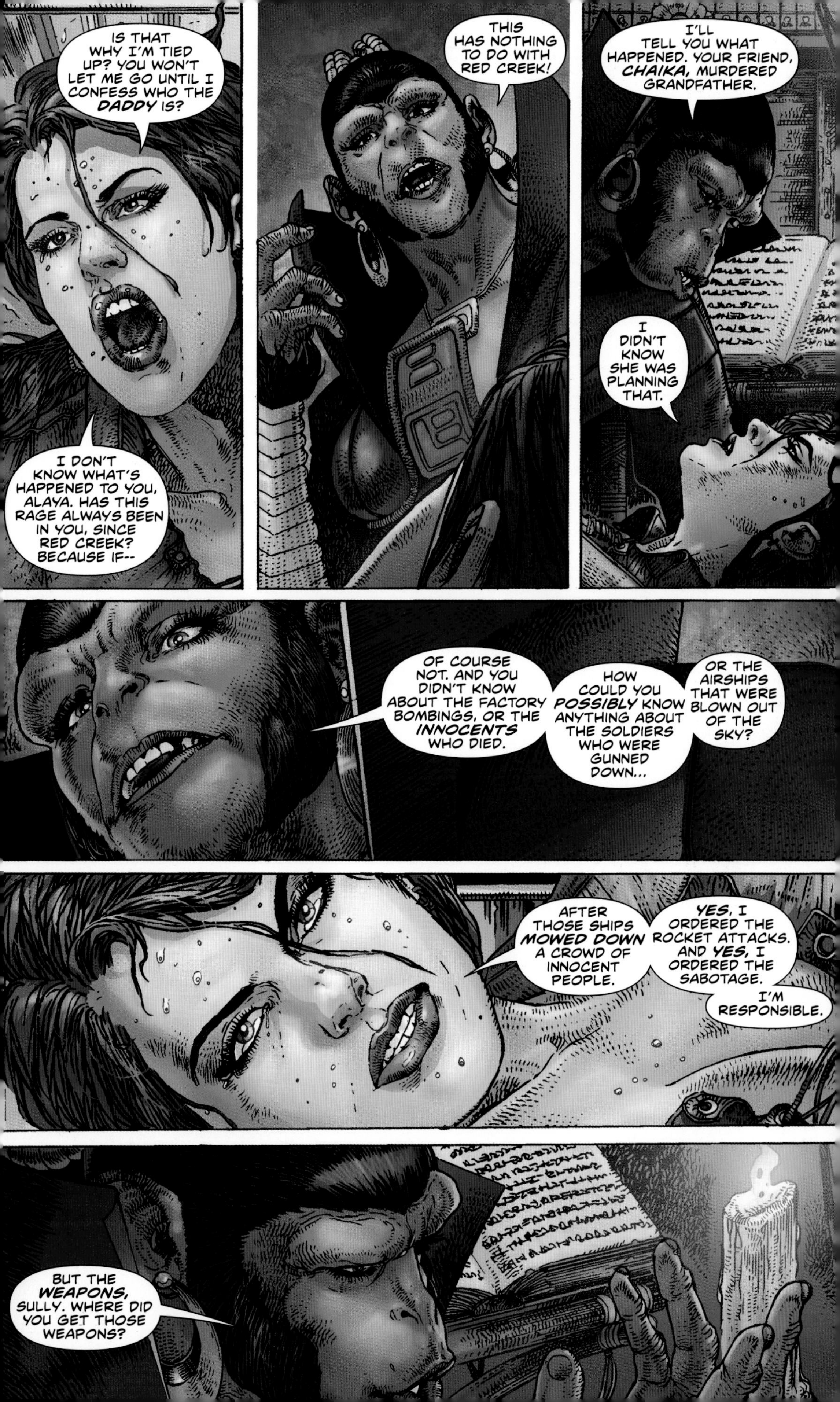
IS THAT WHY I'M TIED UP? YOU WON'T LET ME GO UNTIL I CONFESS WHO THE *DADDY* IS?
I DON'T KNOW WHAT'S HAPPENED TO YOU, ALAYA. HAS THIS RAGE ALWAYS BEEN IN YOU, SINCE RED CREEK? BECAUSE IF--
THIS HAS NOTHING TO DO WITH RED CREEK!
I'LL TELL YOU WHAT HAPPENED. YOUR FRIEND, *CHAIKA,* MURDERED GRANDFATHER.
I DIDN'T KNOW SHE WAS PLANNING THAT.
OF COURSE NOT. AND YOU DIDN'T KNOW ABOUT THE FACTORY BOMBINGS, OR THE *INNOCENTS* WHO DIED.
HOW COULD YOU *POSSIBLY* KNOW ANYTHING ABOUT THE SOLDIERS WHO WERE GUNNED DOWN...
OR THE AIRSHIPS THAT WERE BLOWN OUT OF THE SKY?
AFTER THOSE SHIPS *MOWED DOWN* A CROWD OF INNOCENT PEOPLE.
YES, I ORDERED THE ROCKET ATTACKS. AND *YES*, I ORDERED THE SABOTAGE.
I'M RESPONSIBLE.
BUT THE *WEAPONS,* SULLY. WHERE DID YOU GET THOSE WEAPONS?

SO WHAT'S IT GOING TO BE, THEN? IS THIS WHERE THE TORTURE BEGINS?

VOICE ALAYA?

MY APOLOGIES FOR... INTERRUPTING. NIX HAS IMPORTANT NEWS. HE SENT ME TO FIND YOU.

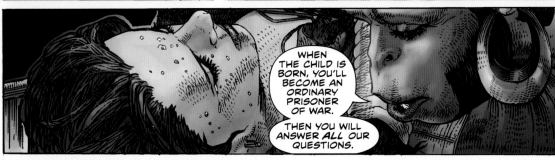

WHEN THE CHILD IS BORN, YOU'LL BECOME AN ORDINARY PRISONER OF WAR.

THEN YOU WILL ANSWER ALL OUR QUESTIONS.

THE JOKE'S ON YOU, ALAYA! THE CHILD HAS NO FATHER!

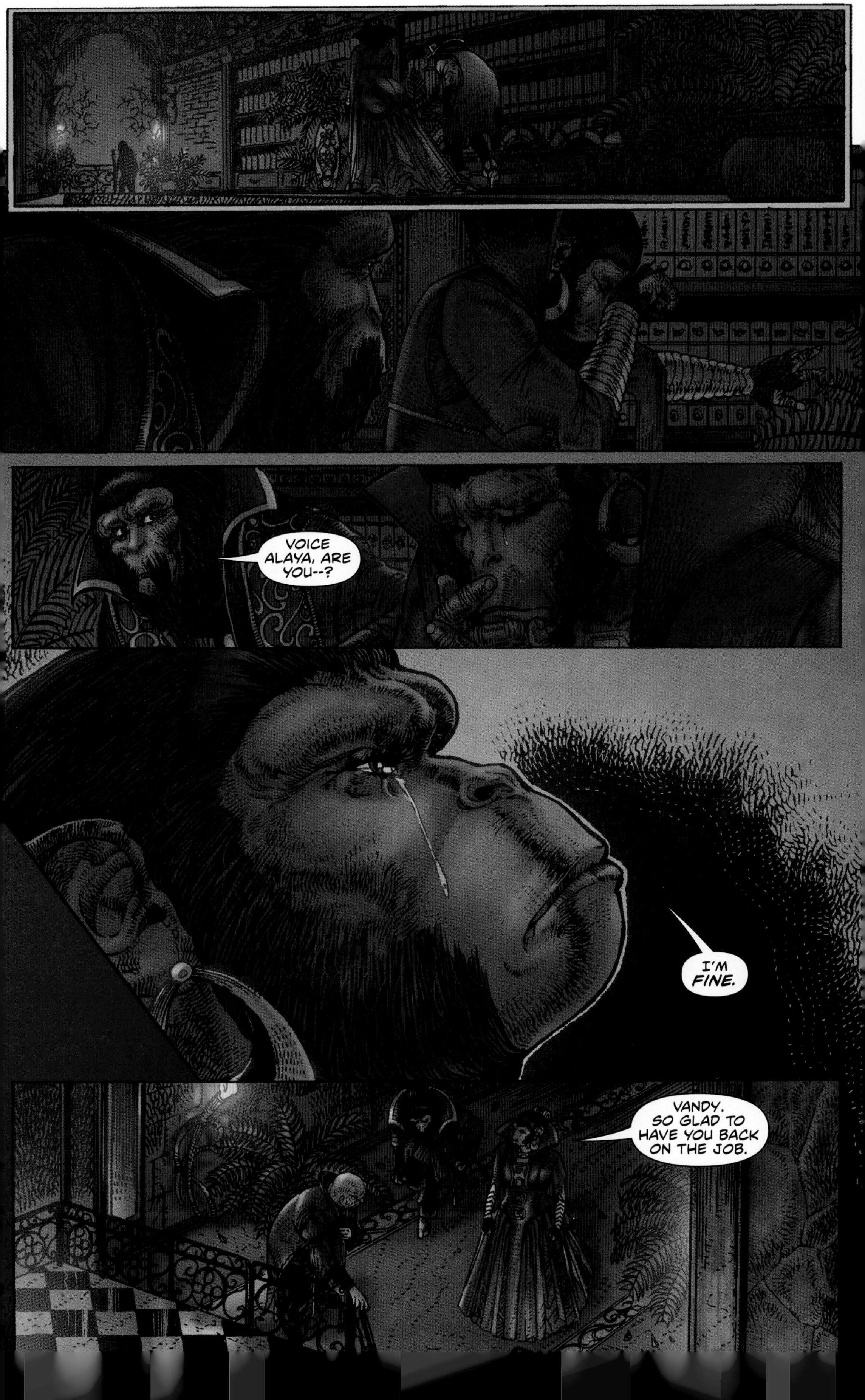
VOICE ALAYA, ARE YOU--?
I'M FINE.
VANDY. SO GLAD TO HAVE YOU BACK ON THE JOB.

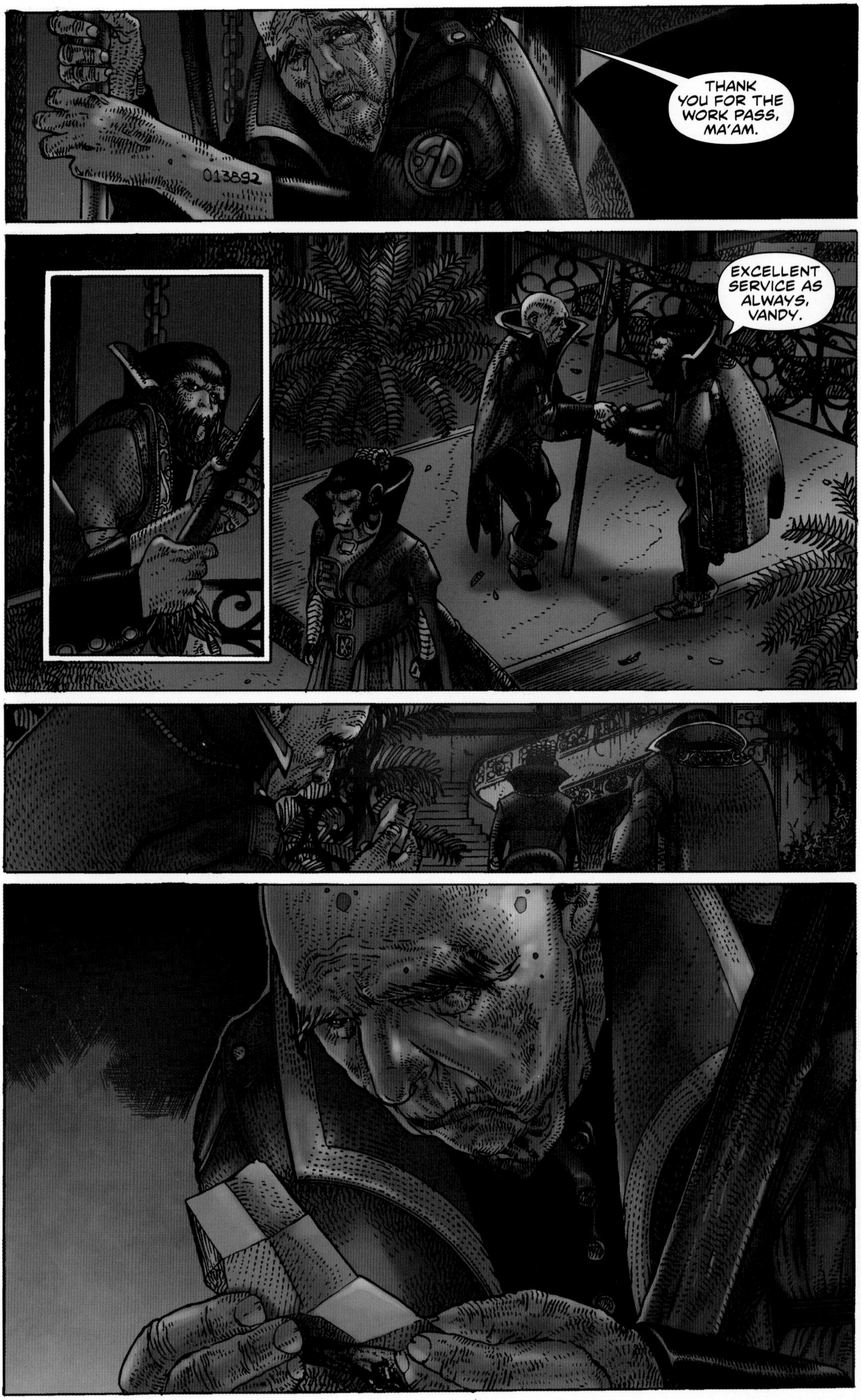
013892
THANK YOU FOR THE WORK PASS, MA'AM.
EXCELLENT SERVICE AS ALWAYS, VANDY.

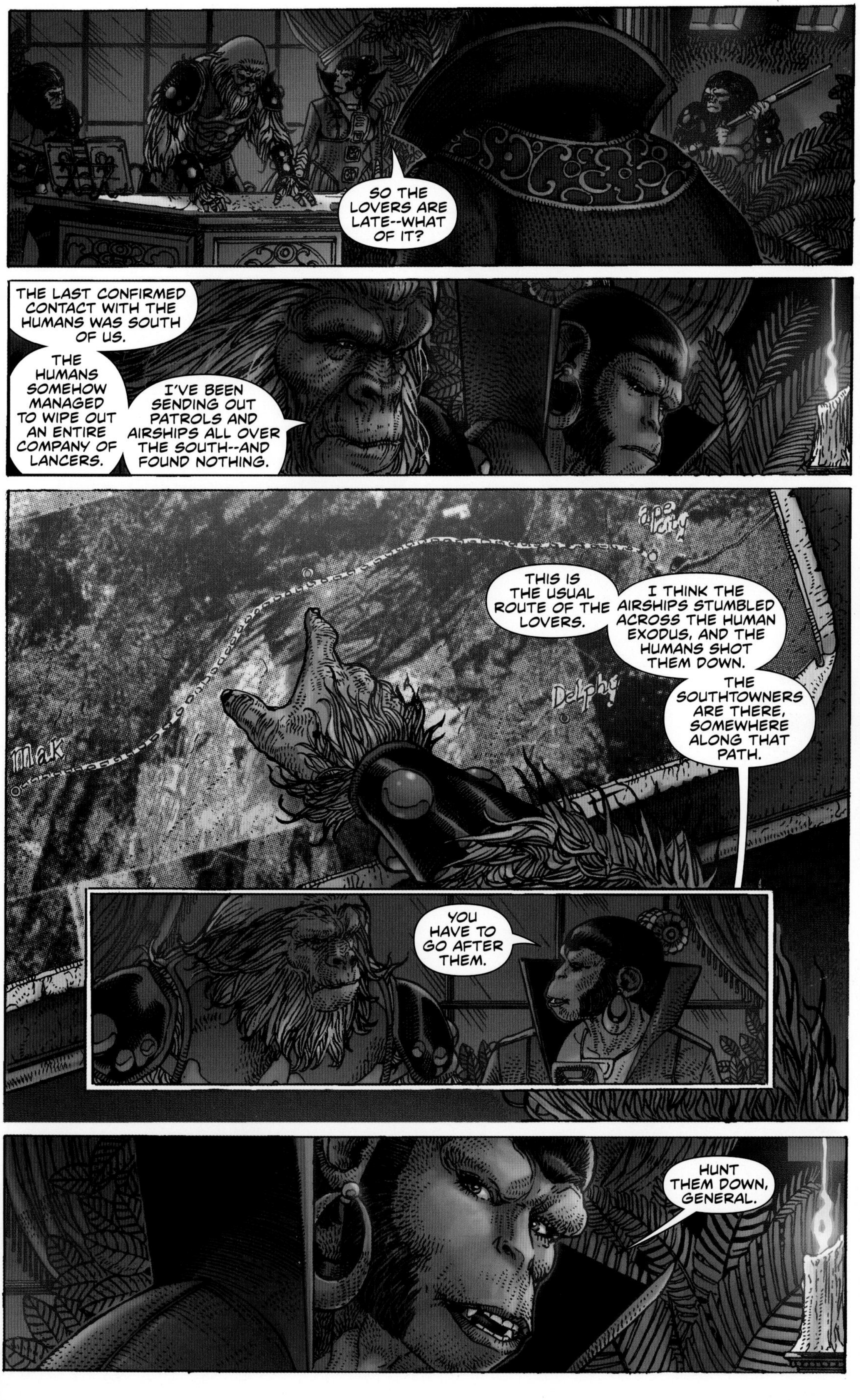
SO THE LOVERS ARE LATE--WHAT OF IT?
THE LAST CONFIRMED CONTACT WITH THE HUMANS WAS SOUTH OF US.
THE HUMANS SOMEHOW MANAGED TO WIPE OUT AN ENTIRE COMPANY OF LANCERS.
I'VE BEEN SENDING OUT PATROLS AND AIRSHIPS ALL OVER THE SOUTH--AND FOUND NOTHING.
ape city
Delphy
THIS IS THE USUAL ROUTE OF THE LOVERS.
I THINK THE AIRSHIPS STUMBLED ACROSS THE HUMAN EXODUS, AND THE HUMANS SHOT THEM DOWN.
THE SOUTHTOWNERS ARE THERE, SOMEWHERE ALONG THAT PATH.
YOU HAVE TO GO AFTER THEM.
HUNT THEM DOWN, GENERAL.

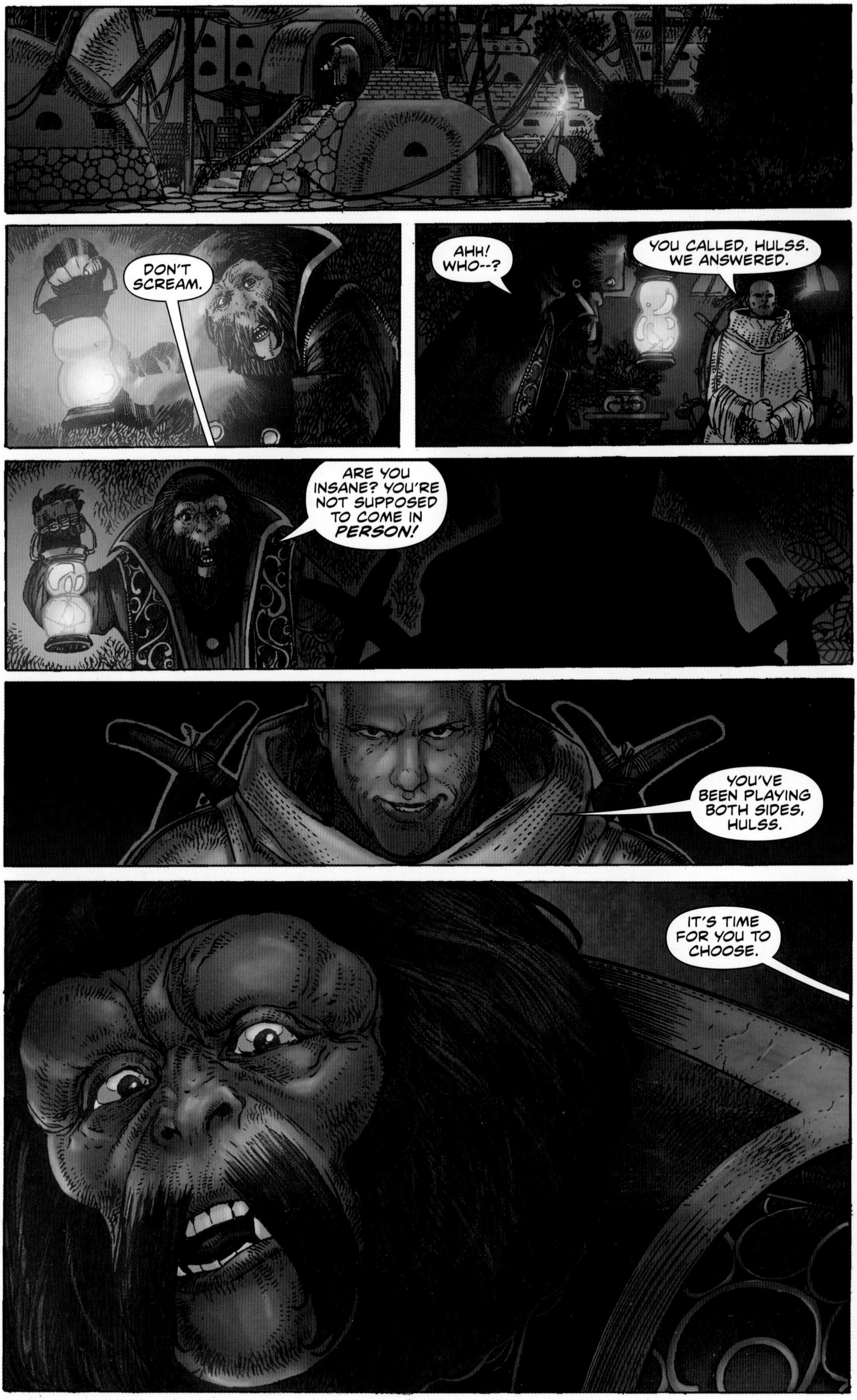
DON'T SCREAM.
AHH! WHO--?
YOU CALLED, HULSS. WE ANSWERED.
ARE YOU INSANE? YOU'RE NOT SUPPOSED TO COME IN PERSON!
YOU'VE BEEN PLAYING BOTH SIDES, HULSS.
IT'S TIME FOR YOU TO CHOOSE.

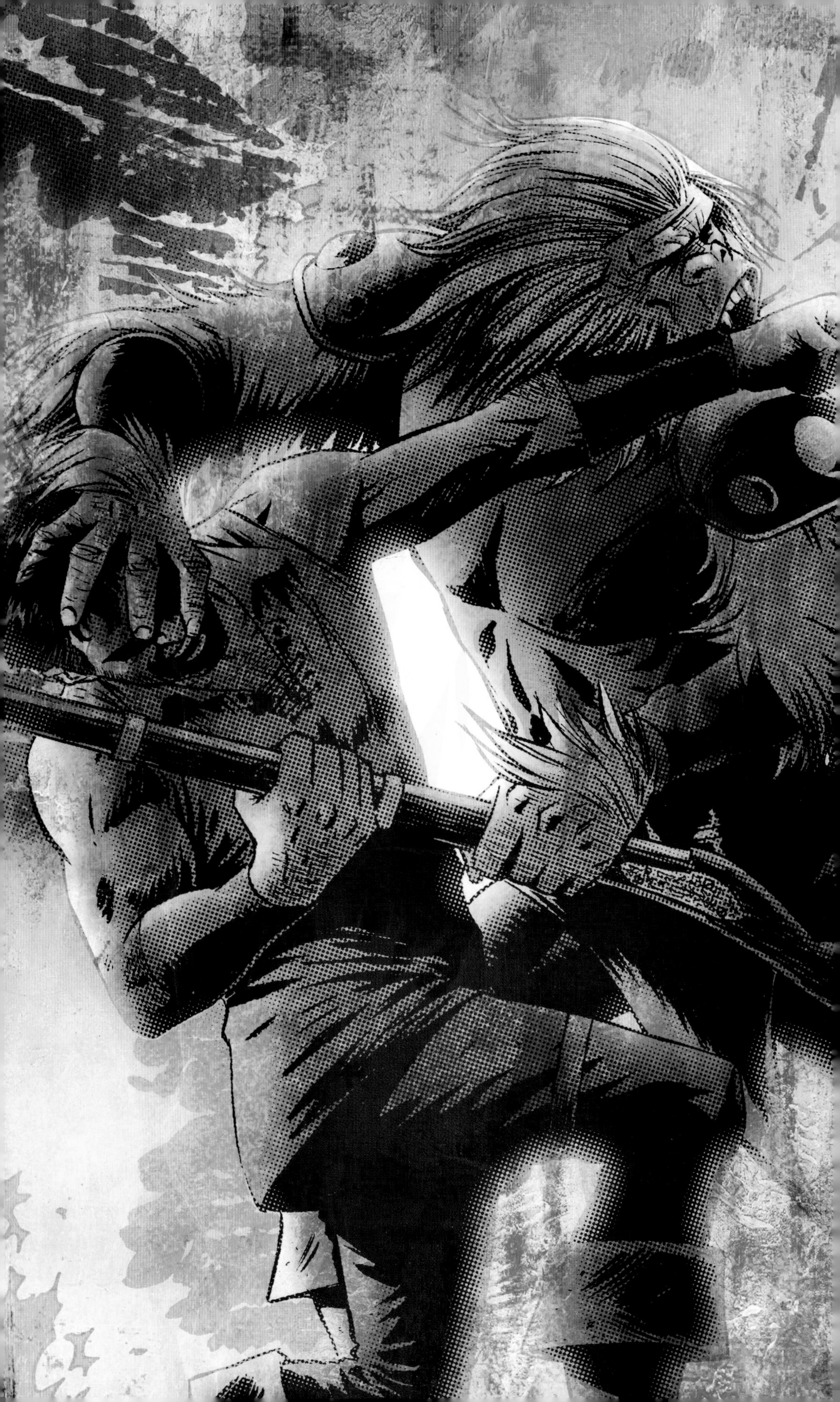

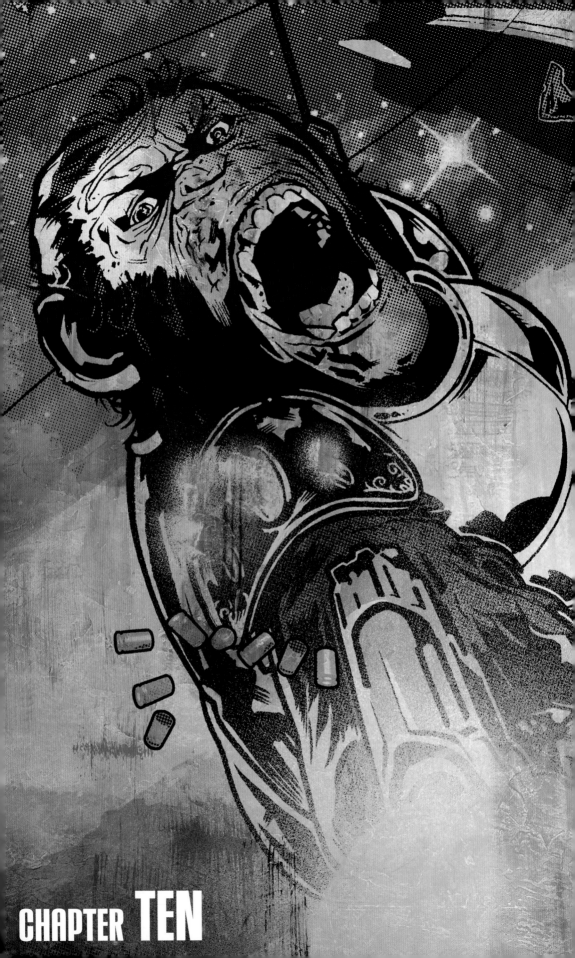

CHAPTER TEN

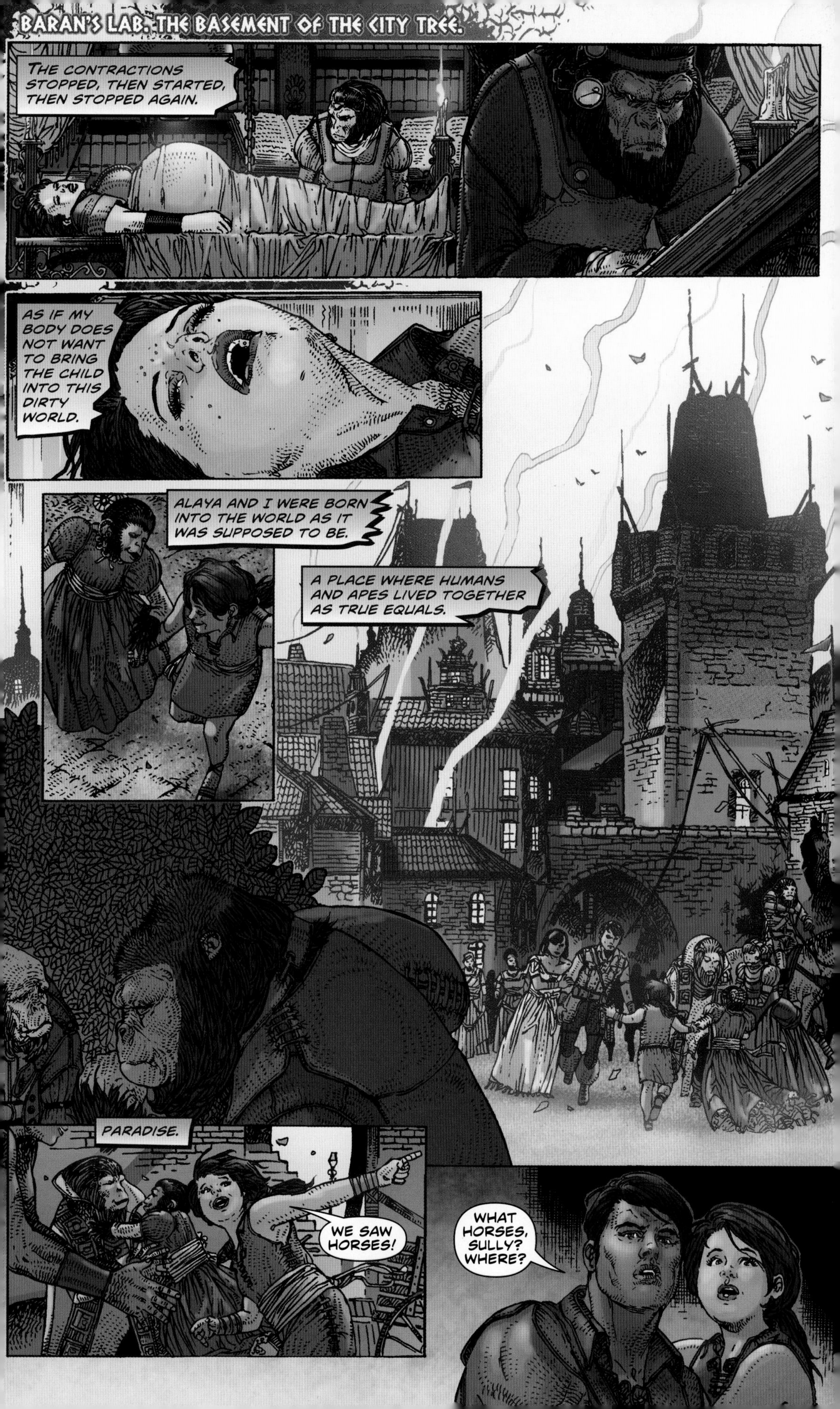
BARAN'S LAB-THE BASEMENT OF THE CITY TREE.
THE CONTRACTIONS STOPPED, THEN STARTED, THEN STOPPED AGAIN.
AS IF MY BODY DOES NOT WANT TO BRING THE CHILD INTO THIS DIRTY WORLD.
ALAYA AND I WERE BORN INTO THE WORLD AS IT WAS SUPPOSED TO BE.
A PLACE WHERE HUMANS AND APES LIVED TOGETHER AS TRUE EQUALS.
PARADISE.
WE SAW HORSES!
WHAT HORSES, SULLY? WHERE?

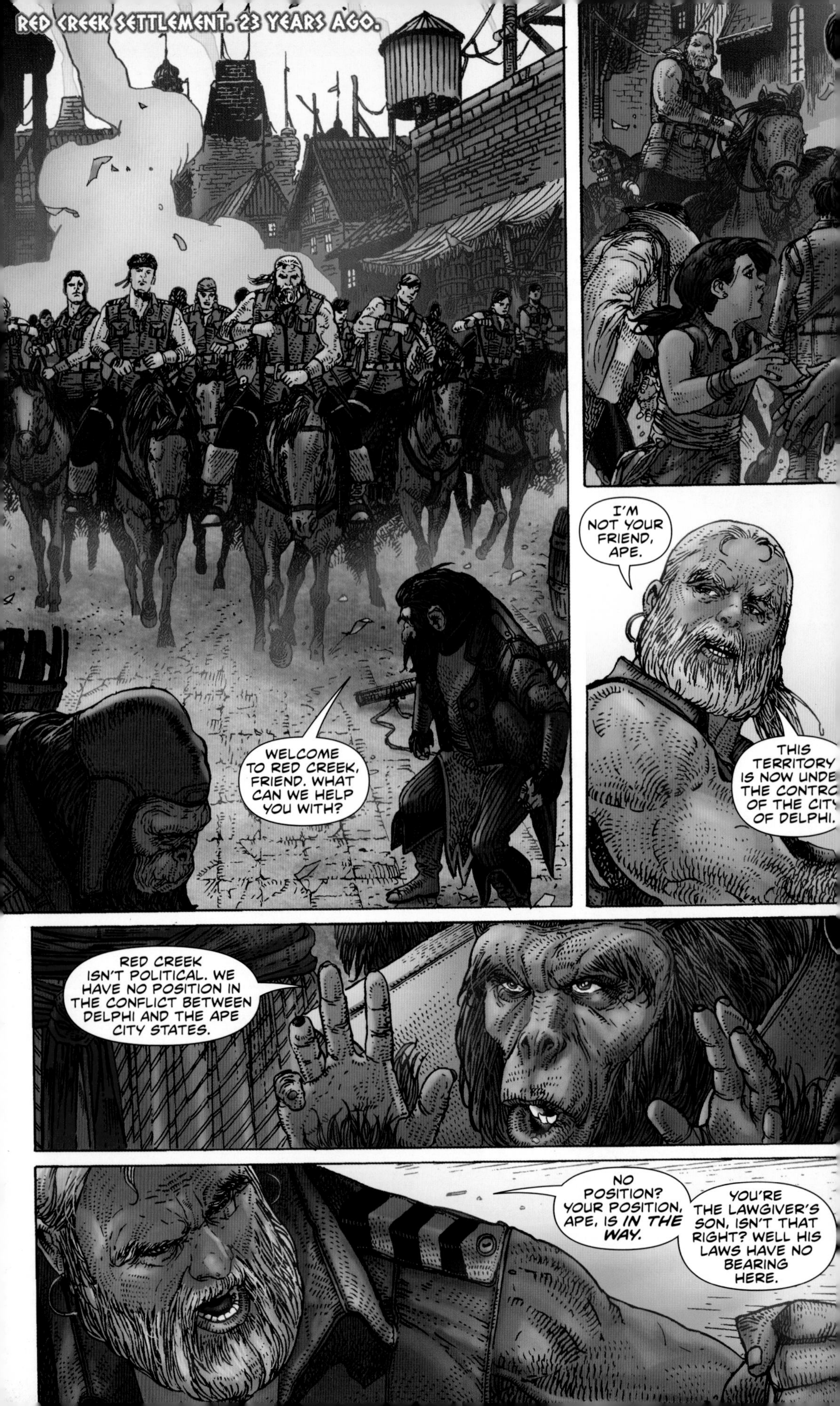
RED CREEK SETTLEMENT. 23 YEARS AGO.
WELCOME TO RED CREEK, FRIEND. WHAT CAN WE HELP YOU WITH?
I'M NOT YOUR FRIEND, APE.
THIS TERRITORY IS NOW UNDE THE CONTRO OF THE CIT OF DELPHI.
RED CREEK ISN'T POLITICAL. WE HAVE NO POSITION IN THE CONFLICT BETWEEN DELPHI AND THE APE CITY STATES.
NO POSITION? YOUR POSITION, APE, IS *IN THE WAY.*
YOU'RE THE LAWGIVER'S SON, ISN'T THAT RIGHT? WELL HIS LAWS HAVE NO BEARING HERE.

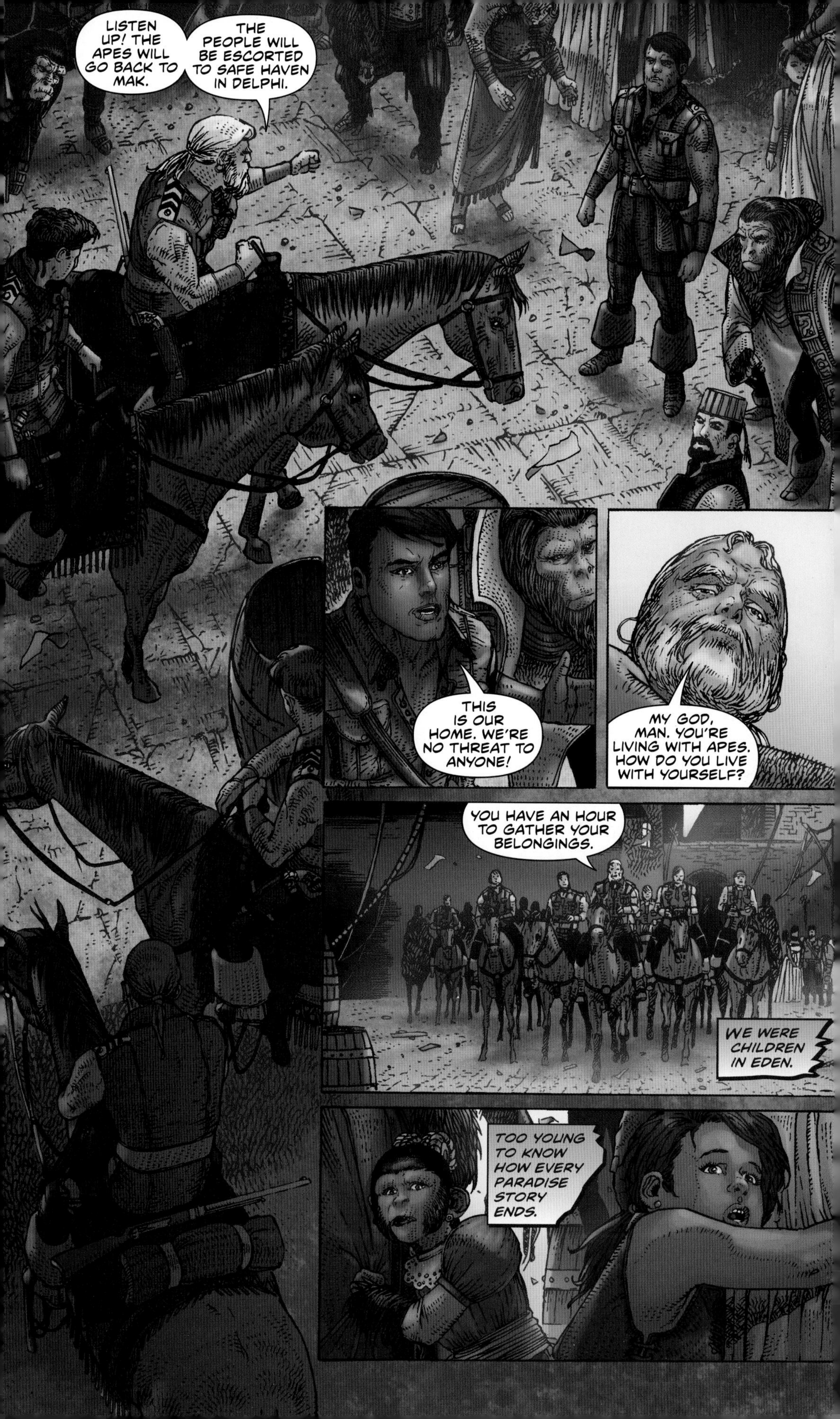
LISTEN UP! THE APES WILL GO BACK TO MAK.
THE PEOPLE WILL BE ESCORTED TO SAFE HAVEN IN DELPHI.
THIS IS OUR HOME. WE'RE NO THREAT TO ANYONE!
MY GOD, MAN. YOU'RE LIVING WITH APES. HOW DO YOU LIVE WITH YOURSELF?
YOU HAVE AN HOUR TO GATHER YOUR BELONGINGS.
WE WERE CHILDREN IN EDEN.
TOO YOUNG TO KNOW HOW EVERY PARADISE STORY ENDS.

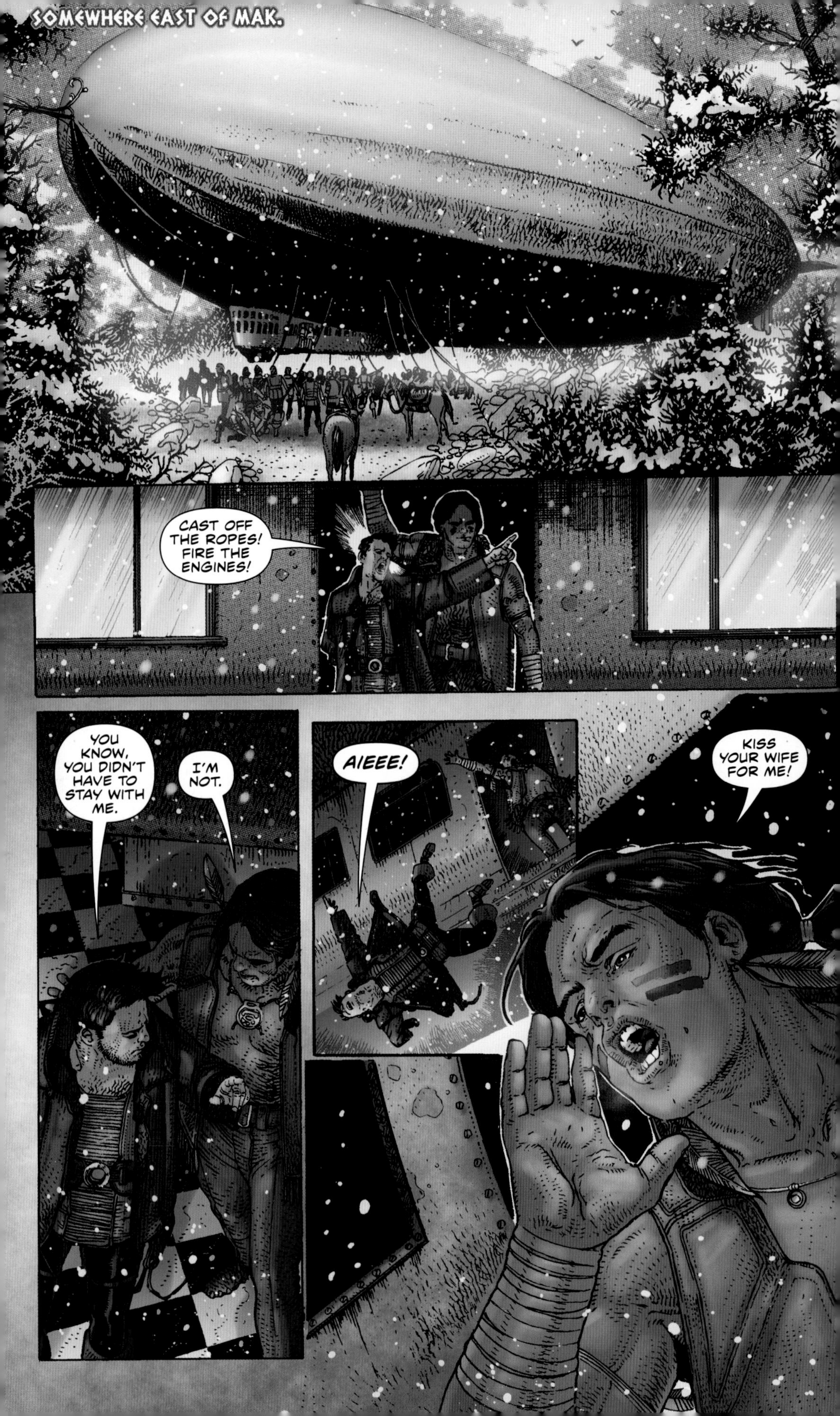
SOMEWHERE EAST OF MAK.
CAST OFF THE ROPES! FIRE THE ENGINES!
YOU KNOW, YOU DIDN'T HAVE TO STAY WITH ME.
I'M NOT.
AIEEE!
KISS YOUR WIFE FOR ME!

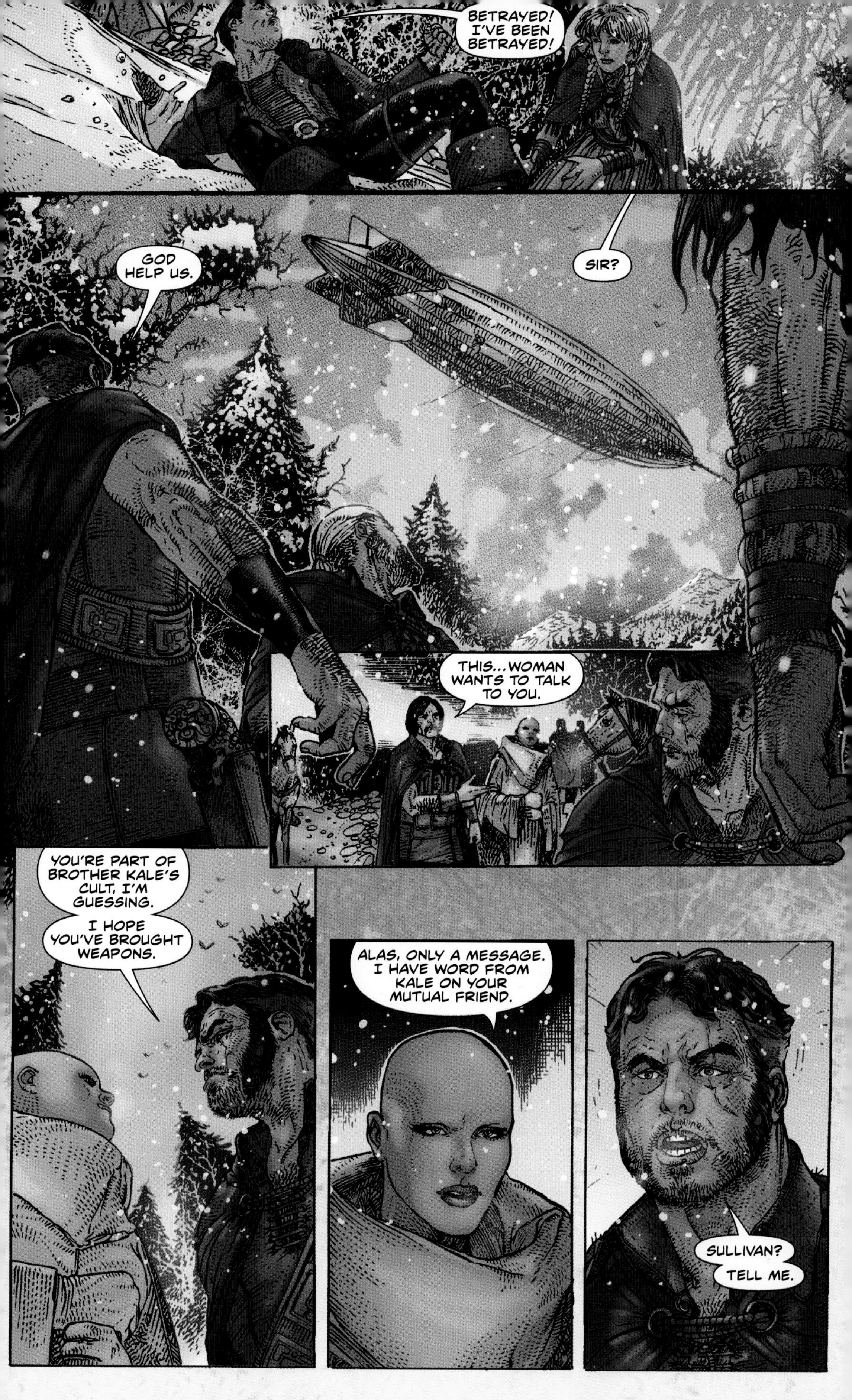
BETRAYED! I'VE BEEN BETRAYED!
GOD HELP US.
SIR?
THIS...WOMAN WANTS TO TALK TO YOU.
YOU'RE PART OF BROTHER KALE'S CULT, I'M GUESSING.
I HOPE YOU'VE BROUGHT WEAPONS.
ALAS, ONLY A MESSAGE. I HAVE WORD FROM KALE ON YOUR MUTUAL FRIEND.
SULLIVAN?
TELL ME.

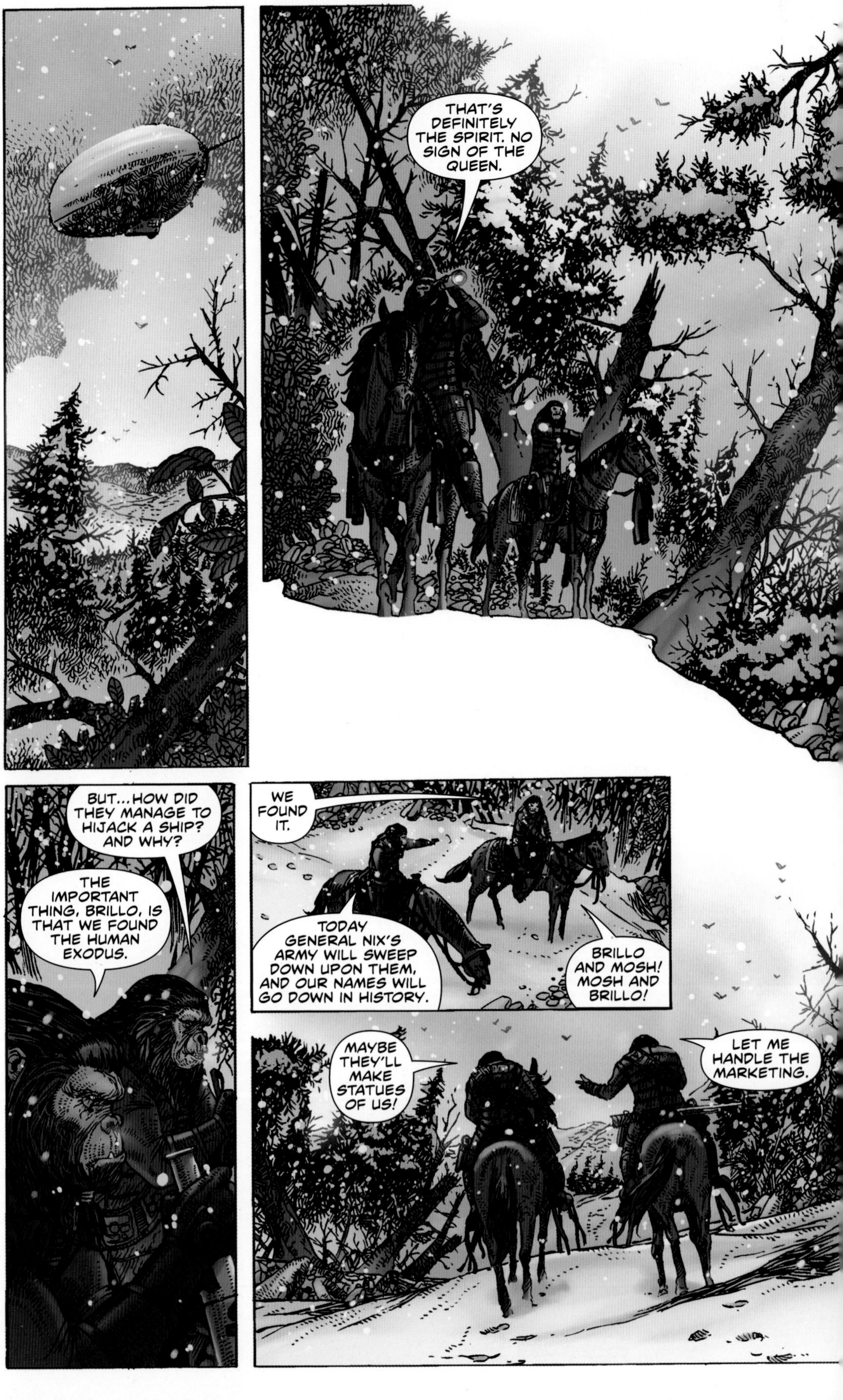
THAT'S DEFINITELY THE SPIRIT. NO SIGN OF THE QUEEN.
BUT...HOW DID THEY MANAGE TO HIJACK A SHIP? AND WHY?
THE IMPORTANT THING, BRILLO, IS THAT WE FOUND THE HUMAN EXODUS.
WE FOUND IT.
TODAY GENERAL NIX'S ARMY WILL SWEEP DOWN UPON THEM, AND OUR NAMES WILL GO DOWN IN HISTORY.
BRILLO AND MOSH! MOSH AND BRILLO!
MAYBE THEY'LL MAKE STATUES OF US!
LET ME HANDLE THE MARKETING.

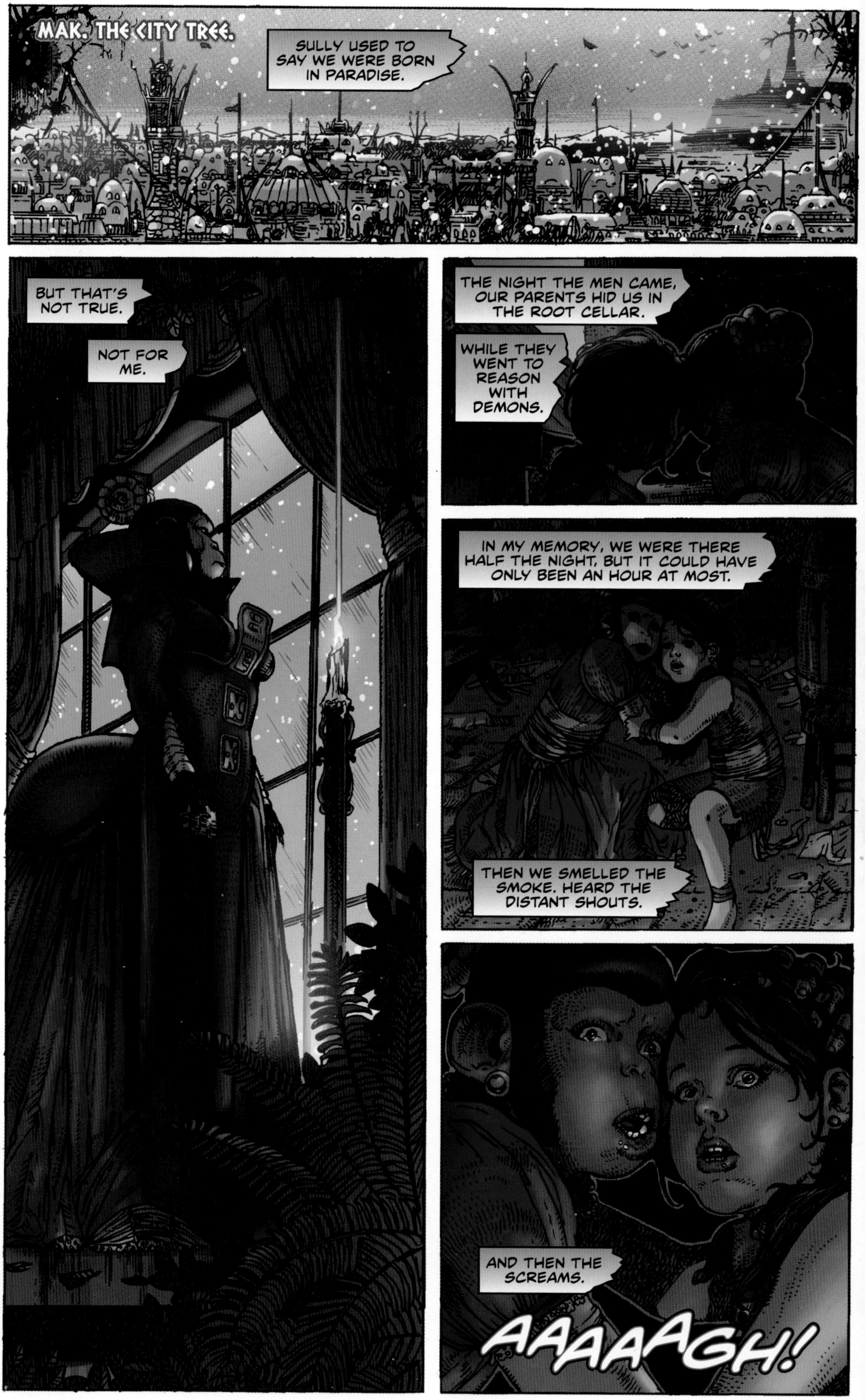
MAK. THE CITY TREE.
SULLY USED TO SAY WE WERE BORN IN PARADISE.
BUT THAT'S NOT TRUE.
NOT FOR ME.
THE NIGHT THE MEN CAME, OUR PARENTS HID US IN THE ROOT CELLAR.
WHILE THEY WENT TO REASON WITH DEMONS.
IN MY MEMORY, WE WERE THERE HALF THE NIGHT, BUT IT COULD HAVE ONLY BEEN AN HOUR AT MOST.
THEN WE SMELLED THE SMOKE. HEARD THE DISTANT SHOUTS.
AND THEN THE SCREAMS.
AAAAAGH!

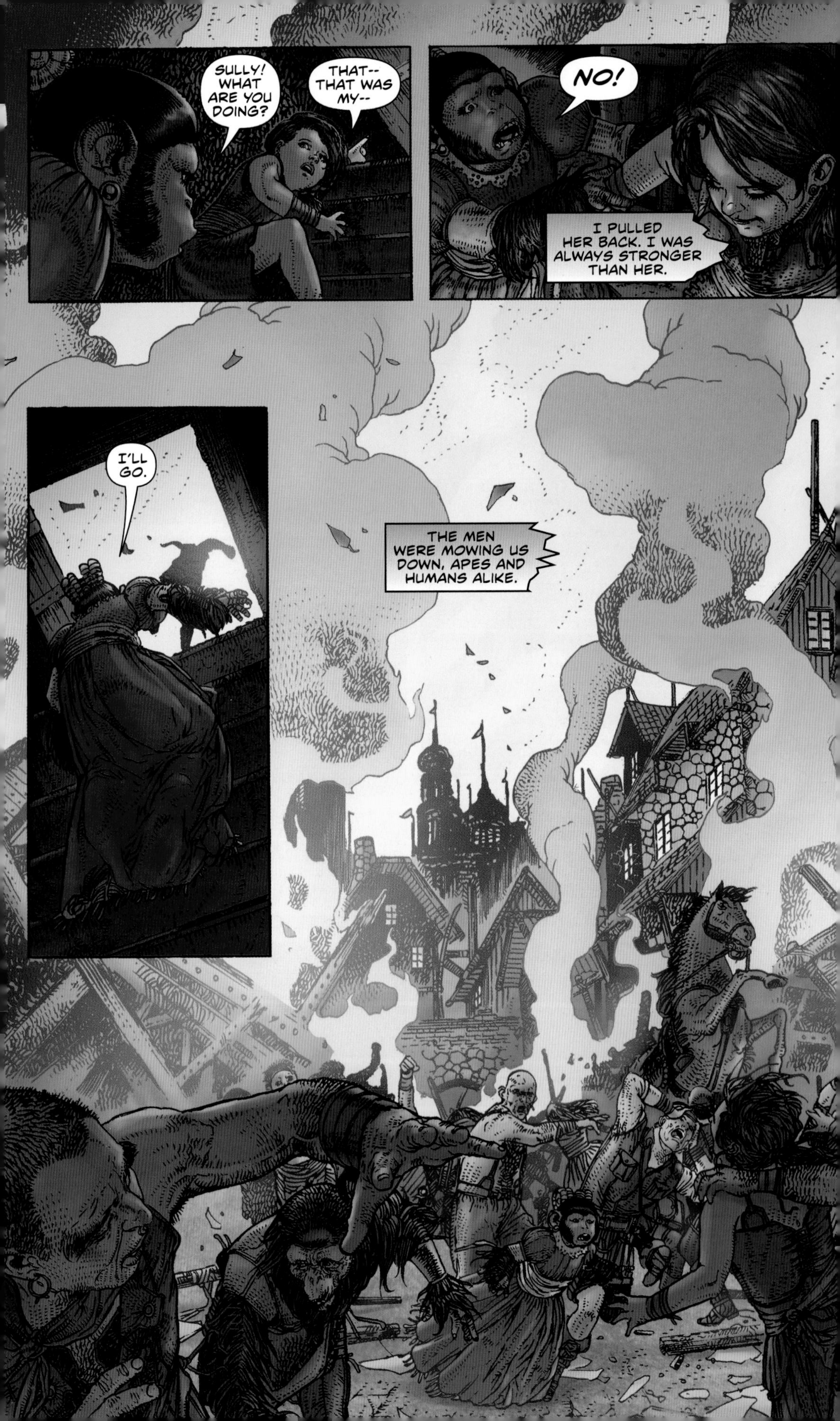
SULLY! WHAT ARE YOU DOING?
THAT-- THAT WAS MY--
NO!
I PULLED HER BACK. I WAS ALWAYS STRONGER THAN HER.
I'LL GO.
THE MEN WERE MOWING US DOWN, APES AND HUMANS ALIKE.

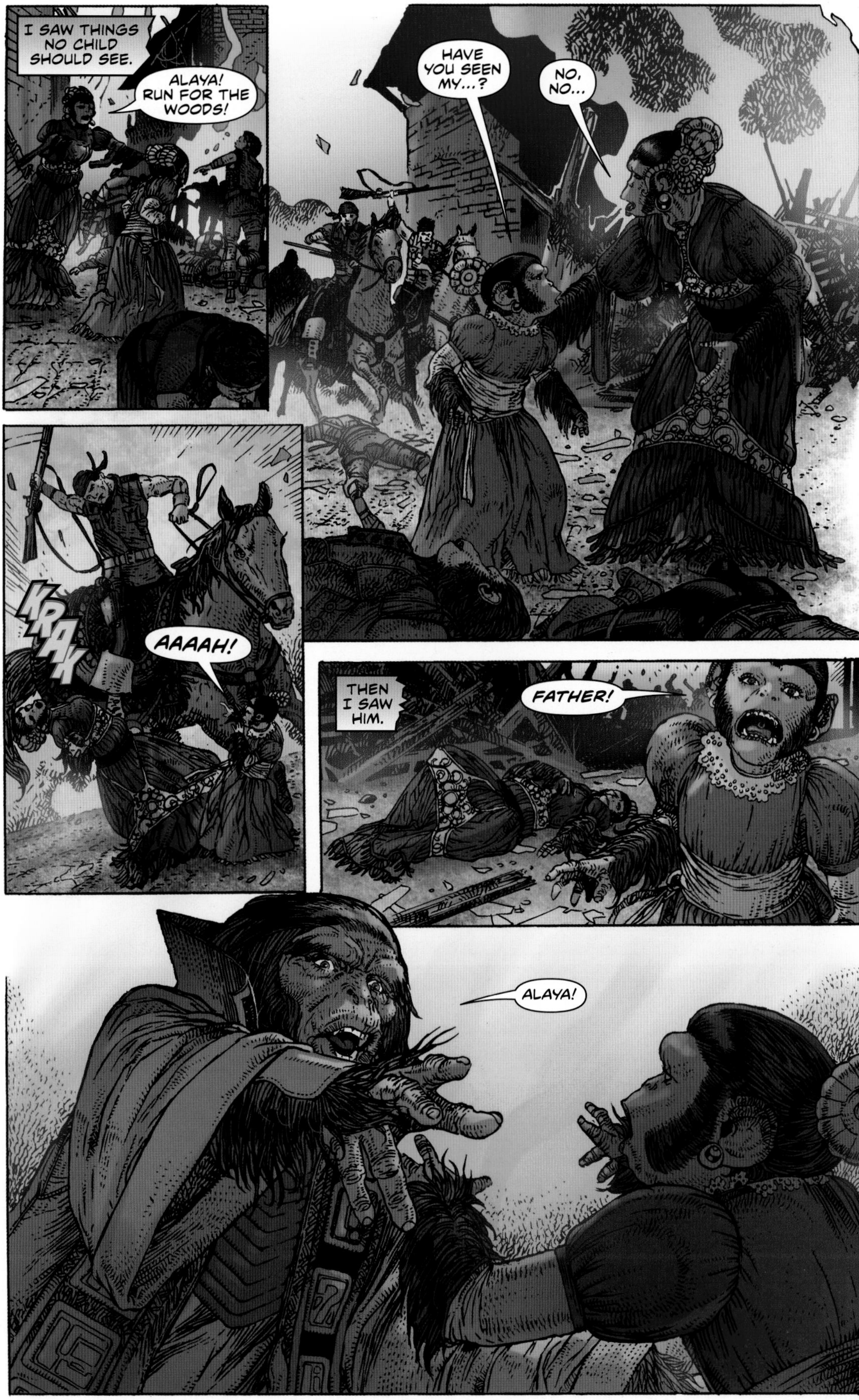
I SAW THINGS NO CHILD SHOULD SEE.
ALAYA! RUN FOR THE WOODS!
HAVE YOU SEEN MY...?
NO, NO...
KRAK
AAAAH!
THEN I SAW HIM.
FATHER!
ALAYA!

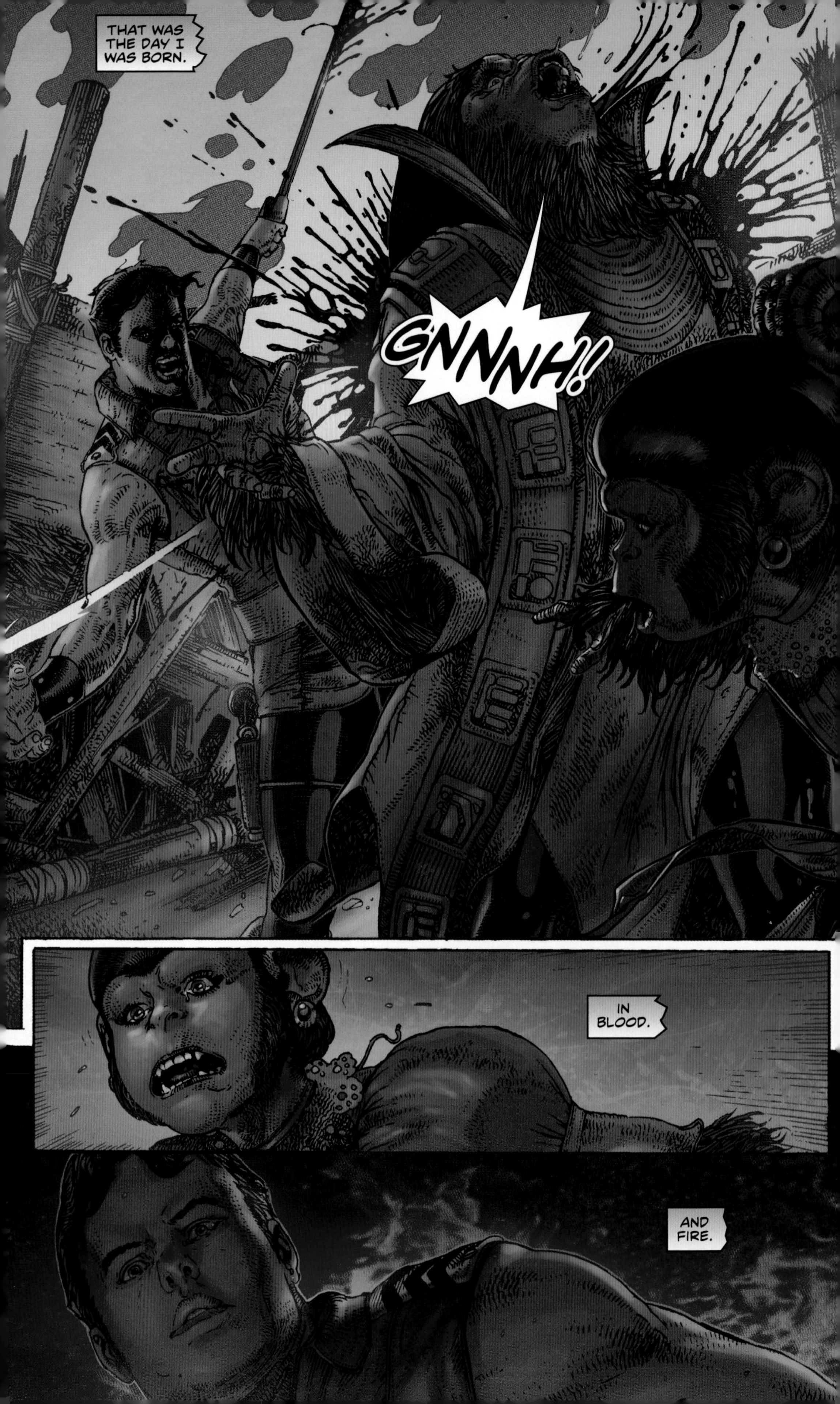
THAT WAS THE DAY I WAS BORN.
GNNNH!!
IN BLOOD.
AND FIRE.

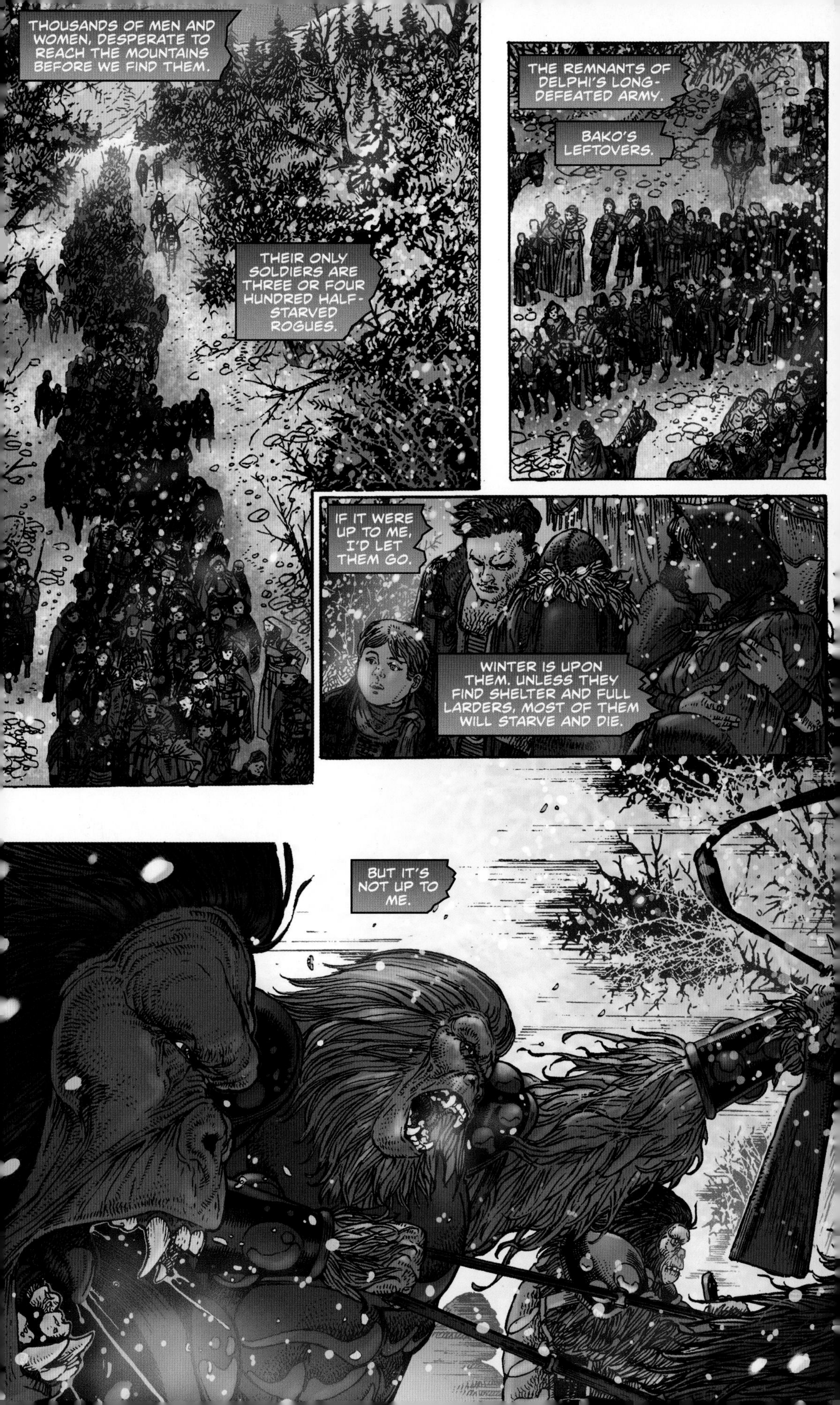
THOUSANDS OF MEN AND WOMEN, DESPERATE TO REACH THE MOUNTAINS BEFORE WE FIND THEM.
THEIR ONLY SOLDIERS ARE THREE OR FOUR HUNDRED HALF-STARVED ROGUES.
THE REMNANTS OF DELPHI'S LONG-DEFEATED ARMY.
BAKO'S LEFTOVERS.
IF IT WERE UP TO ME, I'D LET THEM GO.
WINTER IS UPON THEM. UNLESS THEY FIND SHELTER AND FULL LARDERS, MOST OF THEM WILL STARVE AND DIE.
BUT IT'S NOT UP TO ME.

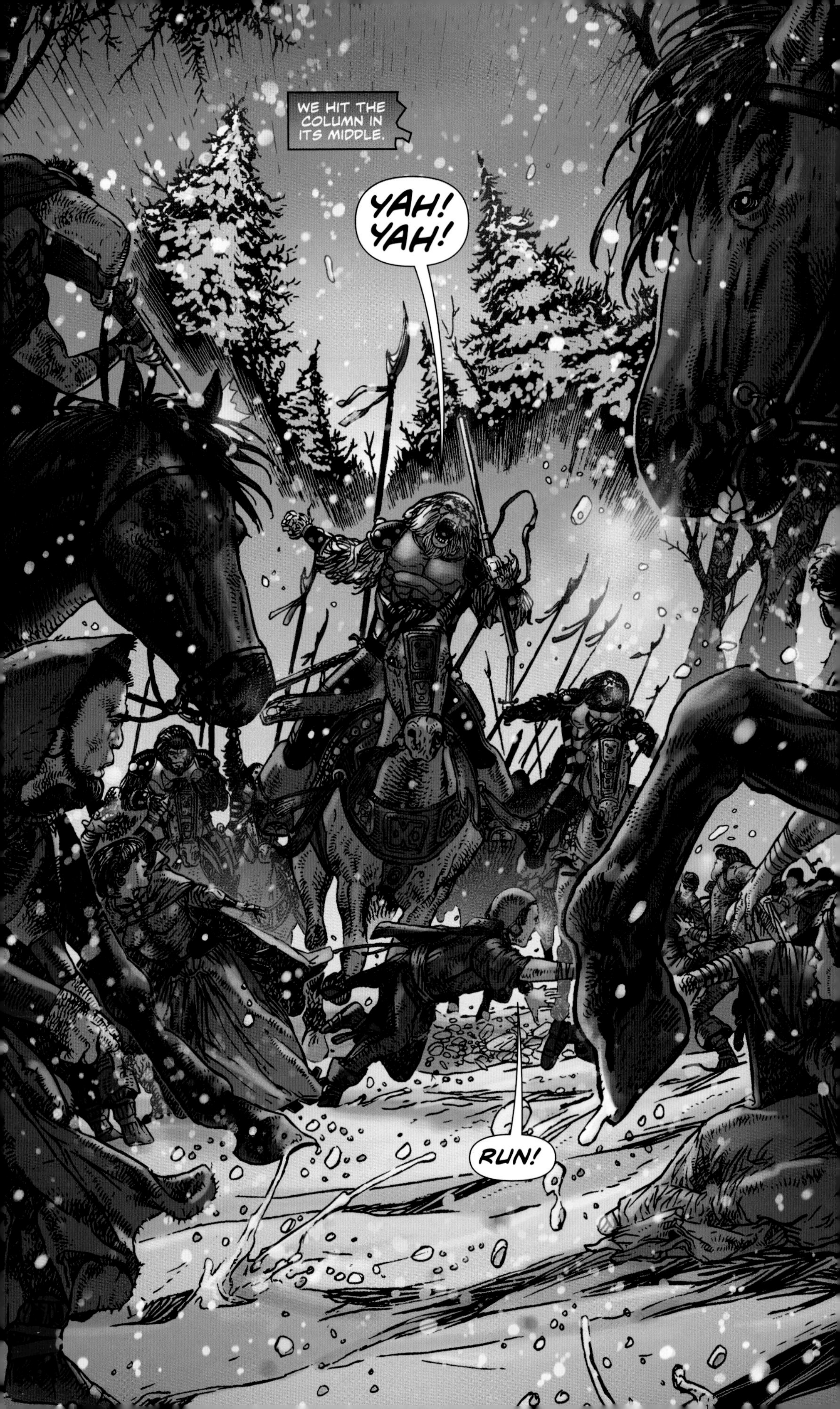
WE HIT THE COLUMN IN ITS MIDDLE.
YAH! YAH!
RUN!

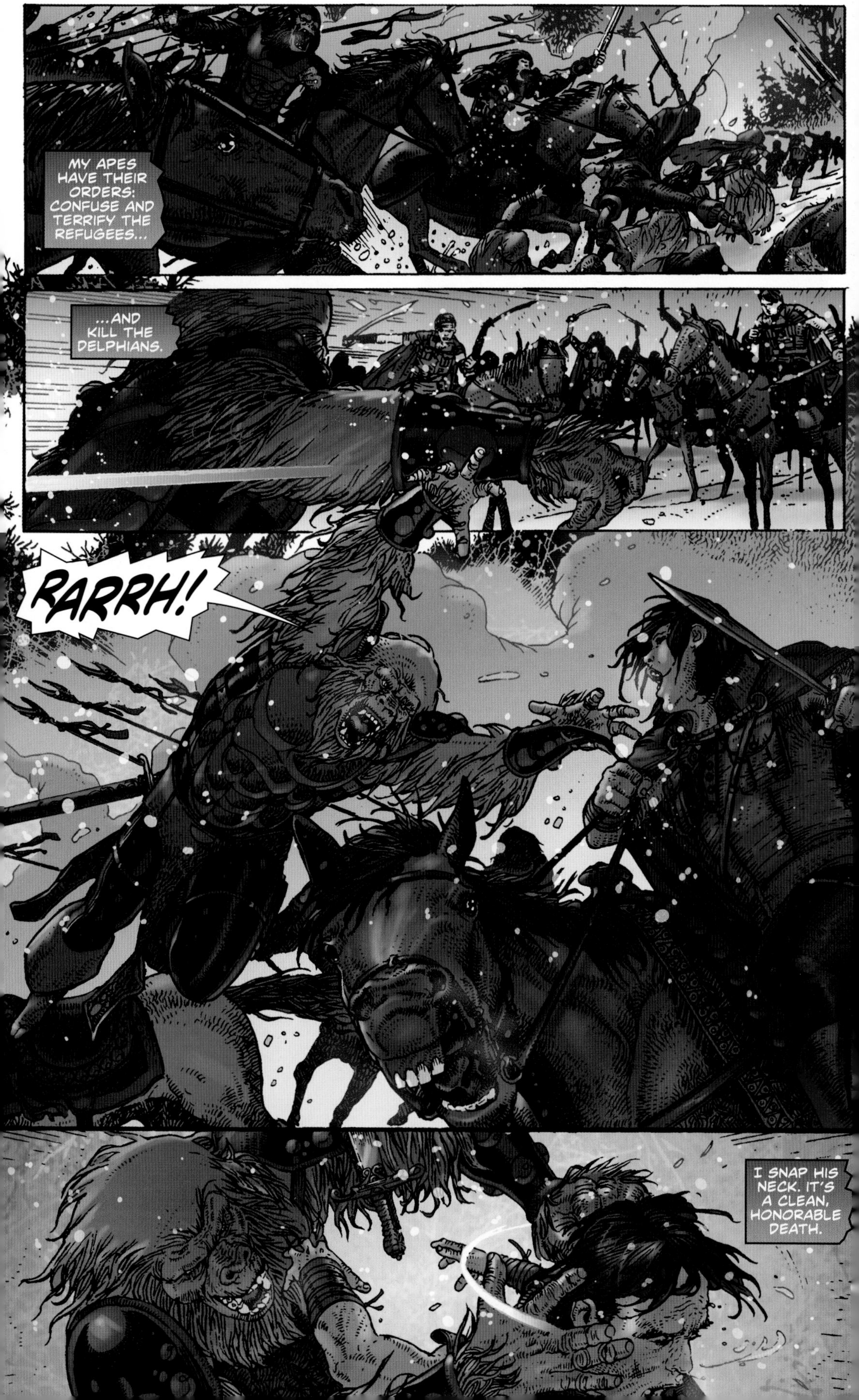
MY APES HAVE THEIR ORDERS: CONFUSE AND TERRIFY THE REFUGEES...
...AND KILL THE DELPHIANS.
RARRH!
I SNAP HIS NECK. IT'S A CLEAN, HONORABLE DEATH.

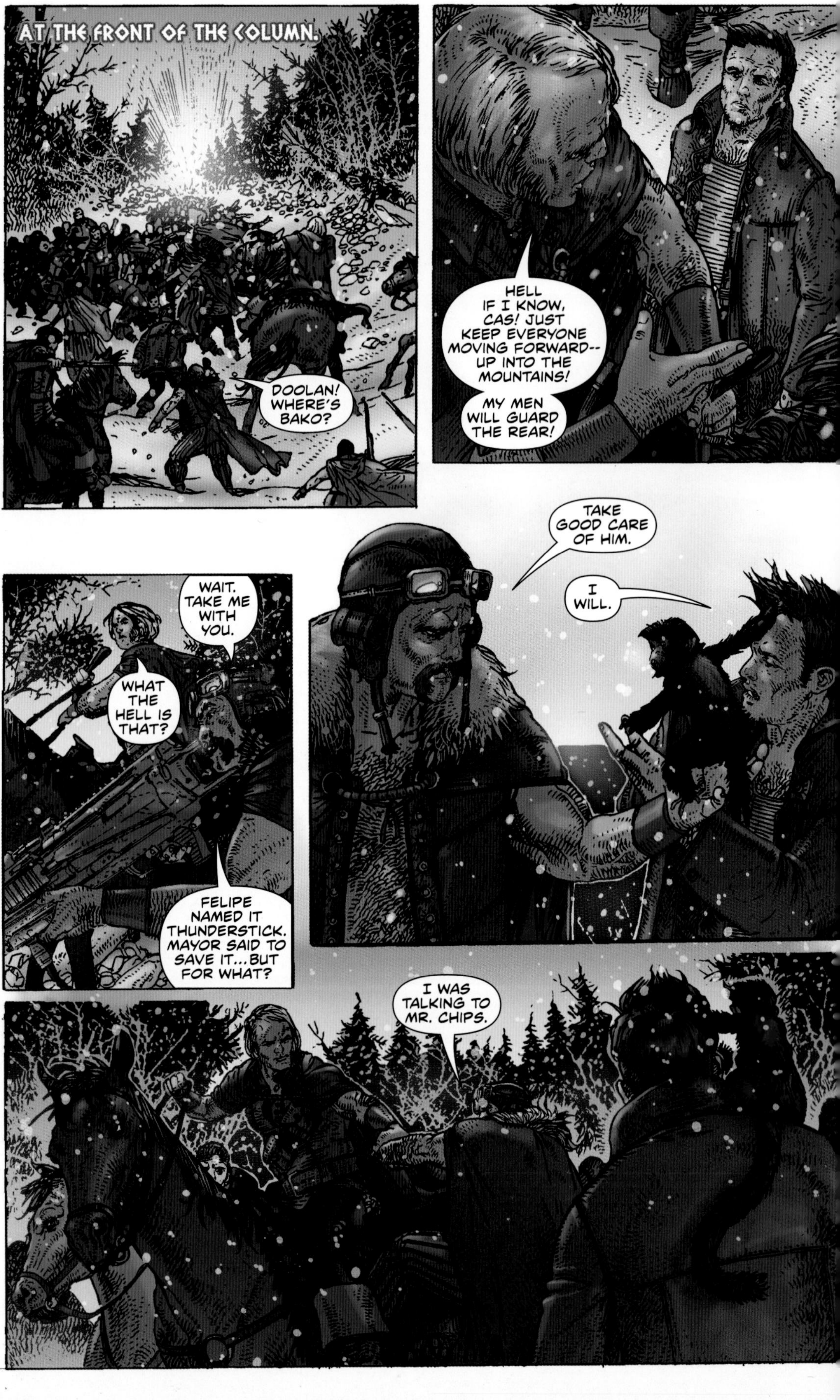
AT THE FRONT OF THE COLUMN.
DOOLAN! WHERE'S BAKO?
HELL IF I KNOW, CAS! JUST KEEP EVERYONE MOVING FORWARD-- UP INTO THE MOUNTAINS!
MY MEN WILL GUARD THE REAR!
WAIT. TAKE ME WITH YOU.
WHAT THE HELL IS THAT?
FELIPE NAMED IT THUNDERSTICK. MAYOR SAID TO SAVE IT...BUT FOR WHAT?
TAKE GOOD CARE OF HIM.
I WILL.
I WAS TALKING TO MR. CHIPS.

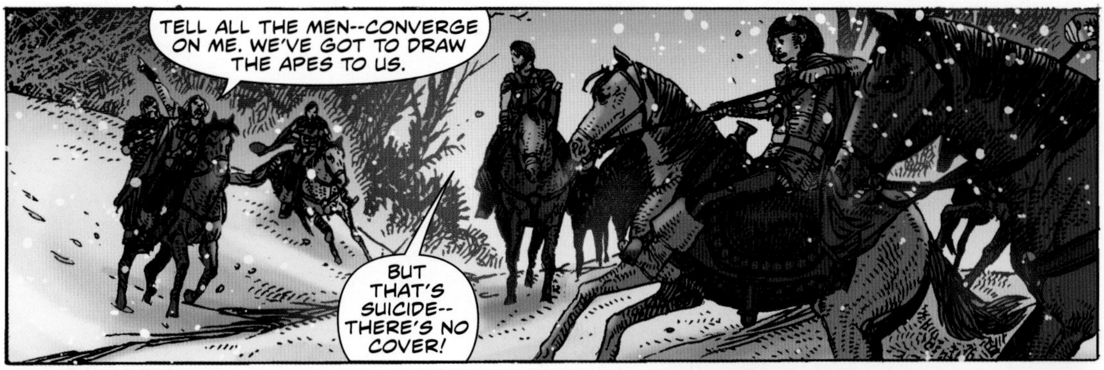
TELL ALL THE MEN--CONVERGE ON ME. WE'VE GOT TO DRAW THE APES TO US.
BUT THAT'S SUICIDE--THERE'S NO COVER!

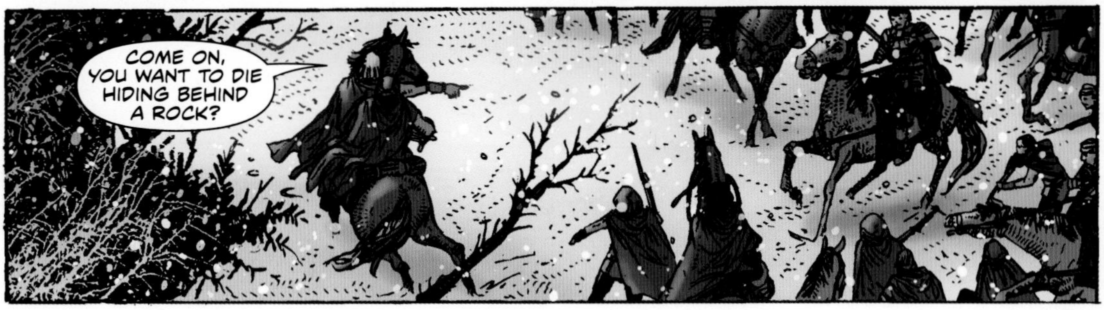
COME ON, YOU WANT TO DIE HIDING BEHIND A ROCK?

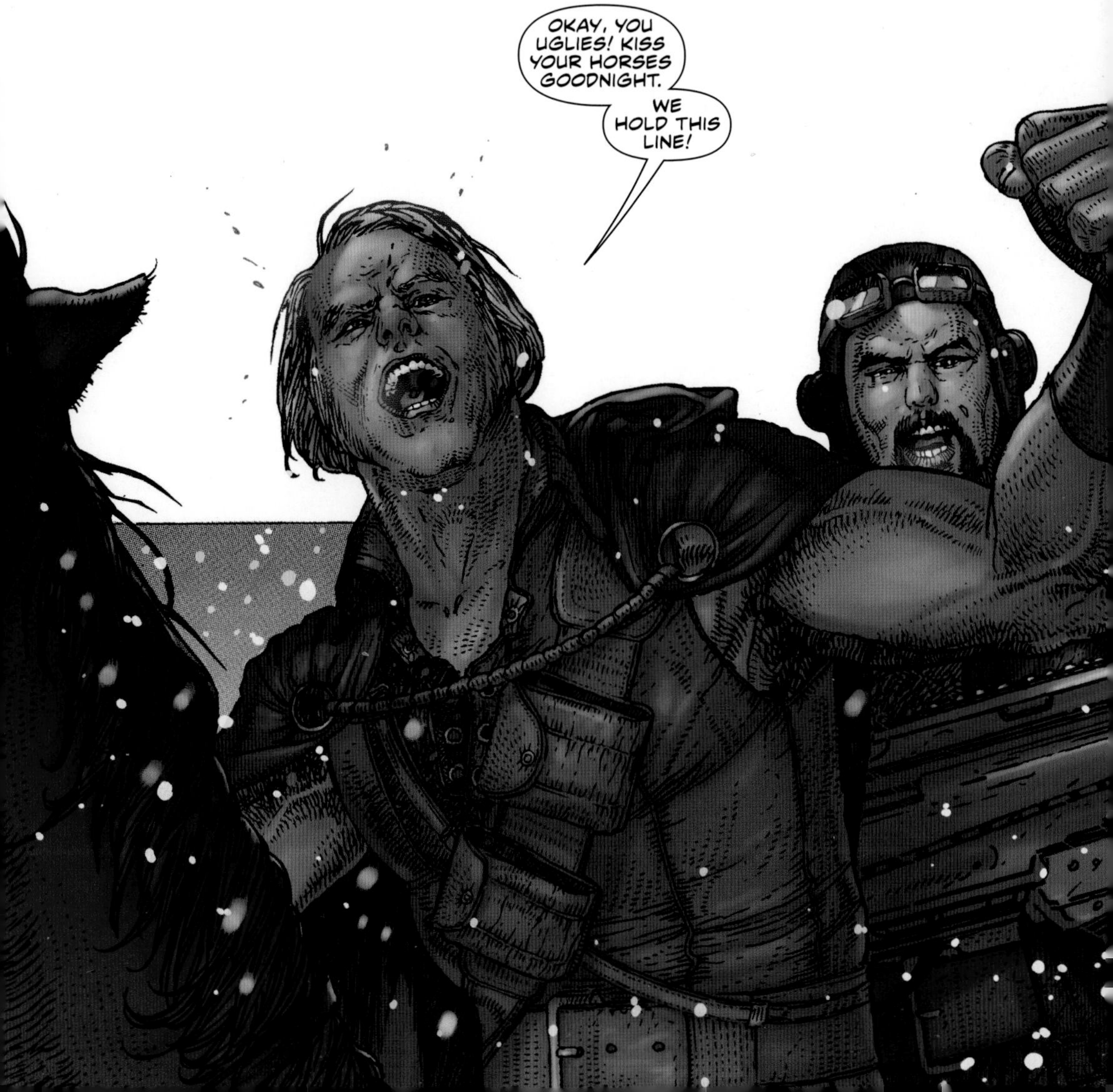
OKAY, YOU UGLIES! KISS YOUR HORSES GOODNIGHT.
WE HOLD THIS LINE!

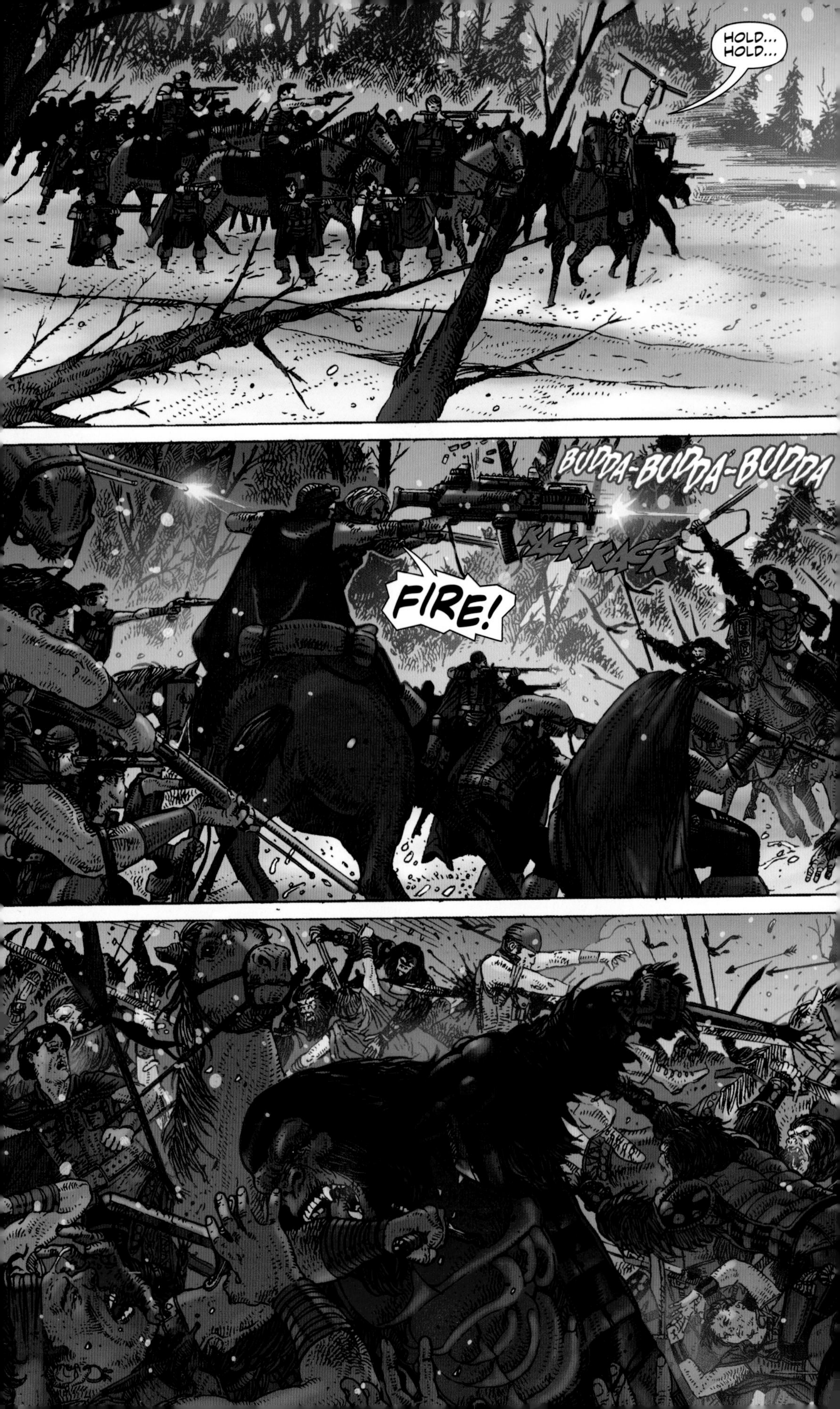
HOLD... HOLD...
BUDDA-BUDDA-BUDDA
KACK KACK
FIRE!

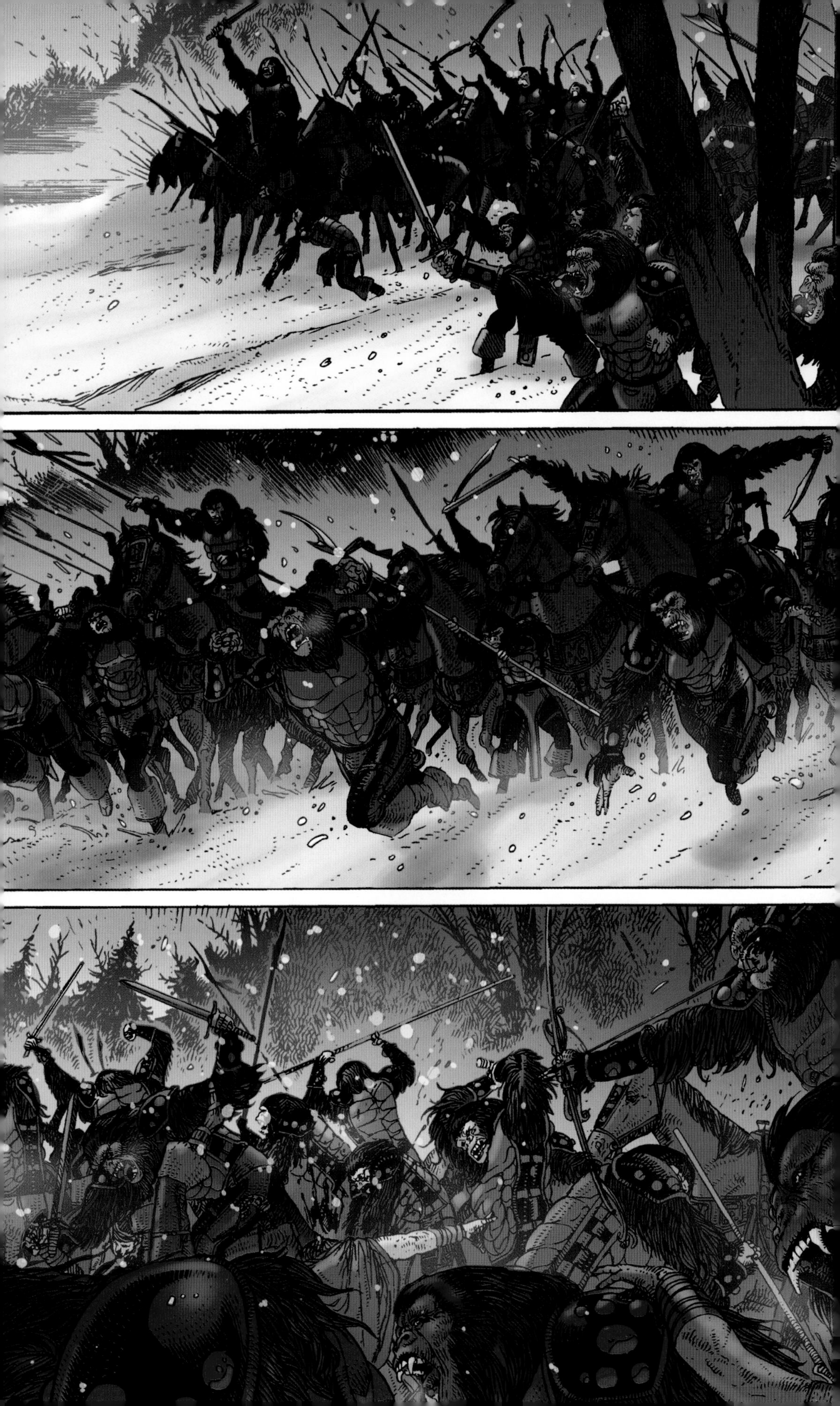

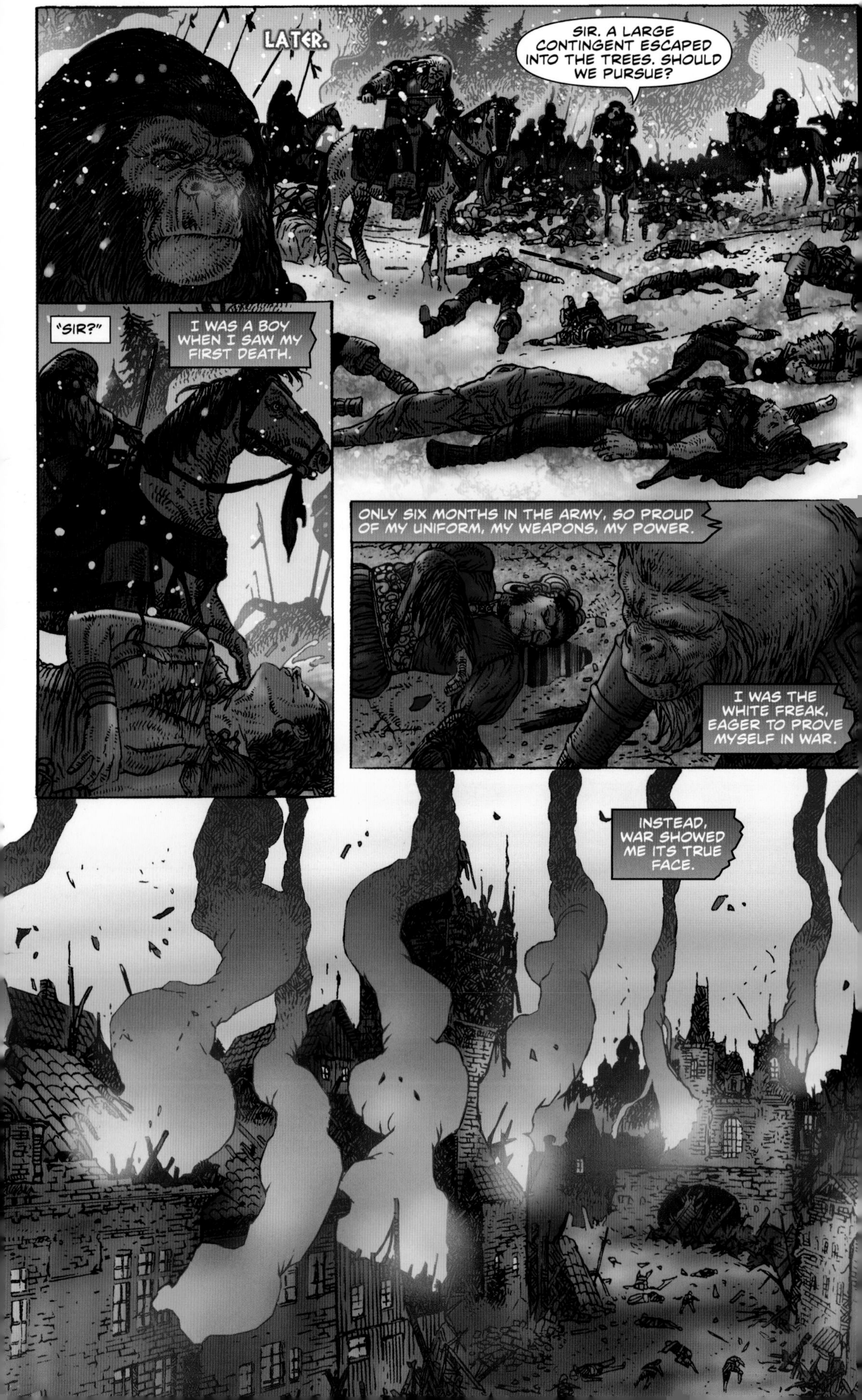

LATER.
SIR. A LARGE CONTINGENT ESCAPED INTO THE TREES. SHOULD WE PURSUE?
"SIR?"
I WAS A BOY WHEN I SAW MY FIRST DEATH.
ONLY SIX MONTHS IN THE ARMY, SO PROUD OF MY UNIFORM, MY WEAPONS, MY POWER.
I WAS THE WHITE FREAK, EAGER TO PROVE MYSELF IN WAR.
INSTEAD, WAR SHOWED ME ITS TRUE FACE.

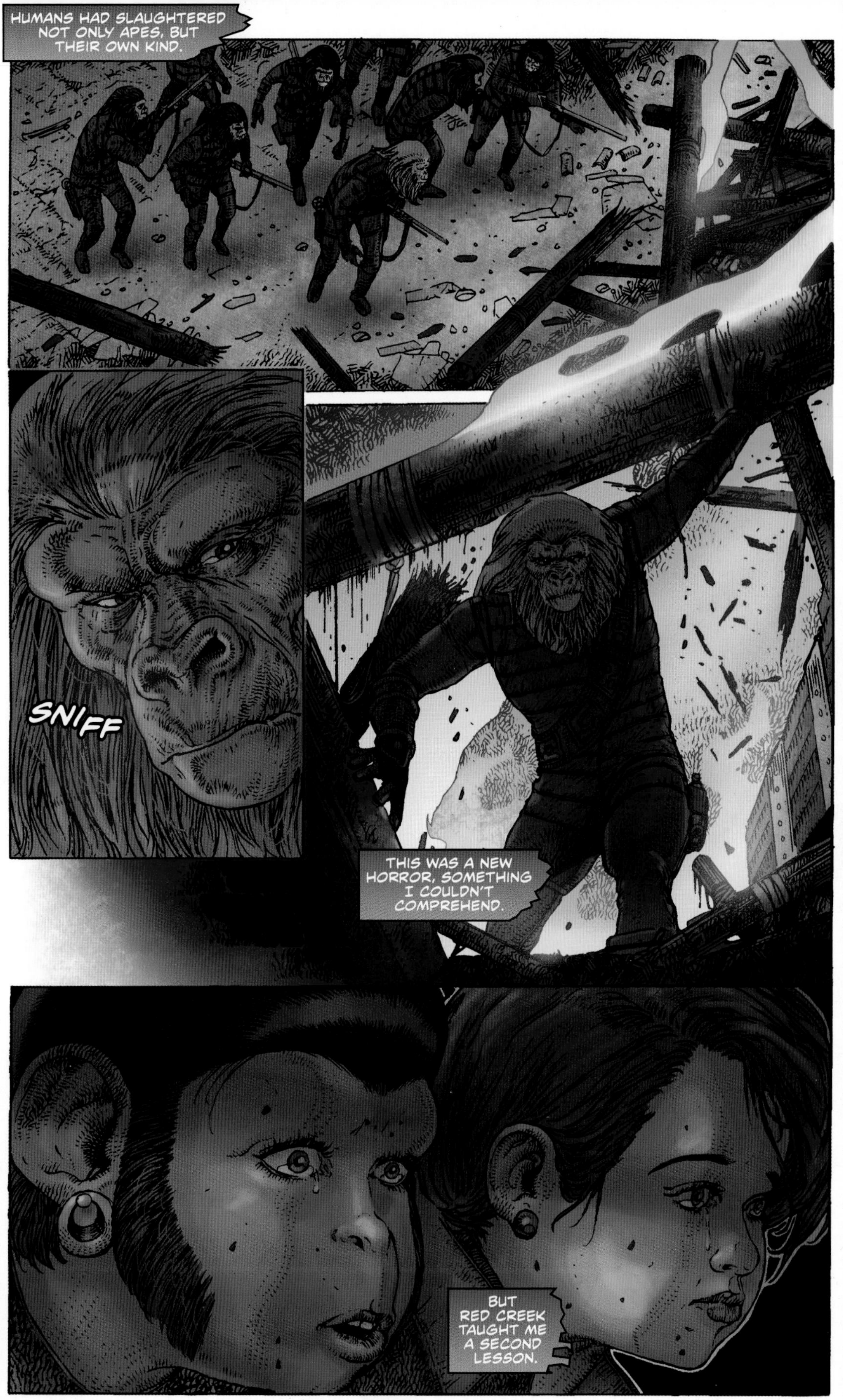
HUMANS HAD SLAUGHTERED NOT ONLY APES, BUT THEIR OWN KIND.
SNIFF
THIS WAS A NEW HORROR, SOMETHING I COULDN'T COMPREHEND.
BUT RED CREEK TAUGHT ME A SECOND LESSON.

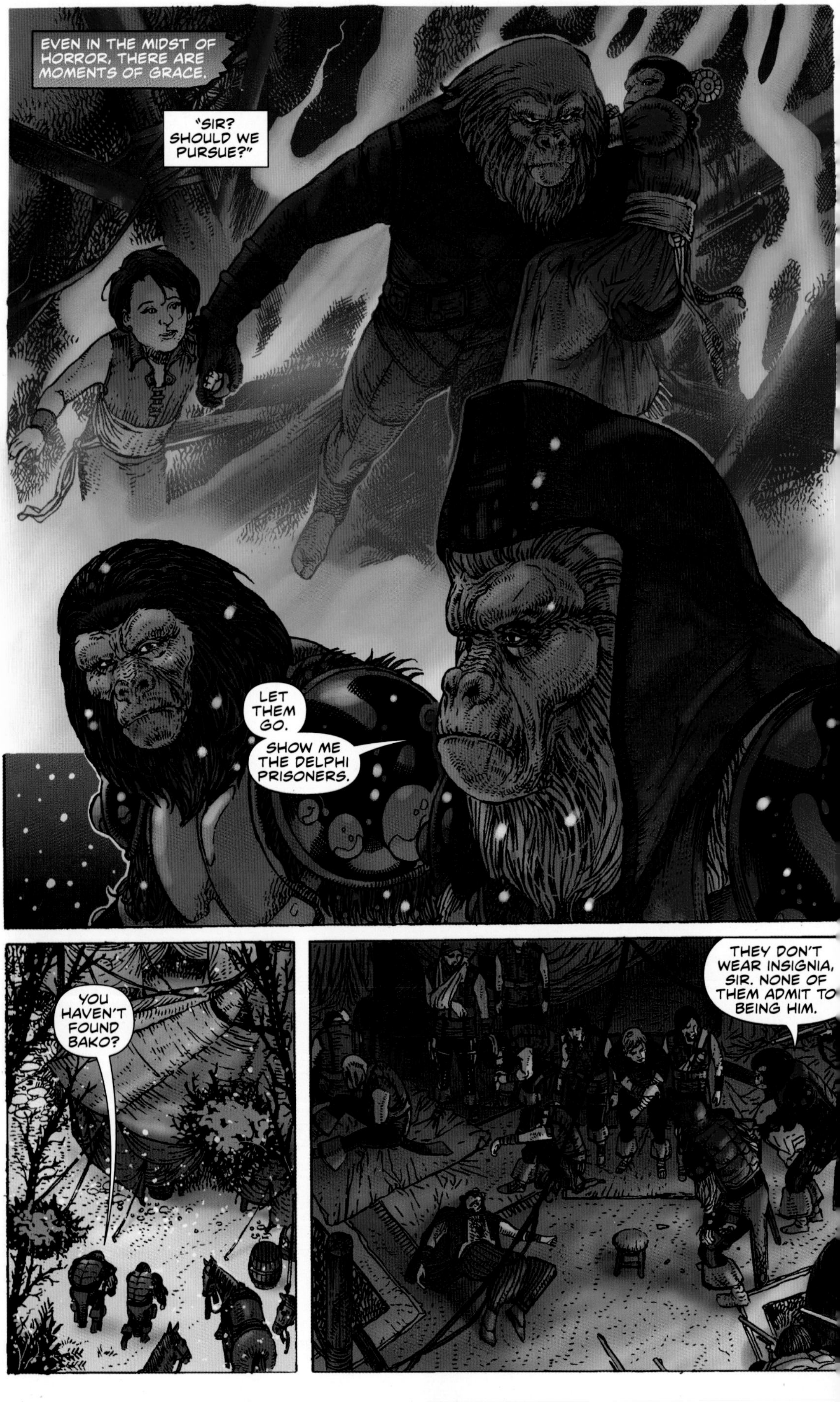
EVEN IN THE MIDST OF HORROR, THERE ARE MOMENTS OF GRACE.
"SIR? SHOULD WE PURSUE?"
LET THEM GO.
SHOW ME THE DELPHI PRISONERS.
YOU HAVEN'T FOUND BAKO?
THEY DON'T WEAR INSIGNIA, SIR. NONE OF THEM ADMIT TO BEING HIM.

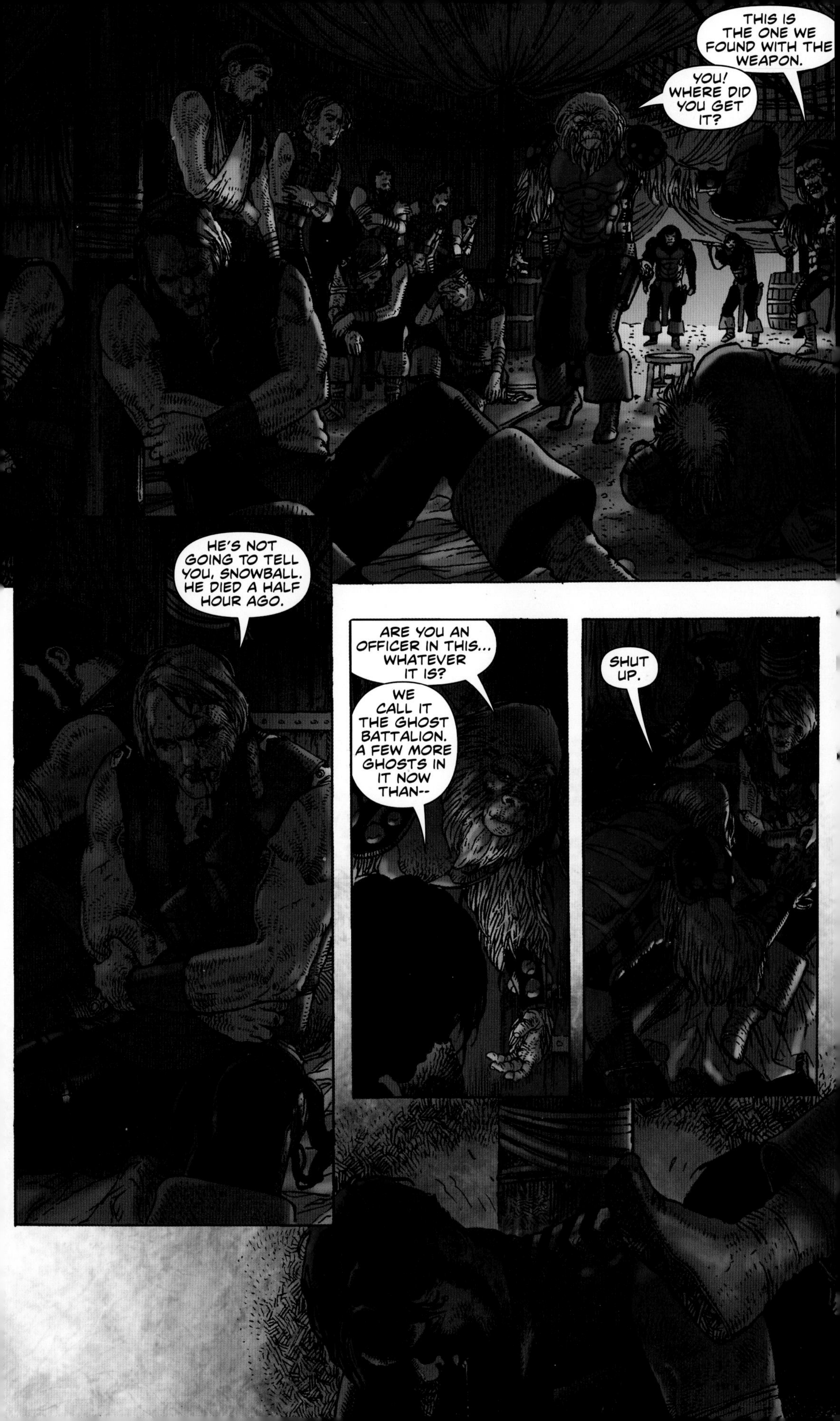
THIS IS THE ONE WE FOUND WITH THE WEAPON.
YOU! WHERE DID YOU GET IT?
HE'S NOT GOING TO TELL YOU, SNOWBALL. HE DIED A HALF HOUR AGO.
ARE YOU AN OFFICER IN THIS... WHATEVER IT IS?
WE CALL IT THE GHOST BATTALION. A FEW MORE GHOSTS IN IT NOW THAN--
SHUT UP.

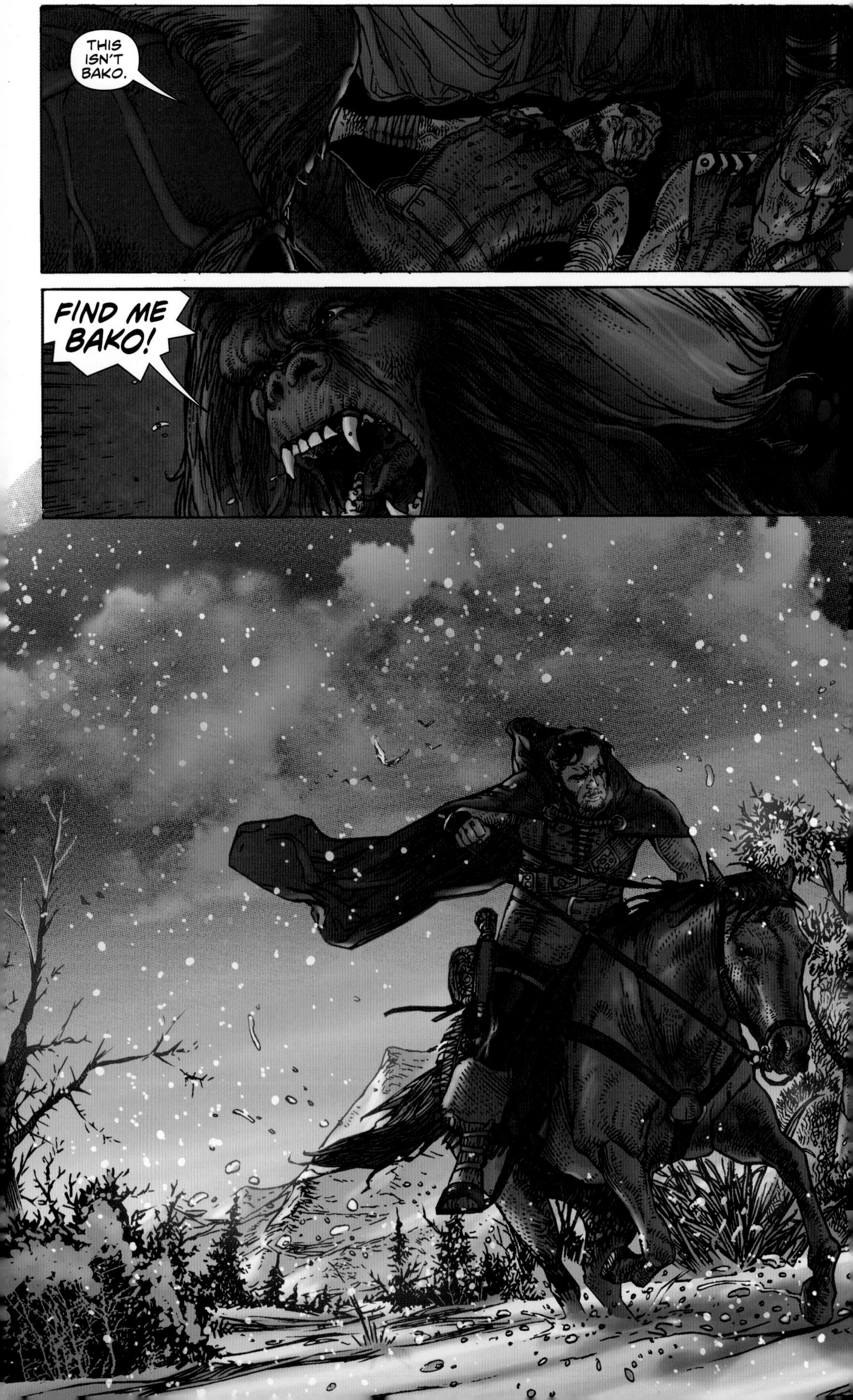
THIS ISN'T BAKO.
FIND ME BAKO!

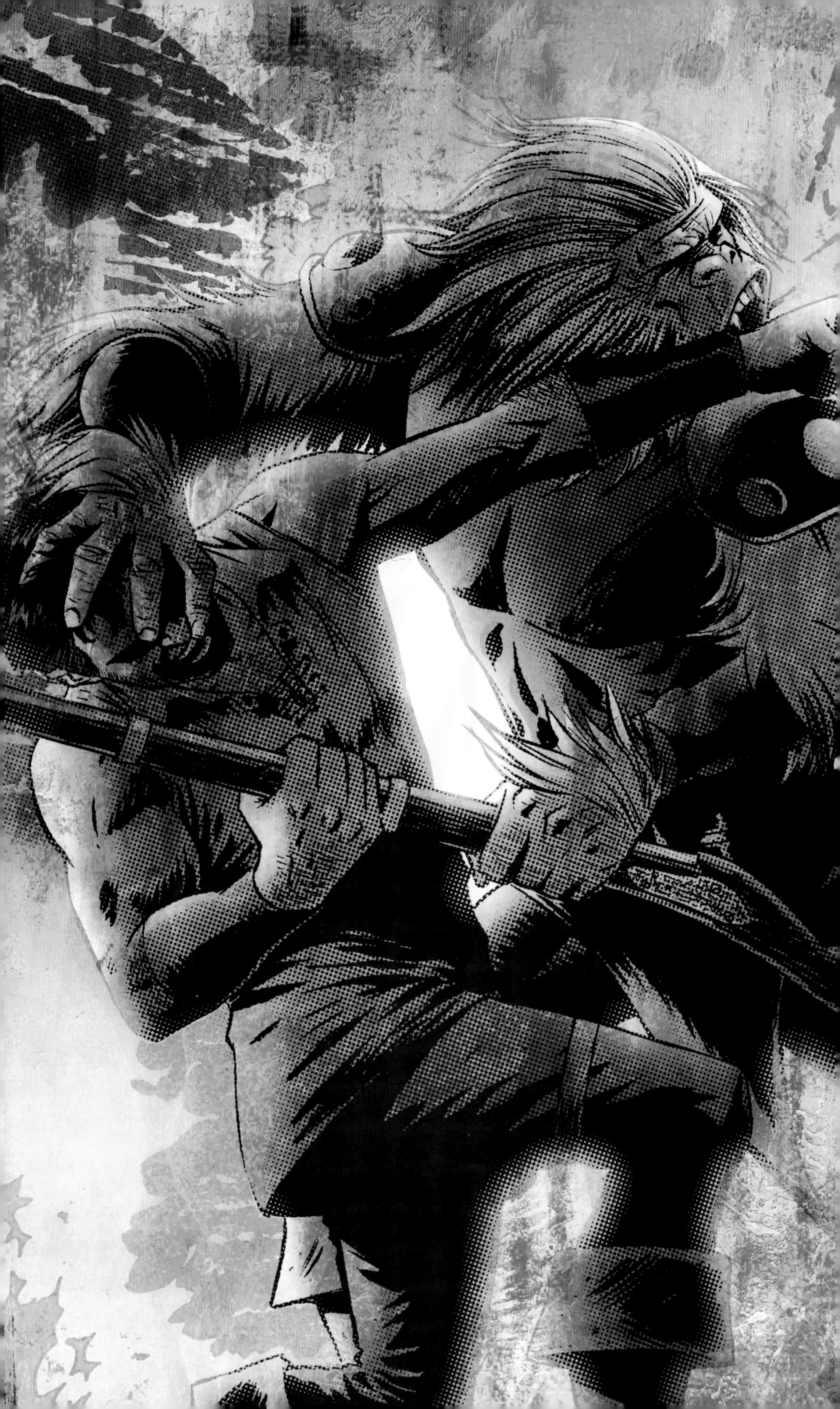

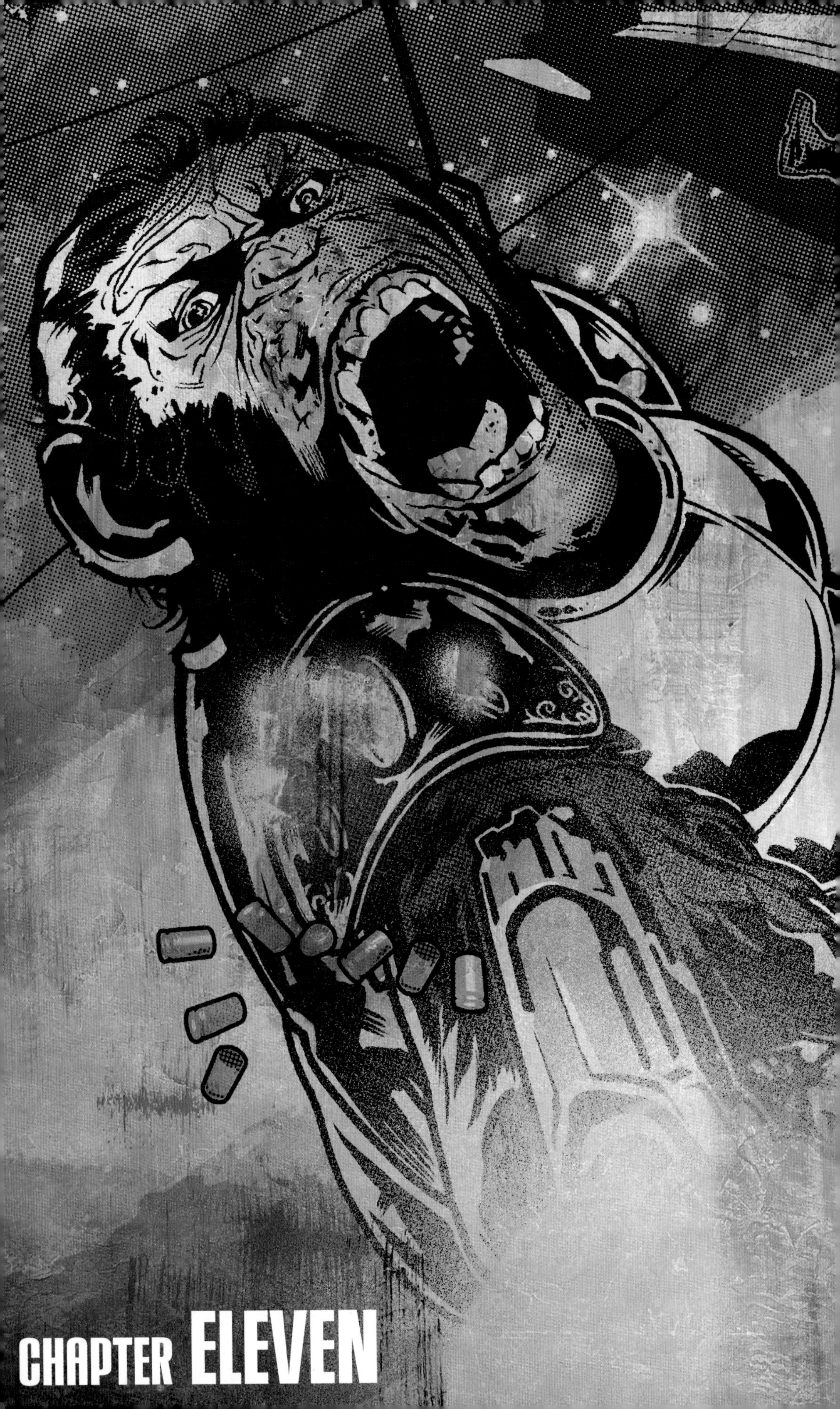

CHAPTER ELEVEN

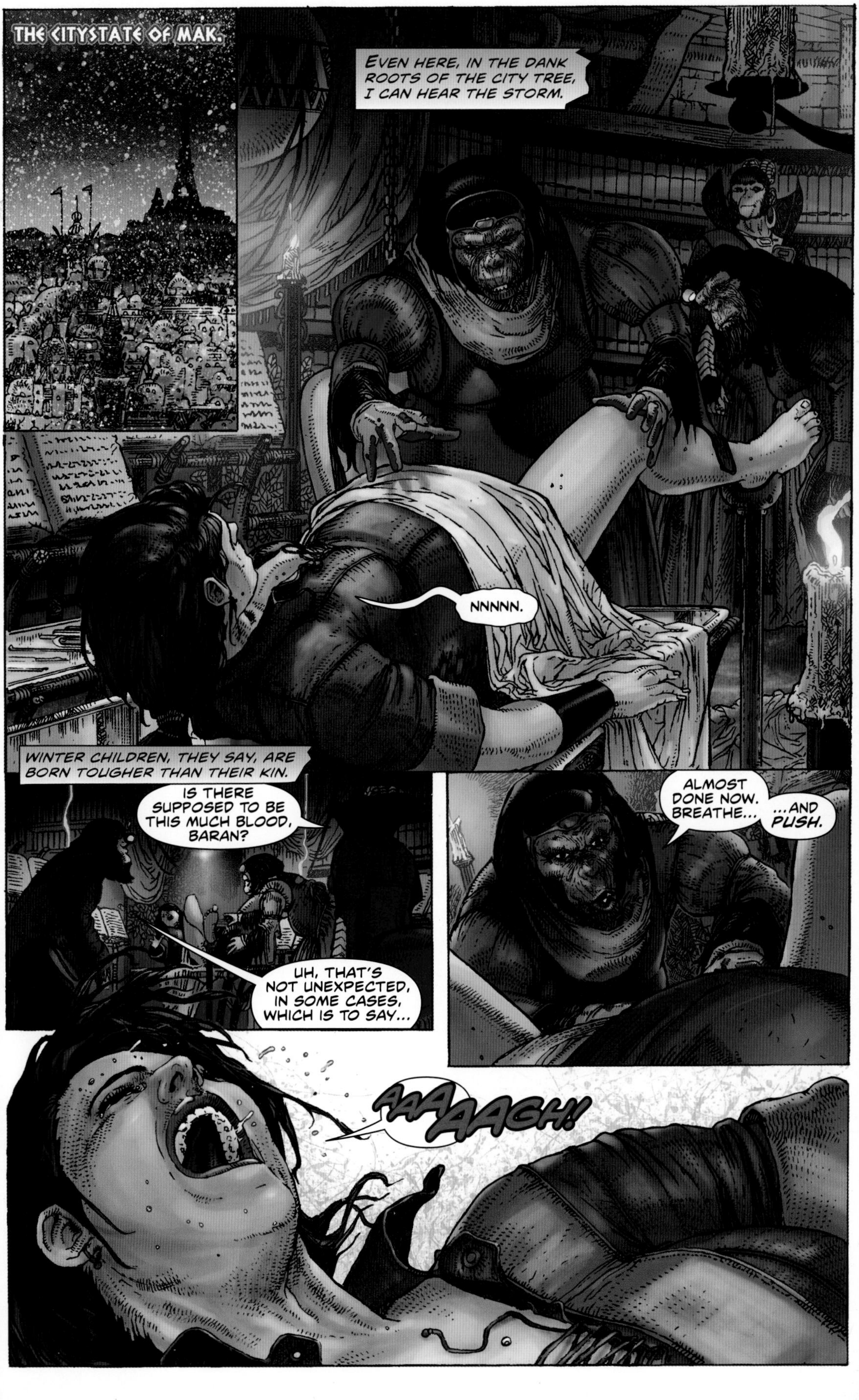
THE CITYSTATE OF MAK.
EVEN HERE, IN THE DANK ROOTS OF THE CITY TREE, I CAN HEAR THE STORM.
NNNNN.
WINTER CHILDREN, THEY SAY, ARE BORN TOUGHER THAN THEIR KIN.
IS THERE SUPPOSED TO BE THIS MUCH BLOOD, BARAN?
UH, THAT'S NOT UNEXPECTED, IN SOME CASES, WHICH IS TO SAY...
ALMOST DONE NOW. BREATHE...
...AND PUSH.
AAAAAAGH!

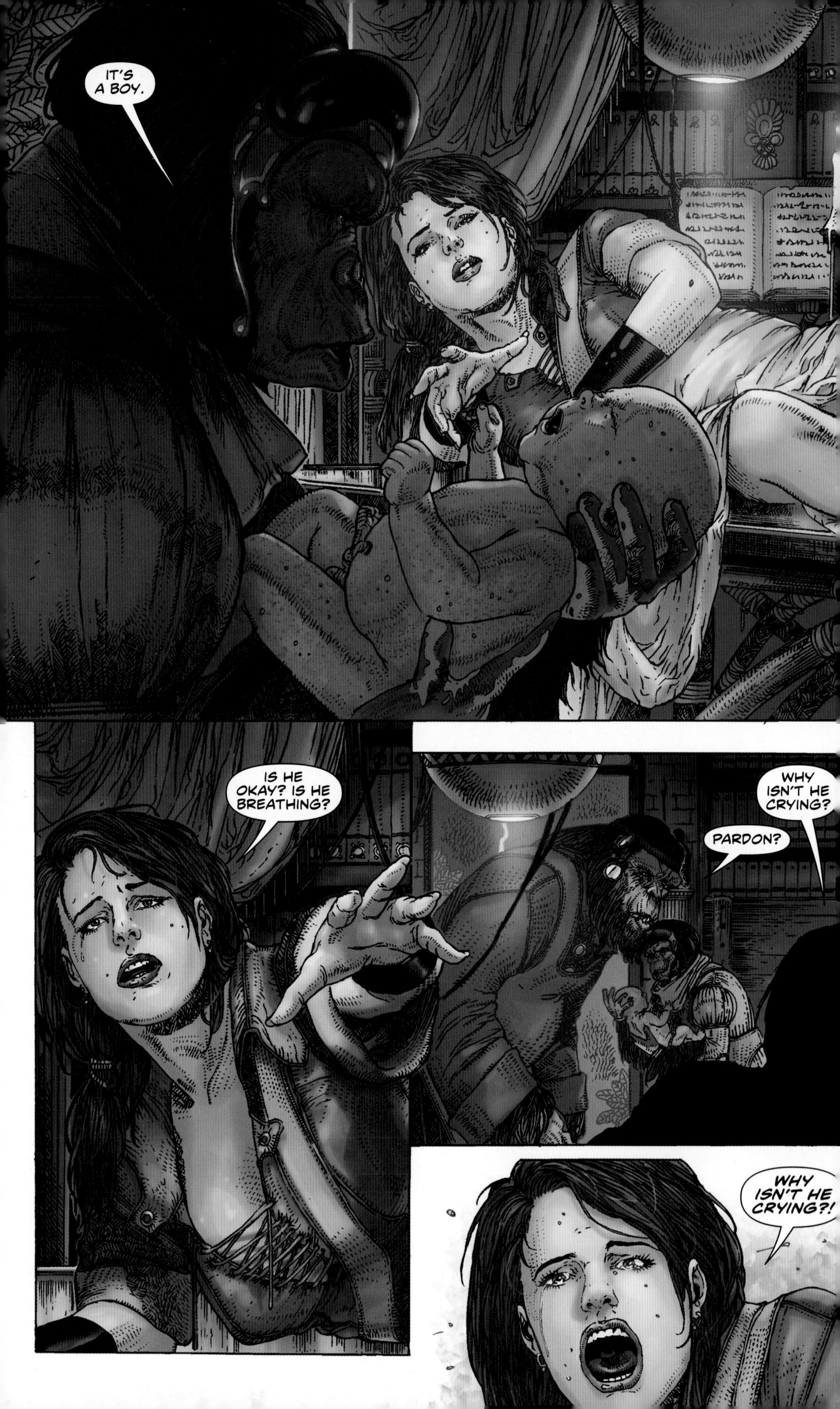
IT'S A BOY.
IS HE OKAY? IS HE BREATHING?
WHY ISN'T HE CRYING?
PARDON?
WHY ISN'T HE CRYING?!

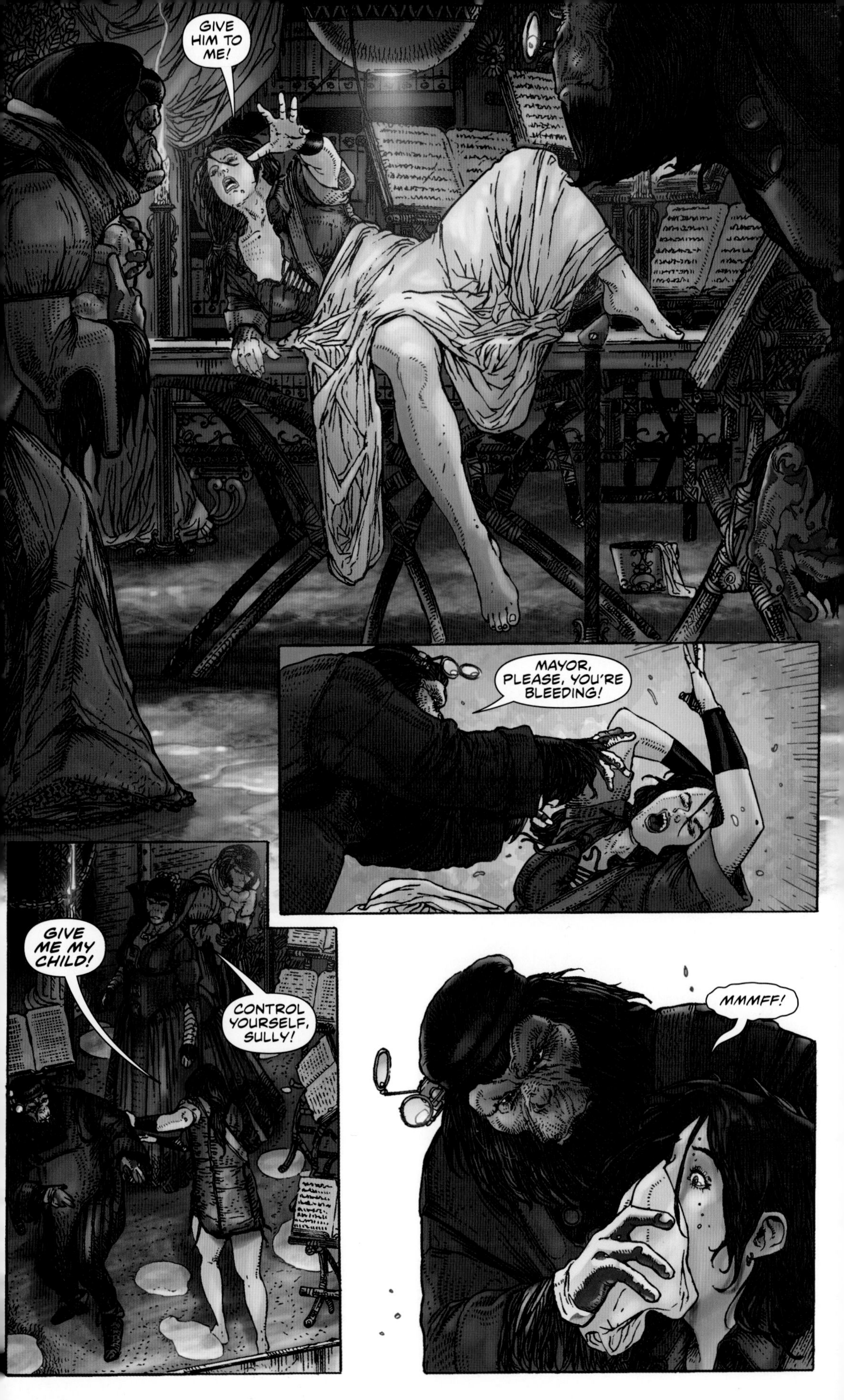
GIVE HIM TO ME!
MAYOR, PLEASE, YOU'RE BLEEDING!
GIVE ME MY CHILD!
CONTROL YOURSELF, SULLY!
MMMFF!

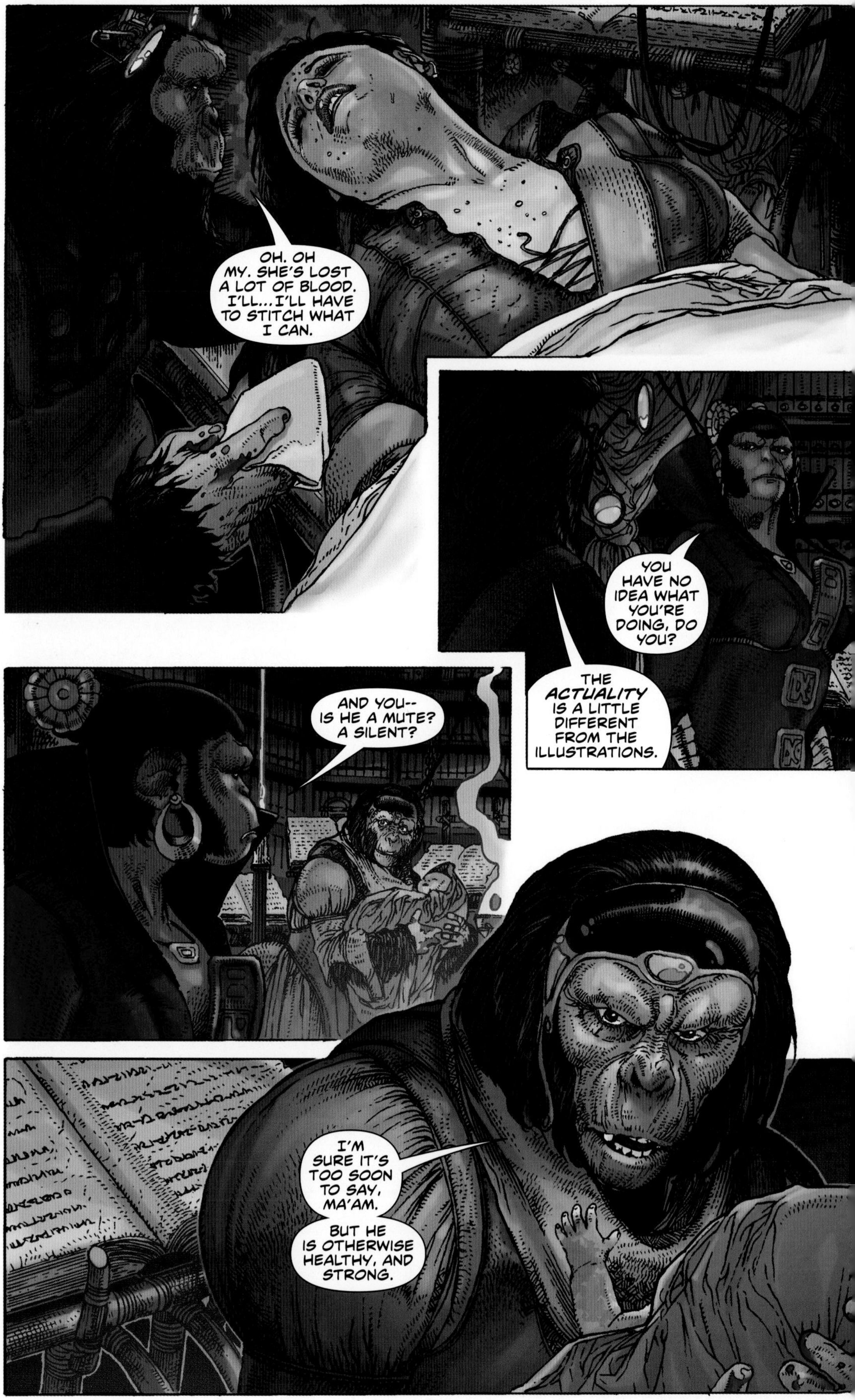
OH. OH MY. SHE'S LOST A LOT OF BLOOD. I'LL...I'LL HAVE TO STITCH WHAT I CAN.
YOU HAVE NO IDEA WHAT YOU'RE DOING, DO YOU?
THE *ACTUALITY* IS A LITTLE DIFFERENT FROM THE ILLUSTRATIONS.
AND YOU-- IS HE A MUTE? A SILENT?
I'M SURE IT'S TOO SOON TO SAY, MA'AM.
BUT HE IS OTHERWISE HEALTHY, AND STRONG.

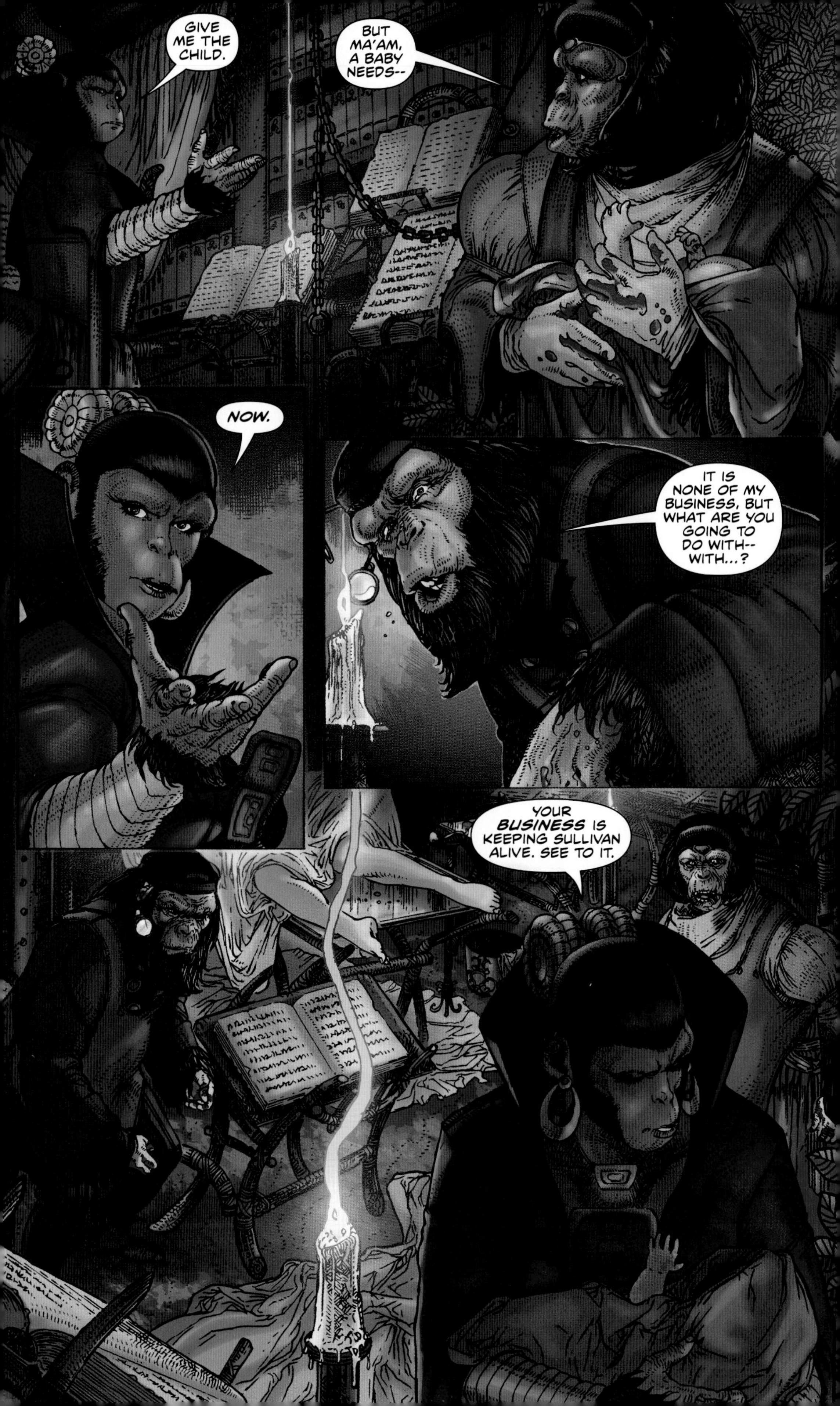
GIVE ME THE CHILD.
BUT MA'AM, A BABY NEEDS--
NOW.
IT IS NONE OF MY BUSINESS, BUT WHAT ARE YOU GOING TO DO WITH-- WITH...?
YOUR *BUSINESS* IS KEEPING SULLIVAN ALIVE. SEE TO IT.

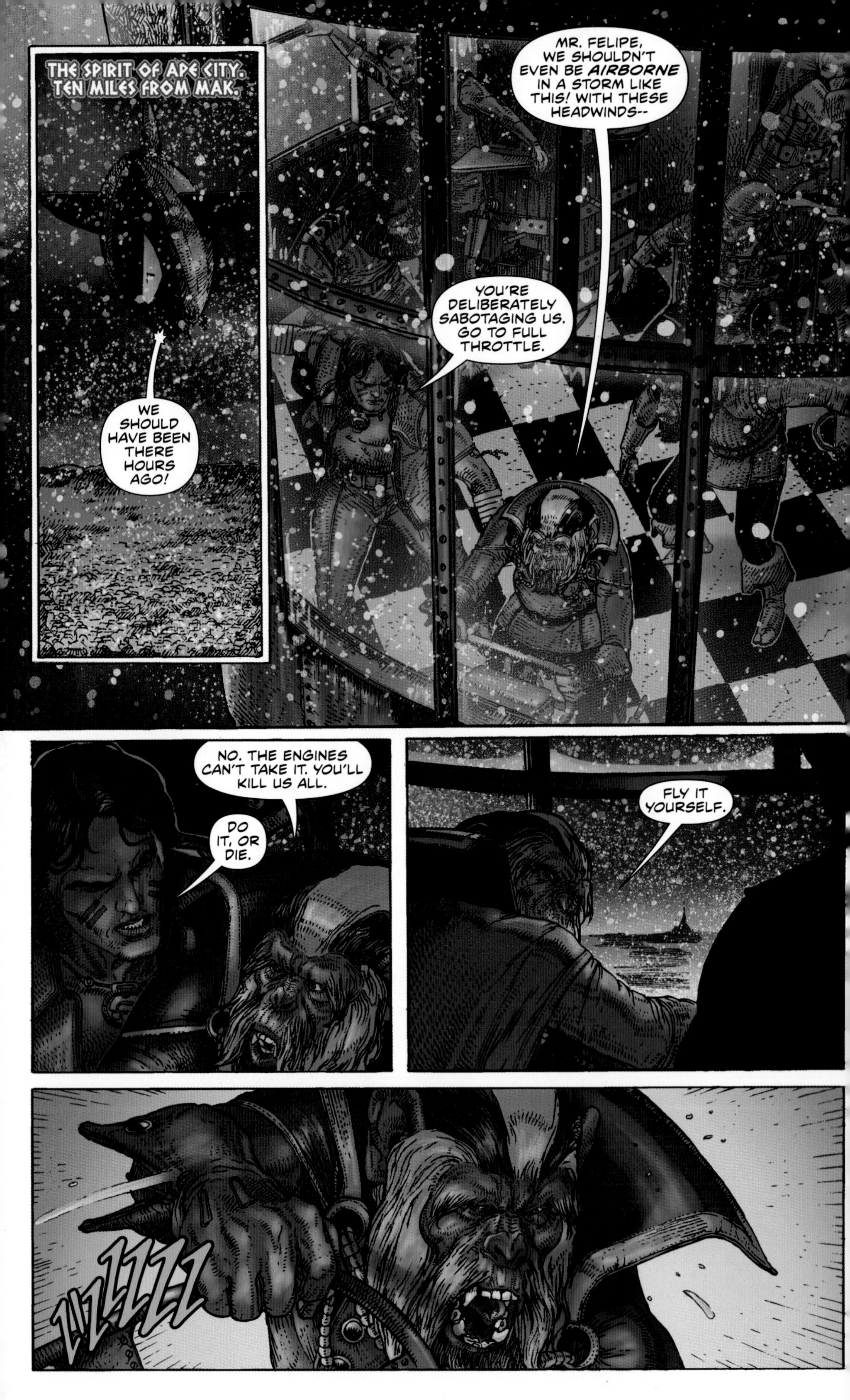
THE SPIRIT OF APE CITY. TEN MILES FROM MAK.
WE SHOULD HAVE BEEN THERE HOURS AGO!
YOU'RE DELIBERATELY SABOTAGING US. GO TO FULL THROTTLE.
MR. FELIPE, WE SHOULDN'T EVEN BE AIRBORNE IN A STORM LIKE THIS! WITH THESE HEADWINDS--
NO. THE ENGINES CAN'T TAKE IT. YOU'LL KILL US ALL.
DO IT, OR DIE.
FLY IT YOURSELF.
ZZZZZZZ

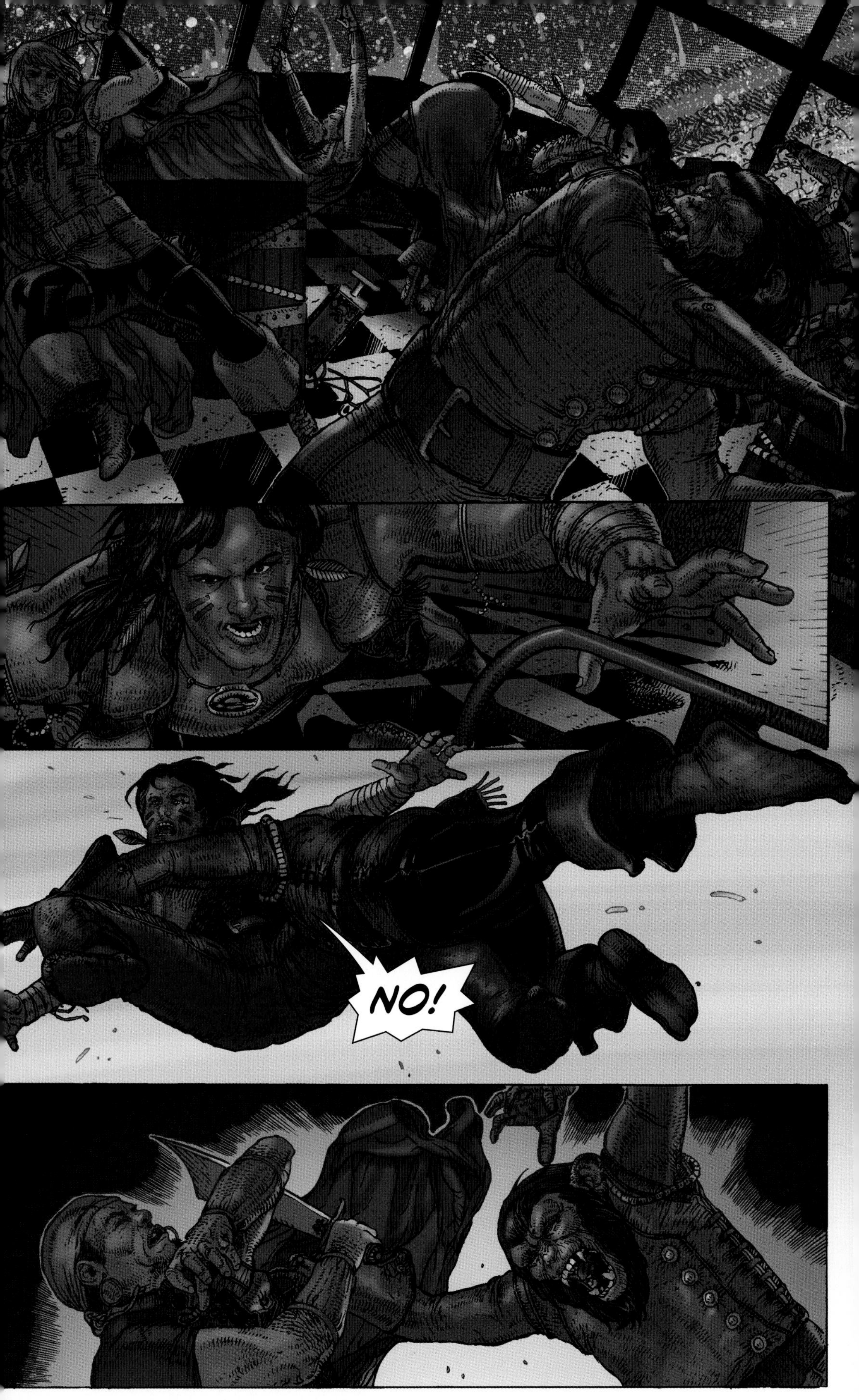
NO!

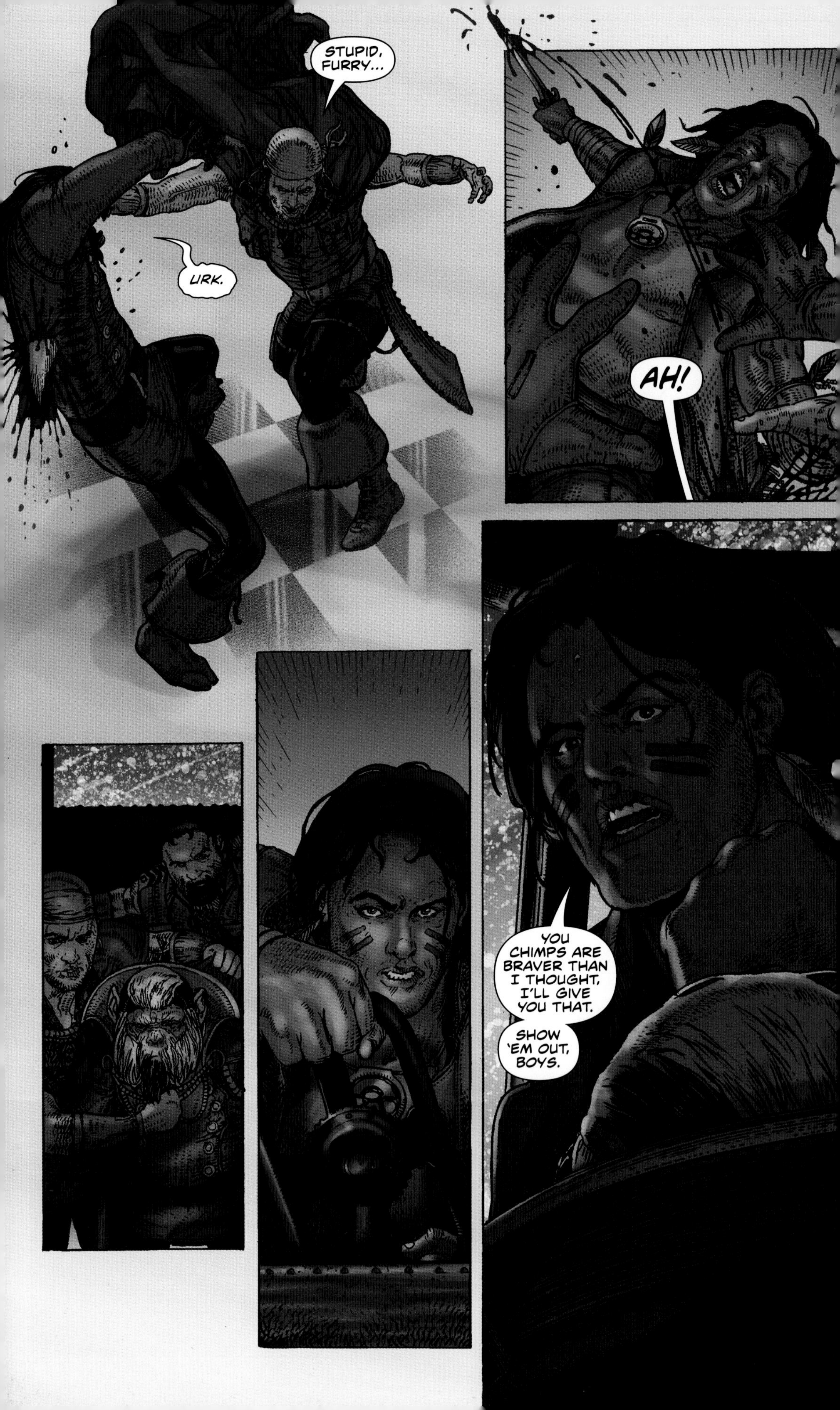
STUPID, FURRY...
URK.
AH!
YOU CHIMPS ARE BRAVER THAN I THOUGHT, I'LL GIVE YOU THAT.
SHOW 'EM OUT, BOYS.

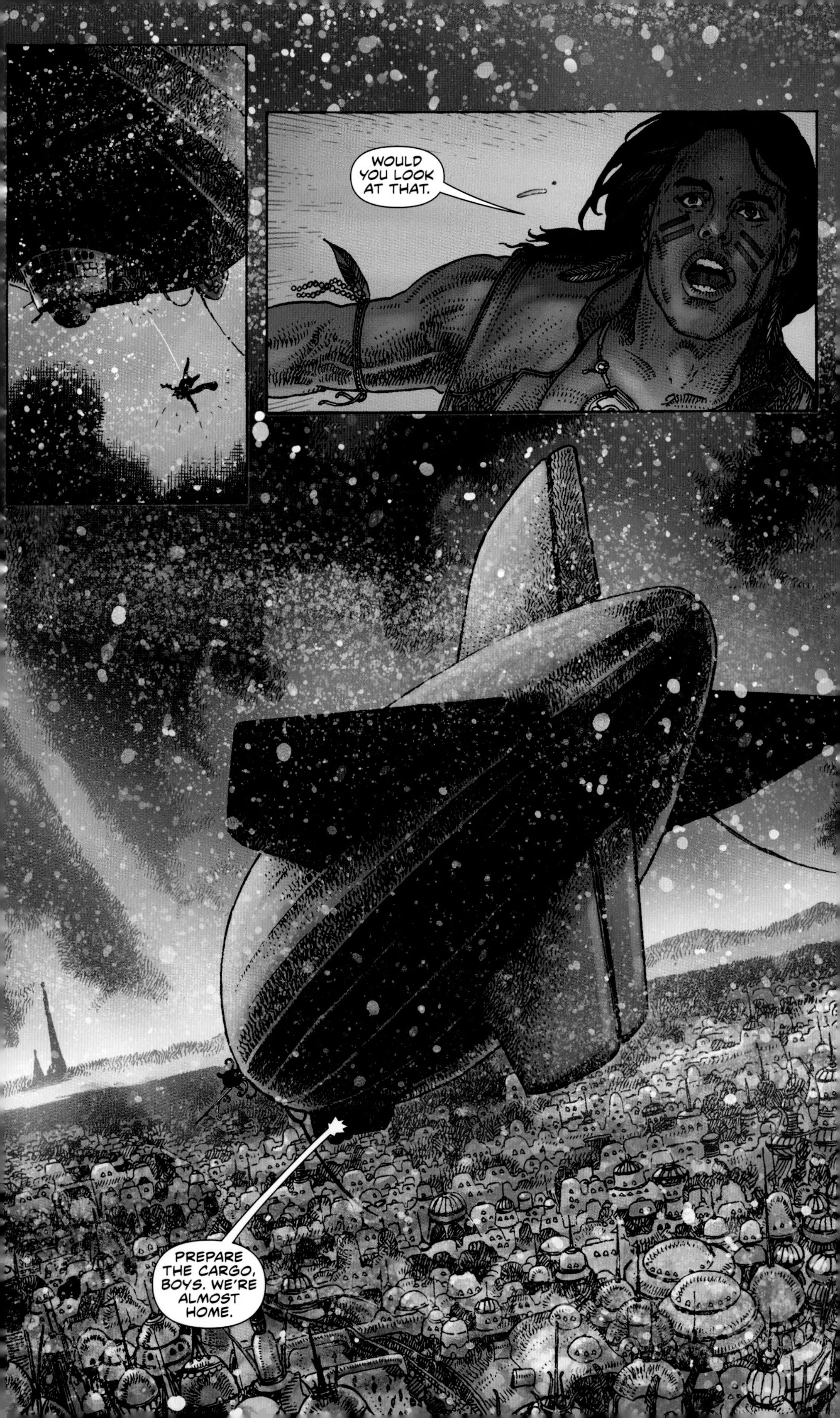
WOULD YOU LOOK AT THAT.
PREPARE THE CARGO, BOYS. WE'RE ALMOST HOME.

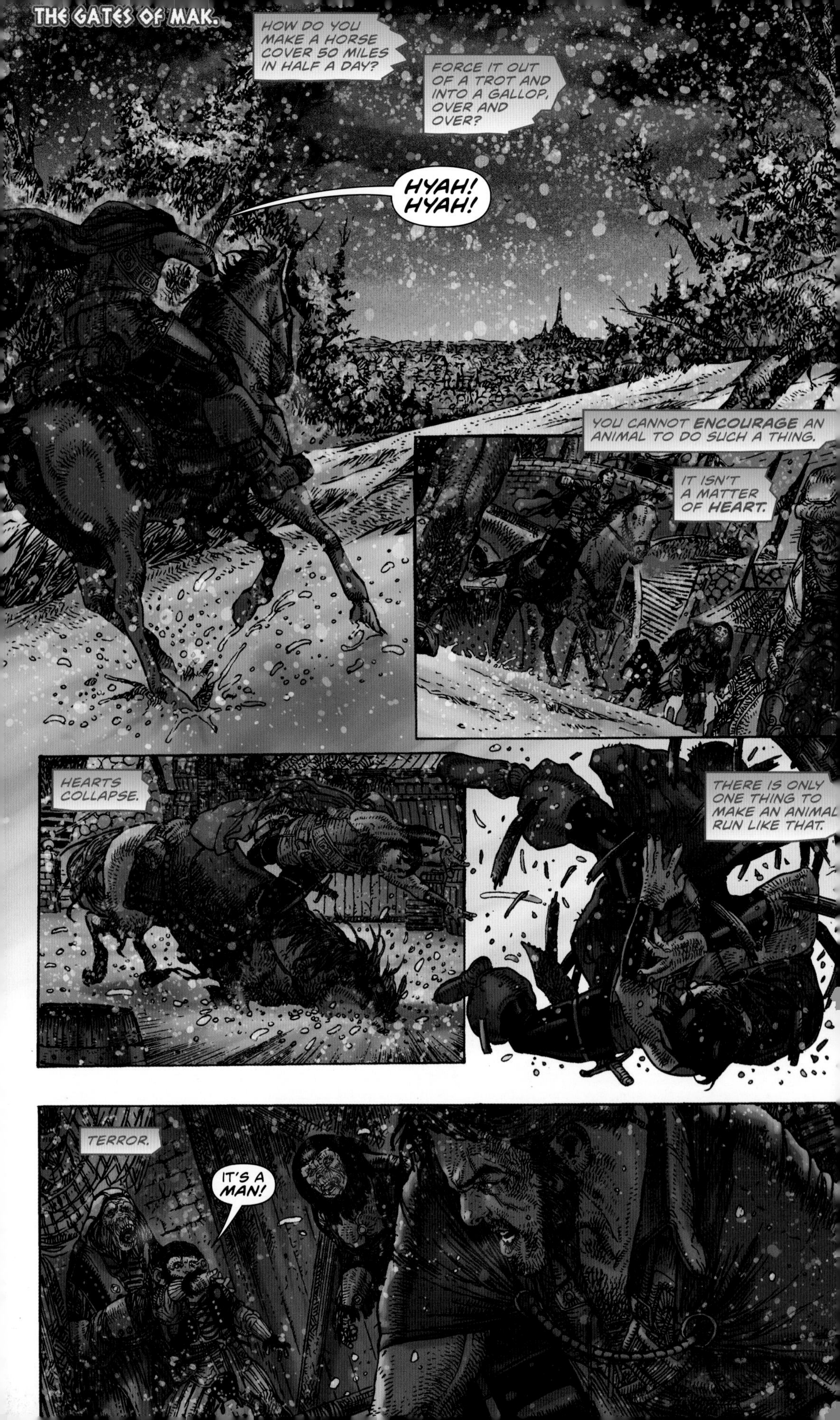
THE GATES OF MAK.
HOW DO YOU MAKE A HORSE COVER 50 MILES IN HALF A DAY?
FORCE IT OUT OF A TROT AND INTO A GALLOP, OVER AND OVER?
HYAH! HYAH!
YOU CANNOT ENCOURAGE AN ANIMAL TO DO SUCH A THING.
IT ISN'T A MATTER OF HEART.
HEARTS COLLAPSE.
THERE IS ONLY ONE THING TO MAKE AN ANIMAL RUN LIKE THAT.
TERROR.
IT'S A MAN!

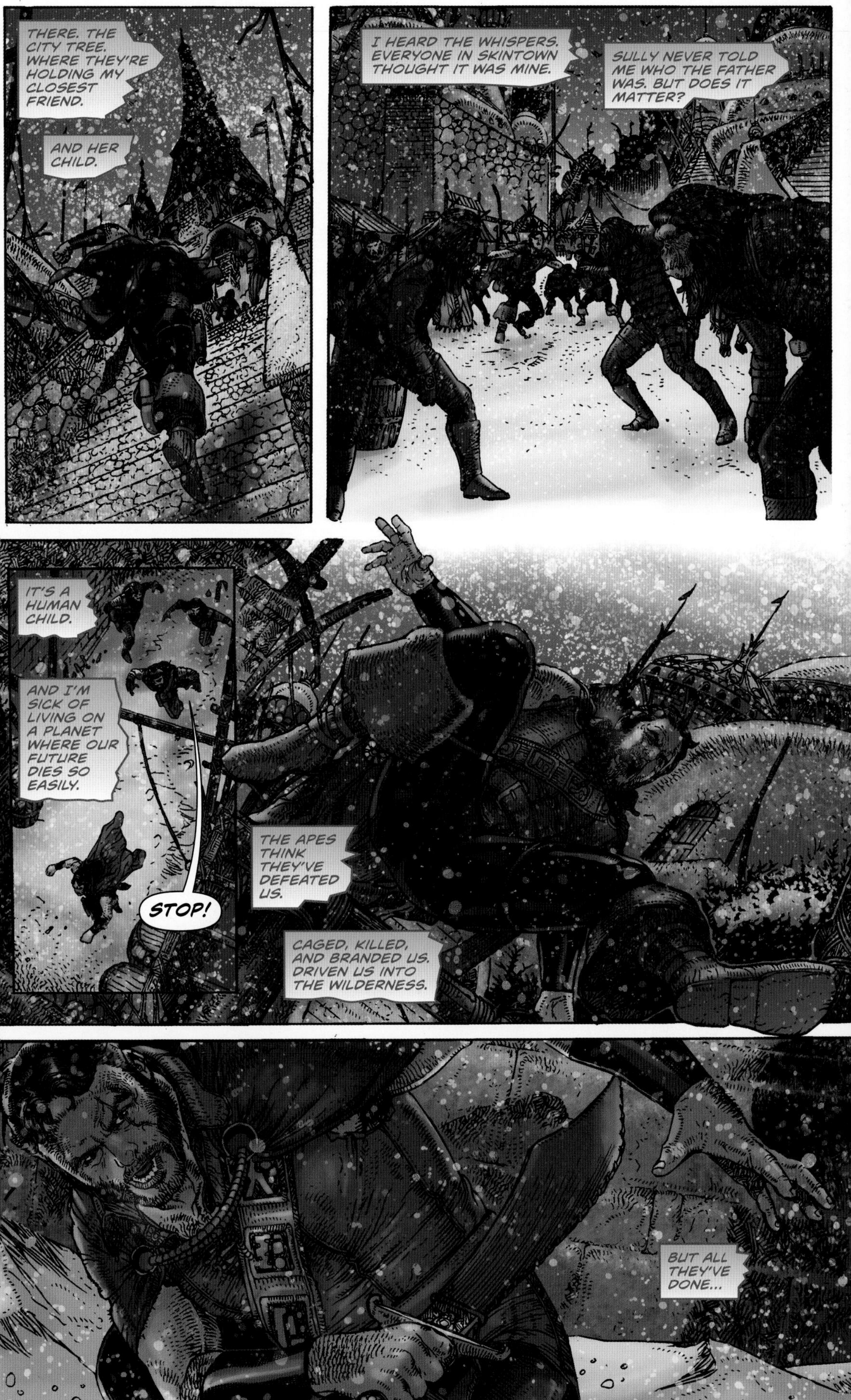
THERE. THE CITY TREE. WHERE THEY'RE HOLDING MY CLOSEST FRIEND.
AND HER CHILD.
I HEARD THE WHISPERS. EVERYONE IN SKINTOWN THOUGHT IT WAS MINE.
SULLY NEVER TOLD ME WHO THE FATHER WAS. BUT DOES IT MATTER?
IT'S A HUMAN CHILD.
AND I'M SICK OF LIVING ON A PLANET WHERE OUR FUTURE DIES SO EASILY.
STOP!
THE APES THINK THEY'VE DEFEATED US.
CAGED, KILLED, AND BRANDED US. DRIVEN US INTO THE WILDERNESS.
BUT ALL THEY'VE DONE...

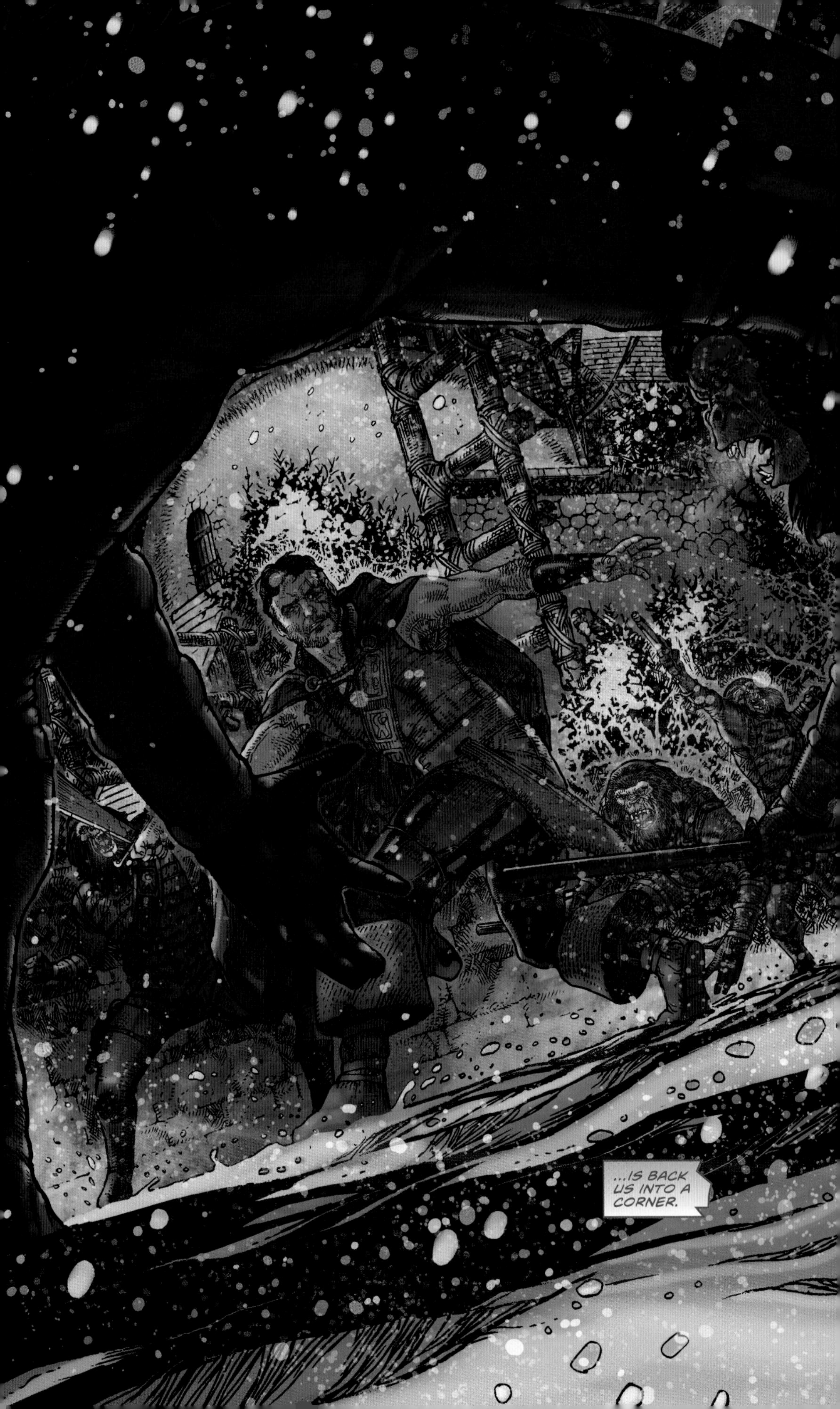
...IS BACK US INTO A CORNER.

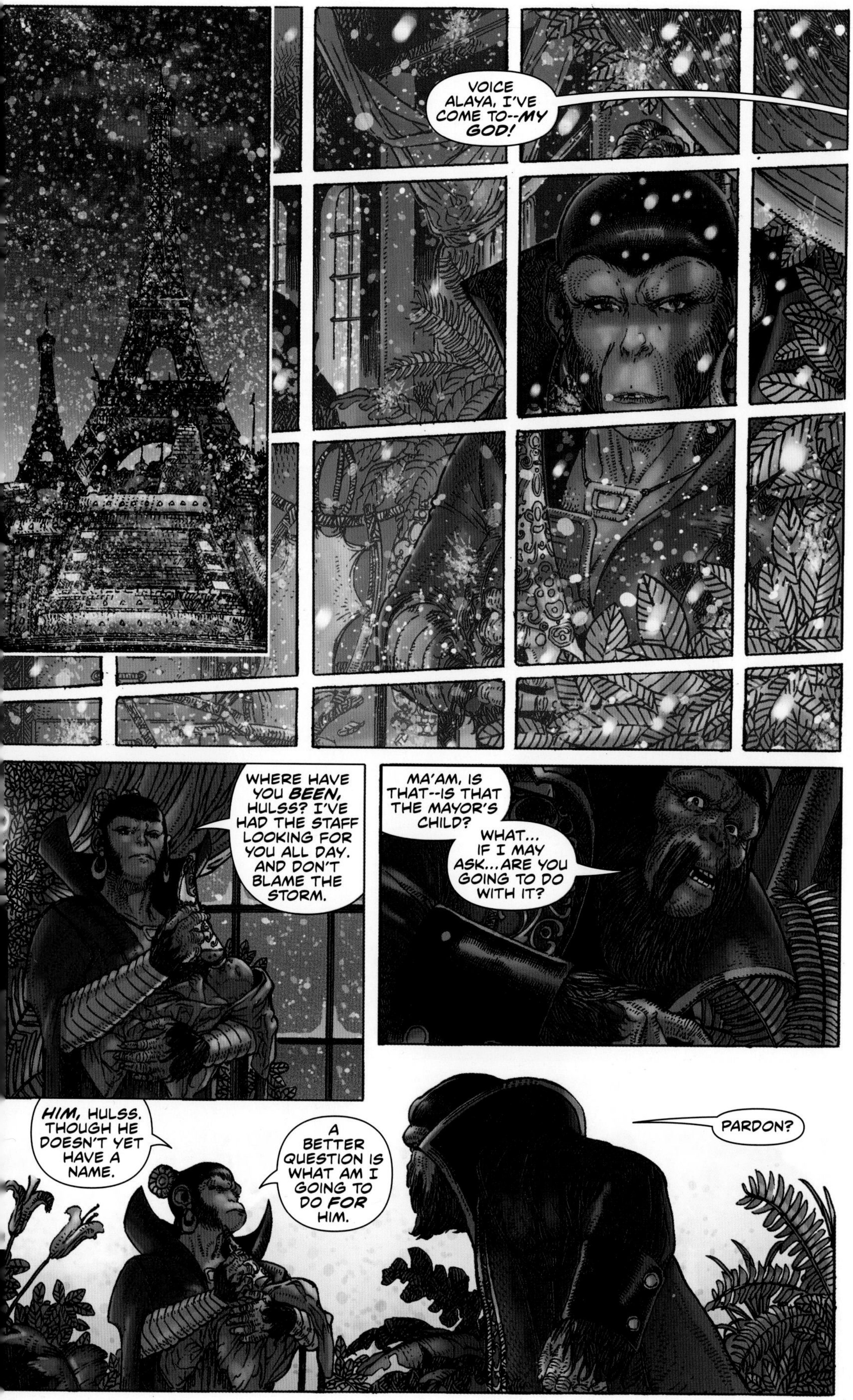
VOICE ALAYA, I'VE COME TO--*MY GOD!*
WHERE HAVE YOU *BEEN,* HULSS? I'VE HAD THE STAFF LOOKING FOR YOU ALL DAY. AND DON'T BLAME THE STORM.
MA'AM, IS THAT--IS THAT THE MAYOR'S CHILD?
WHAT... IF I MAY ASK...ARE YOU GOING TO DO WITH IT?
HIM, HULSS. THOUGH HE DOESN'T YET HAVE A NAME.
A BETTER QUESTION IS WHAT AM I GOING TO DO *FOR* HIM.
PARDON?

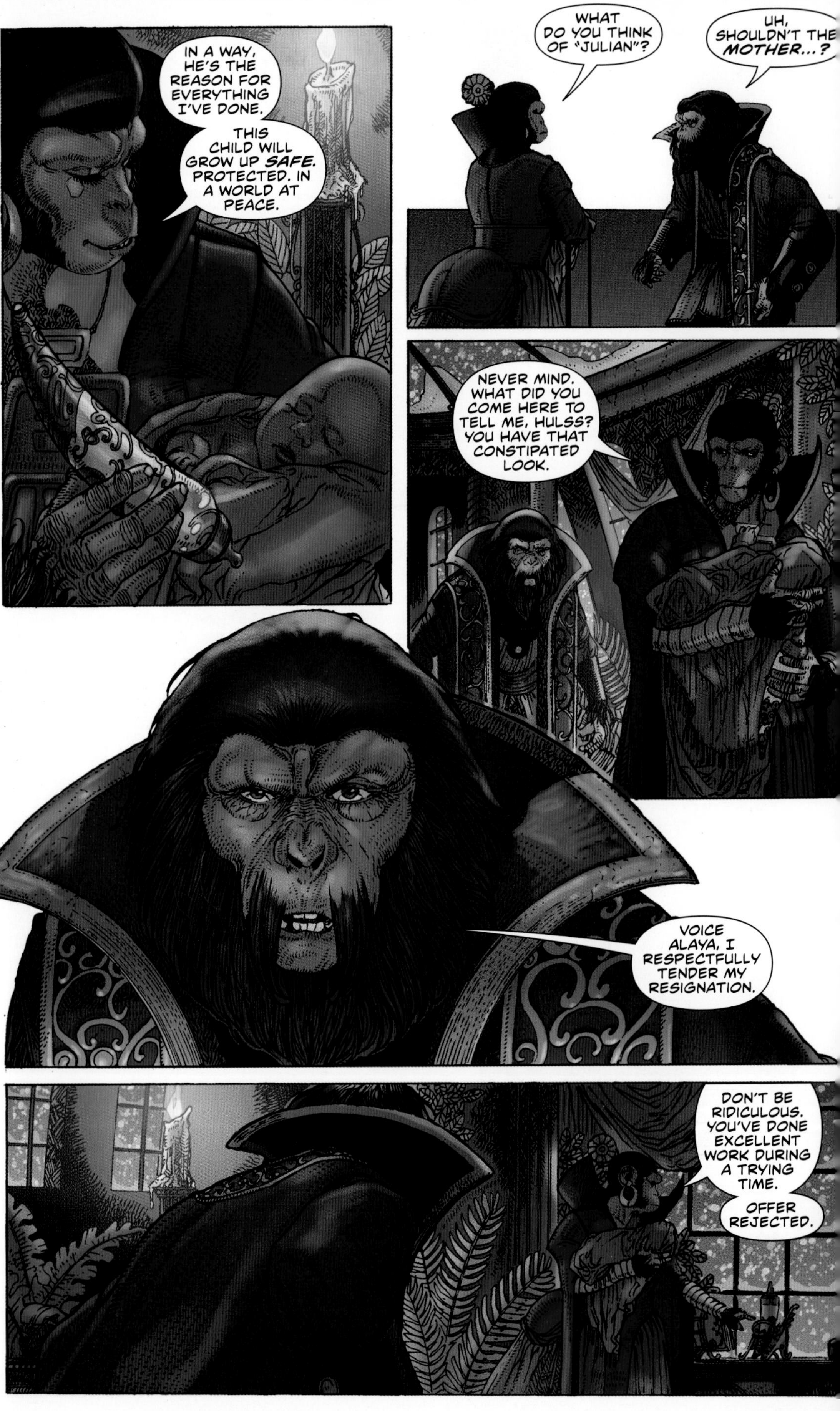
IN A WAY, HE'S THE REASON FOR EVERYTHING I'VE DONE.
THIS CHILD WILL GROW UP *SAFE*. PROTECTED. IN A WORLD AT PEACE.
WHAT DO YOU THINK OF "JULIAN"?
UH, SHOULDN'T THE *MOTHER...?*
NEVER MIND. WHAT DID YOU COME HERE TO TELL ME, HULSS? YOU HAVE THAT CONSTIPATED LOOK.
VOICE ALAYA, I RESPECTFULLY TENDER MY RESIGNATION.
DON'T BE RIDICULOUS. YOU'VE DONE EXCELLENT WORK DURING A TRYING TIME.
OFFER REJECTED.

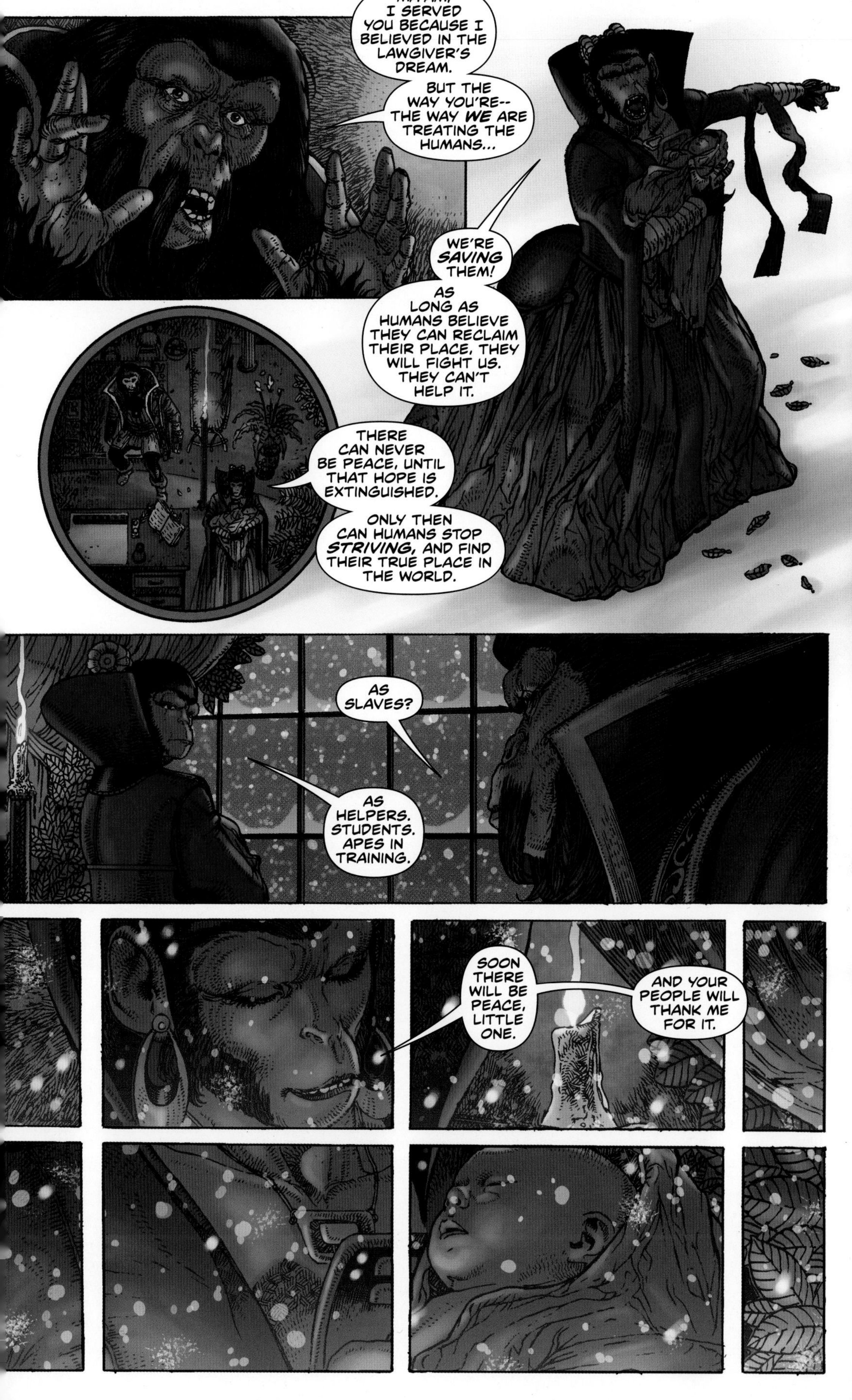
MA'AM, I SERVED YOU BECAUSE I BELIEVED IN THE LAWGIVER'S DREAM.
BUT THE WAY YOU'RE-- THE WAY WE ARE TREATING THE HUMANS...
WE'RE SAVING THEM!
AS LONG AS HUMANS BELIEVE THEY CAN RECLAIM THEIR PLACE, THEY WILL FIGHT US. THEY CAN'T HELP IT.
THERE CAN NEVER BE PEACE, UNTIL THAT HOPE IS EXTINGUISHED.
ONLY THEN CAN HUMANS STOP STRIVING, AND FIND THEIR TRUE PLACE IN THE WORLD.
AS SLAVES?
AS HELPERS. STUDENTS. APES IN TRAINING.
SOON THERE WILL BE PEACE, LITTLE ONE.
AND YOUR PEOPLE WILL THANK ME FOR IT.

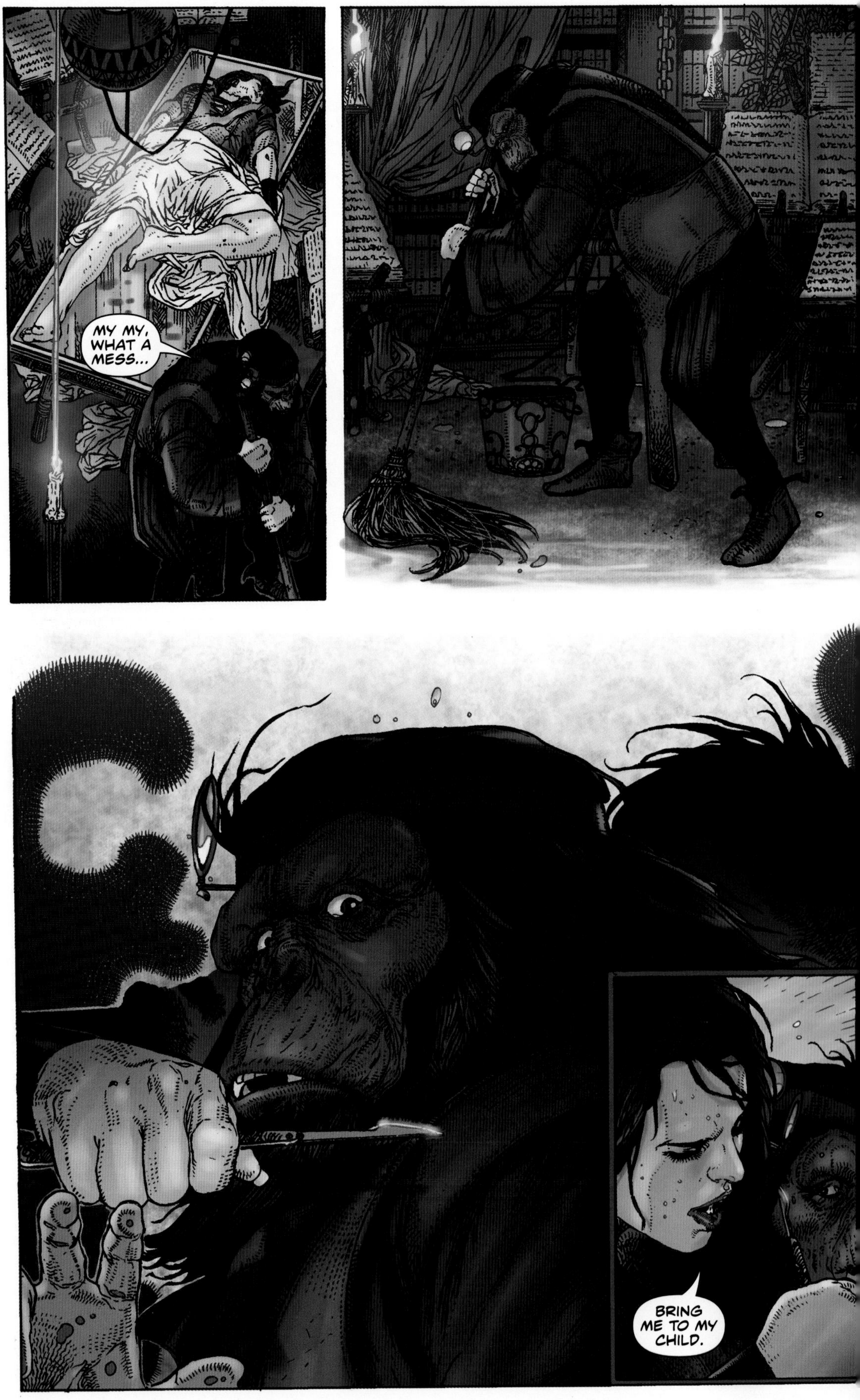
MY MY, WHAT A MESS...
BRING ME TO MY CHILD.

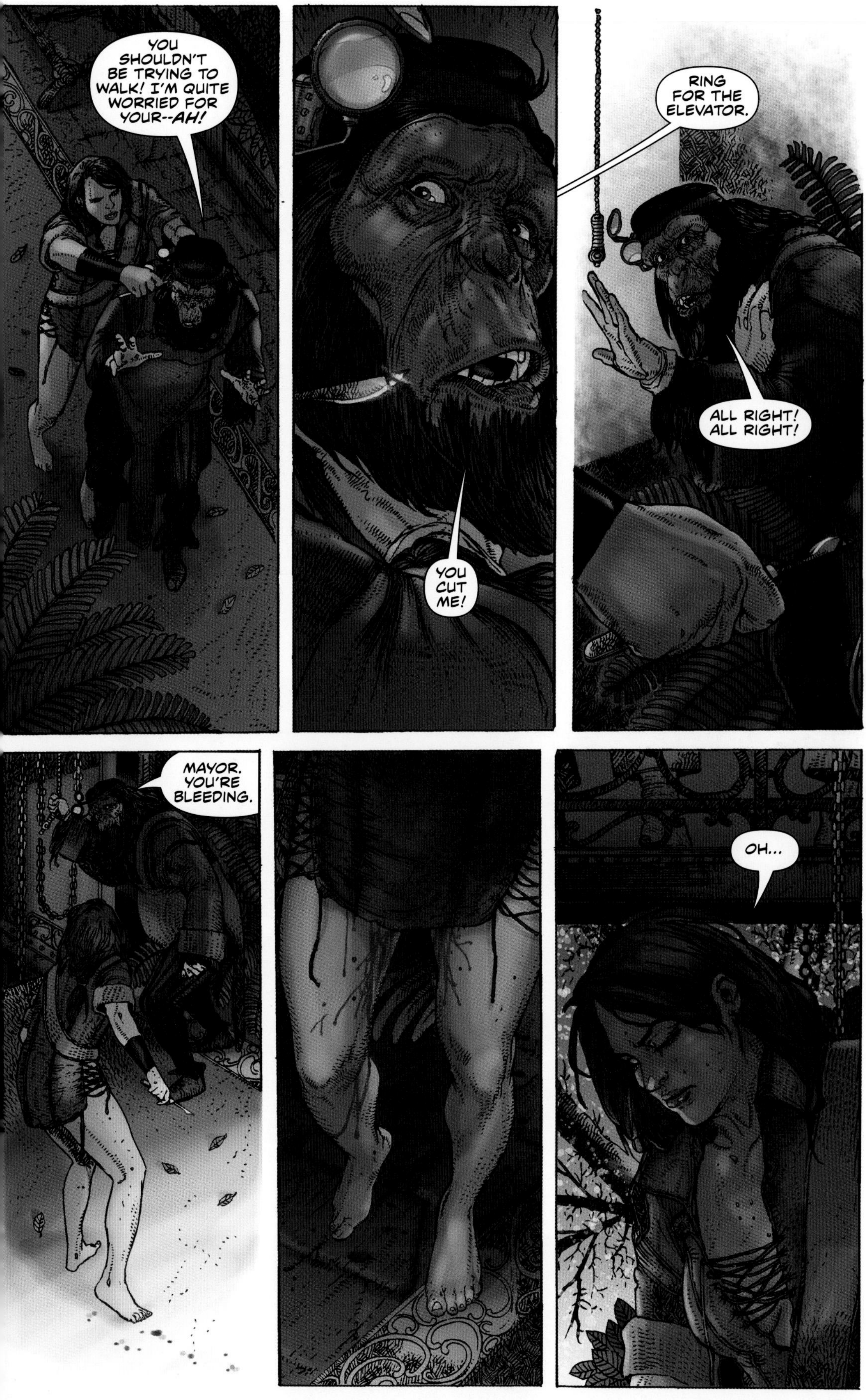
YOU SHOULDN'T BE TRYING TO WALK! I'M QUITE WORRIED FOR YOUR--AH!
YOU CUT ME!
RING FOR THE ELEVATOR.
ALL RIGHT! ALL RIGHT!
MAYOR. YOU'RE BLEEDING.
OH...

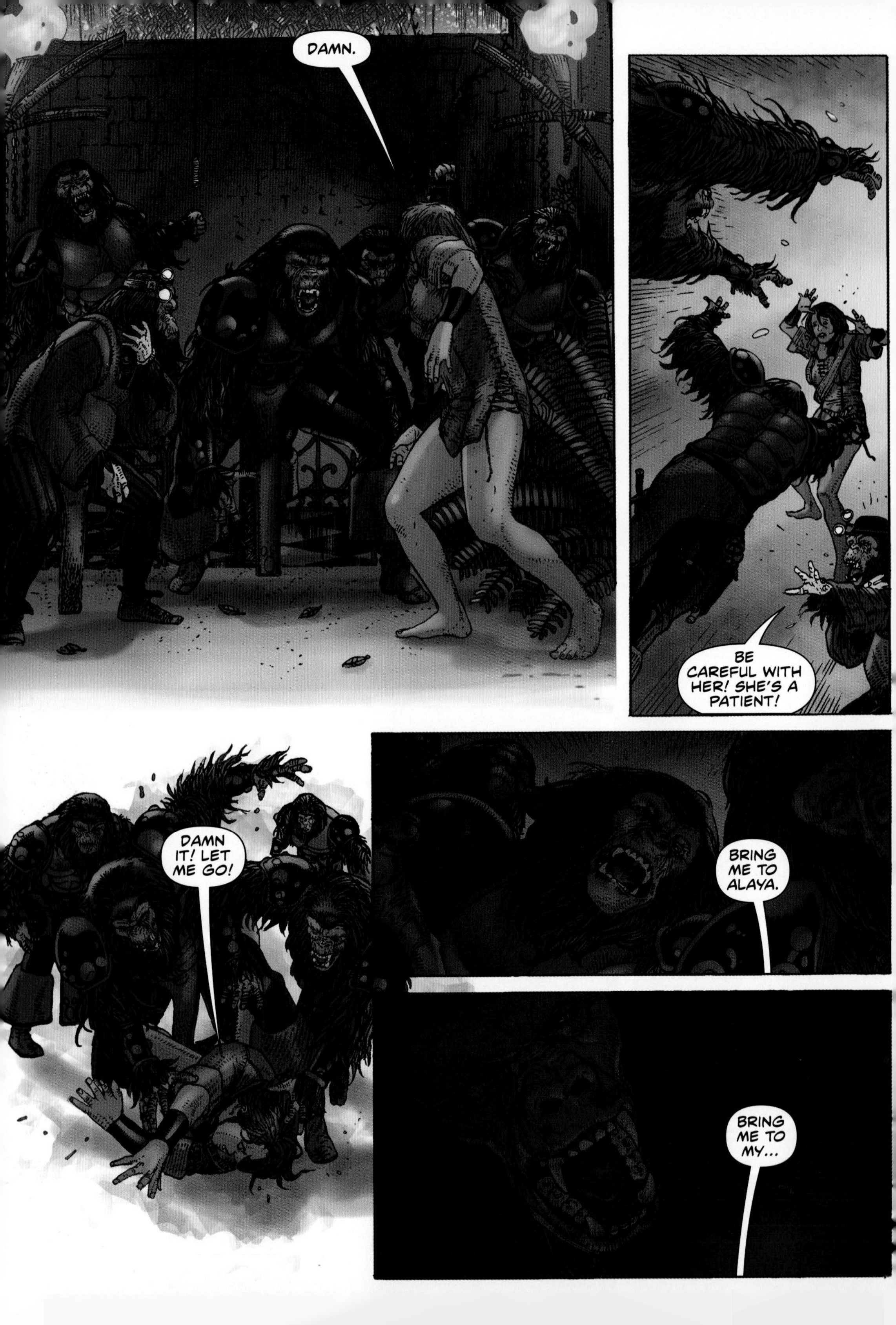
DAMN.
BE CAREFUL WITH HER! SHE'S A PATIENT!
DAMN IT! LET ME GO!
BRING ME TO ALAYA.
BRING ME TO MY...

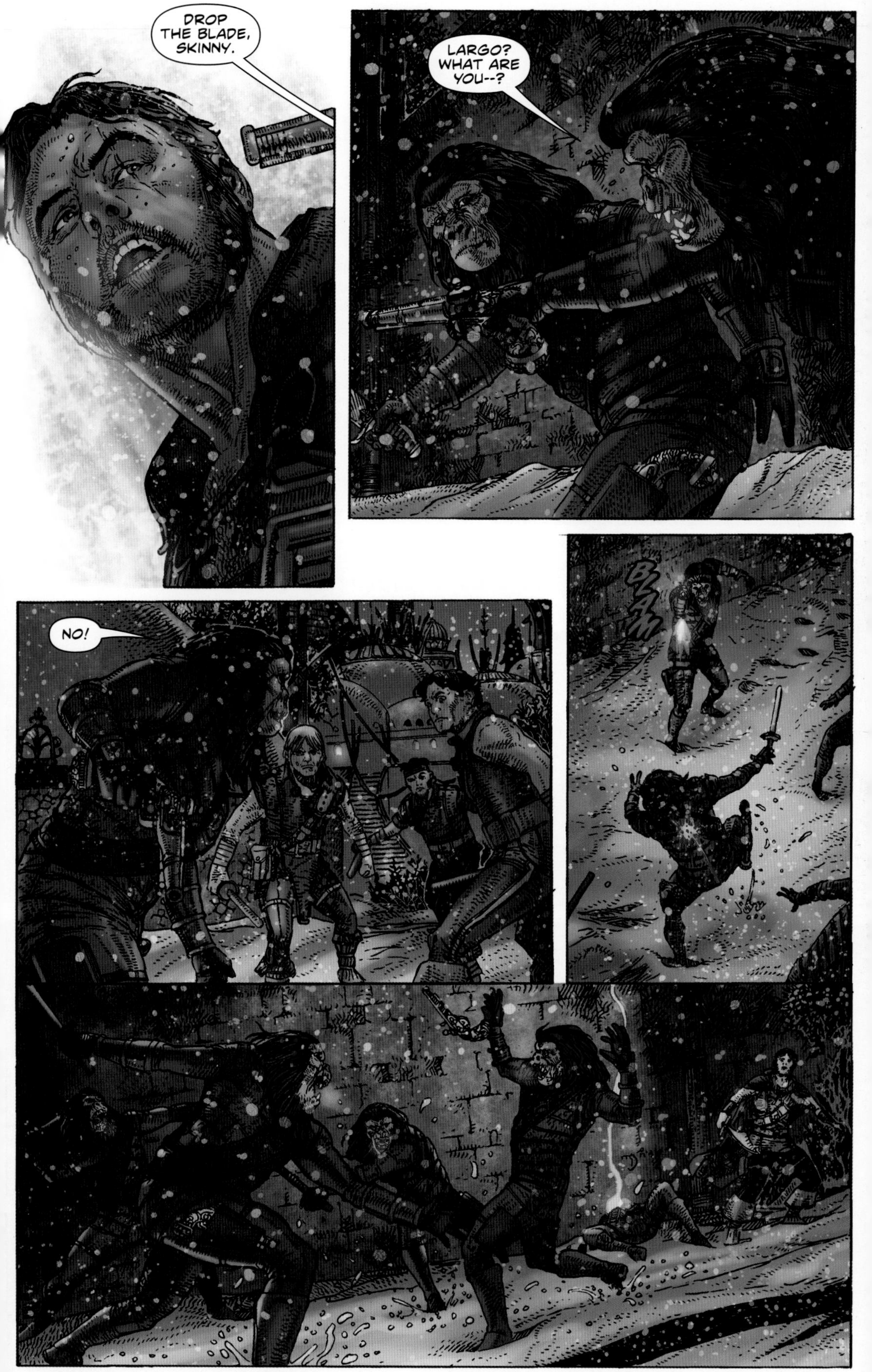
DROP THE BLADE, SKINNY.
LARGO? WHAT ARE YOU--?
BLAM
NO!

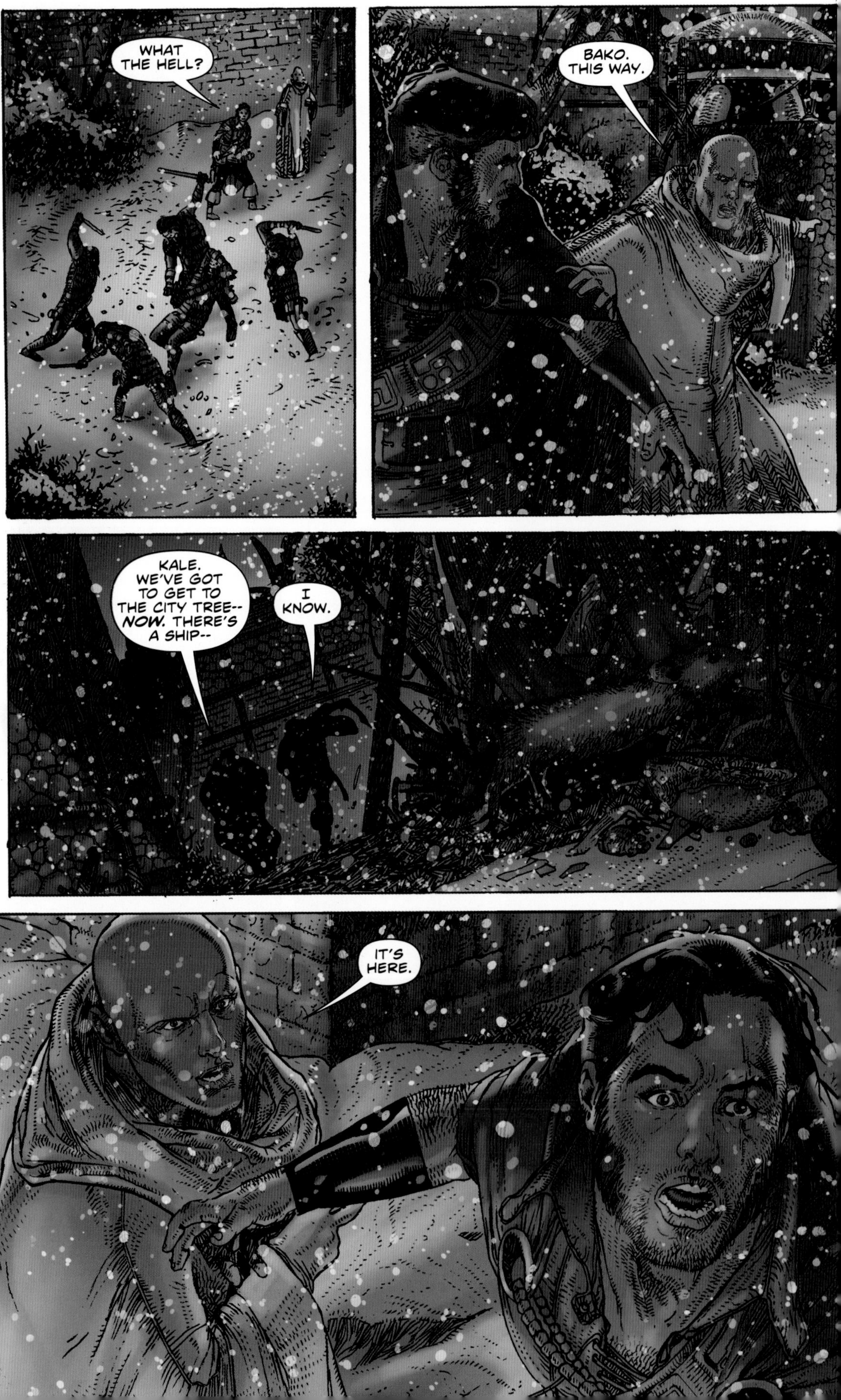
WHAT THE HELL?
BAKO. THIS WAY.
KALE. WE'VE GOT TO GET TO THE CITY TREE-- NOW. THERE'S A SHIP--
I KNOW.
IT'S HERE.

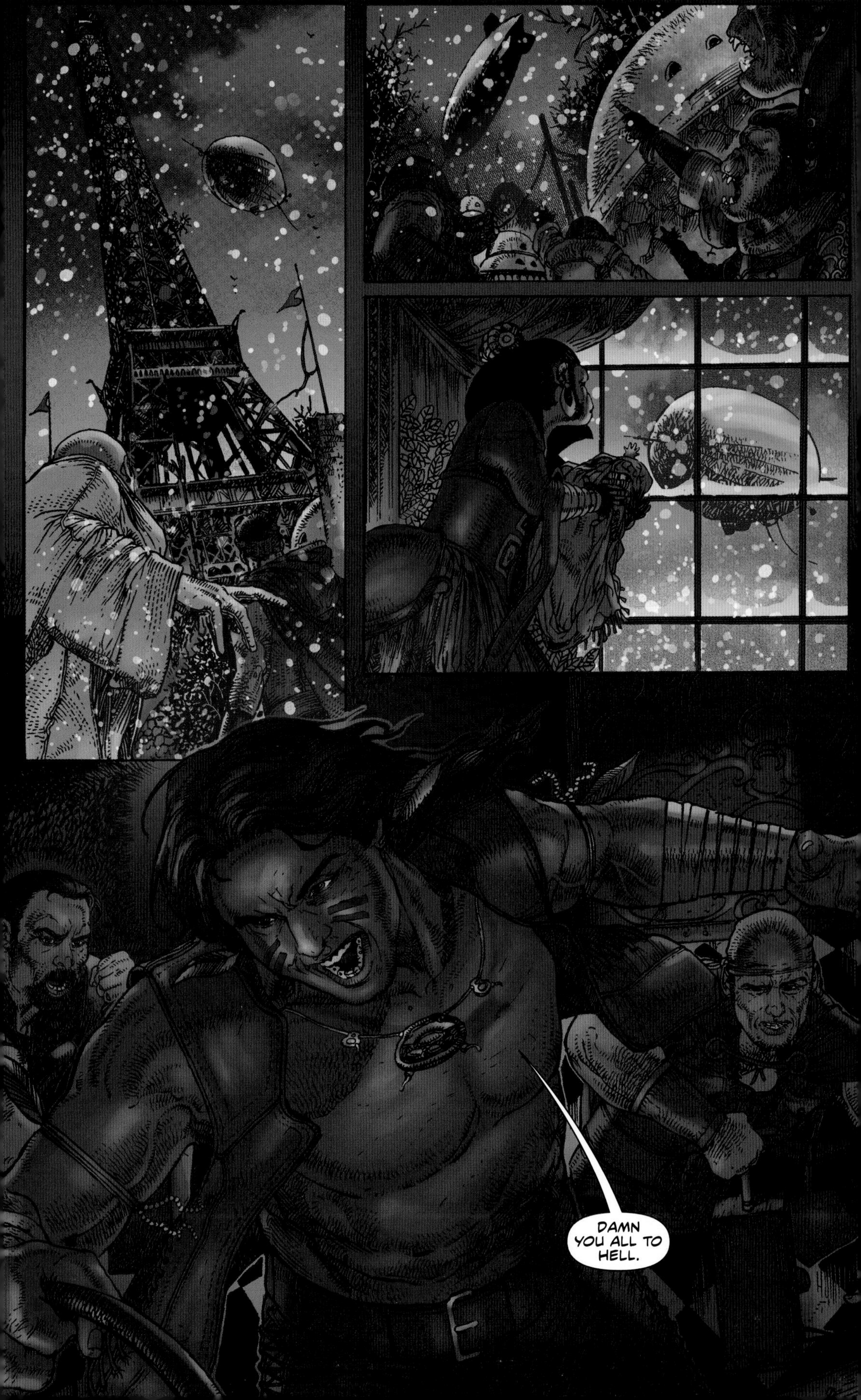
DAMN
YOU ALL TO
HELL.

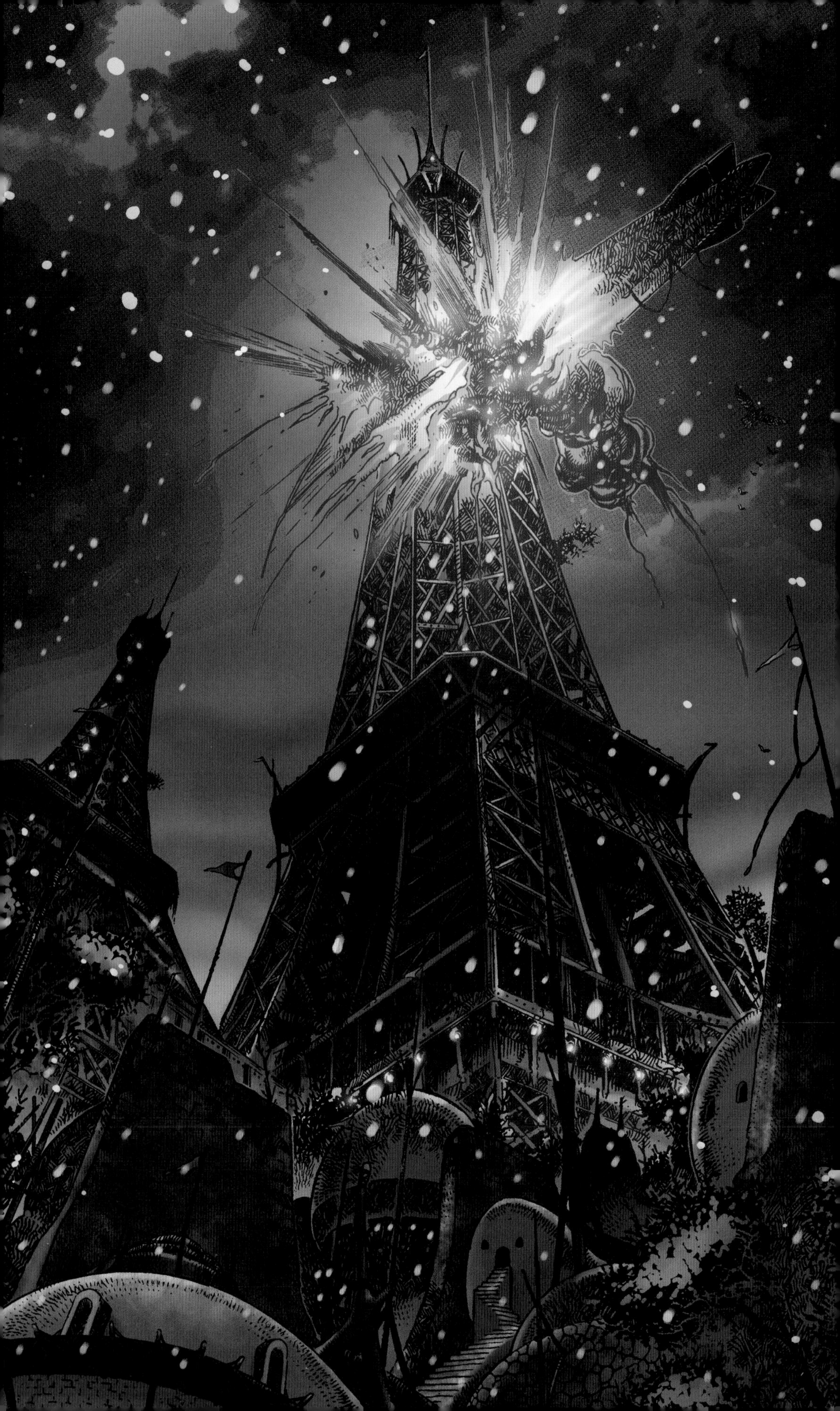

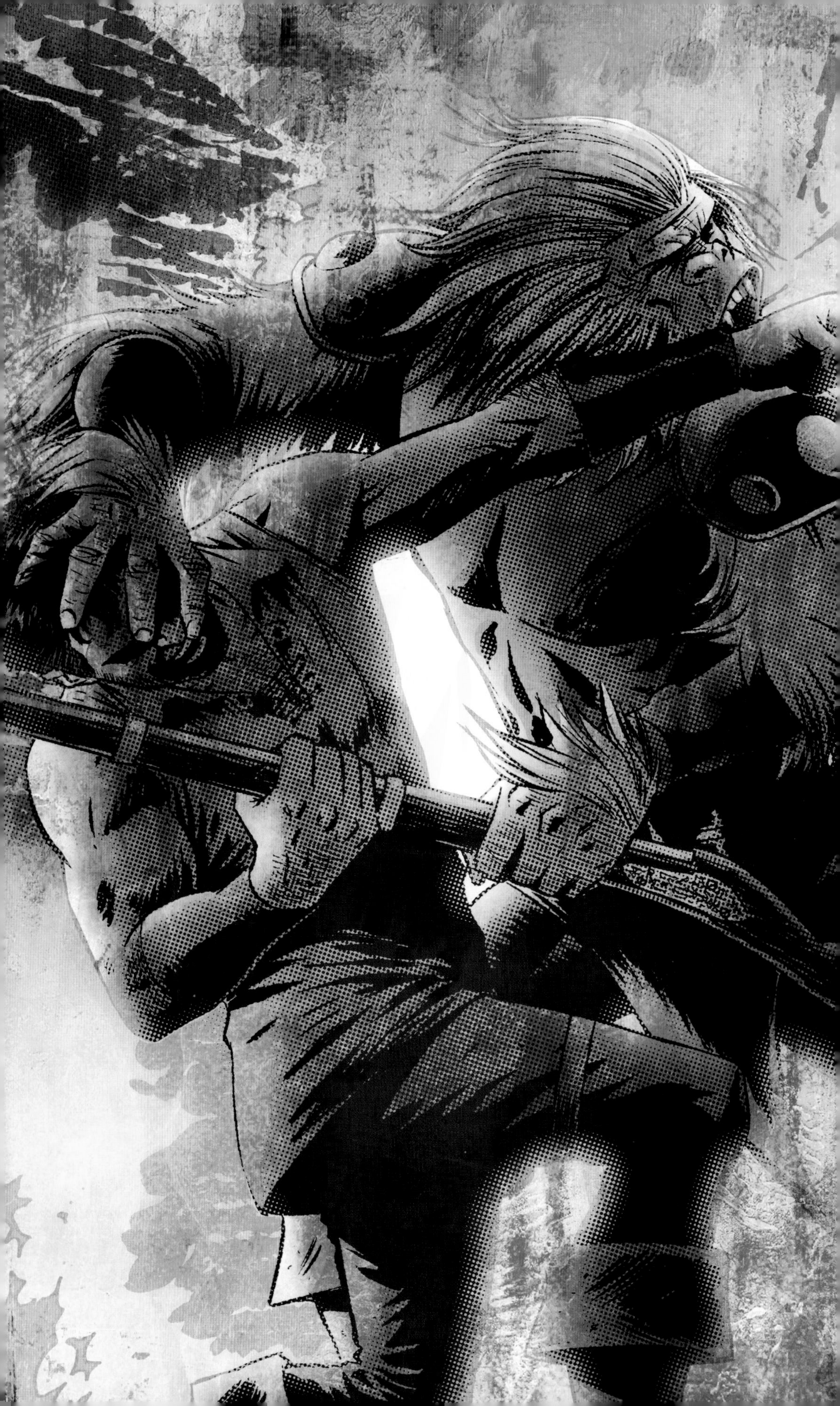

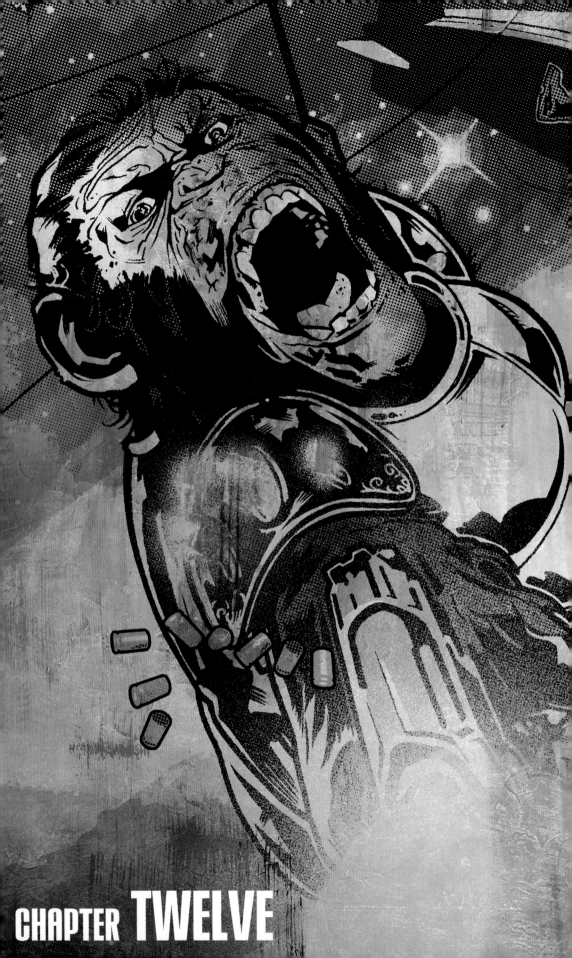

CHAPTER **TWELVE**

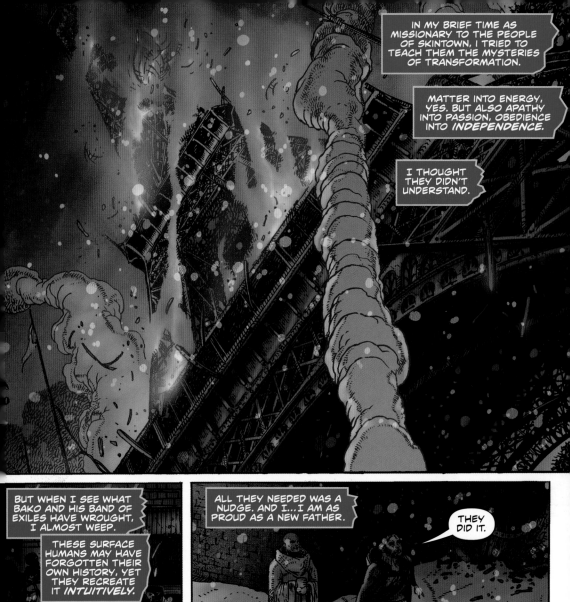

IN MY BRIEF TIME AS MISSIONARY TO THE PEOPLE OF SKINTOWN, I TRIED TO TEACH THEM THE MYSTERIES OF TRANSFORMATION.

MATTER INTO ENERGY, YES. BUT ALSO APATHY INTO PASSION, OBEDIENCE INTO *INDEPENDENCE*.

I THOUGHT THEY DIDN'T UNDERSTAND.

BUT WHEN I SEE WHAT BAKO AND HIS BAND OF EXILES HAVE WROUGHT, I ALMOST WEEP.

THESE SURFACE HUMANS MAY HAVE FORGOTTEN THEIR OWN HISTORY, YET THEY RECREATE IT *INTUITIVELY*.

ALL THEY NEEDED WAS A NUDGE. AND I...I AM AS PROUD AS A NEW FATHER.

THEY DID IT.

THE FRONT ENTRANCE IS TOO PACKED--WE'LL NEVER GET IN.

LET'S TRY THE MAN DOOR.

EVERY APE BUILDING OF SIZE HAS A *MAN DOOR.*

IT'S NOT *ONLY* FOR HUMANS--ALL SERVANTS AND STAFF OF ALL SPECIES USE IT--BUT THE TERM PERSISTS.

HOLD.

AGGH! NOT *AGAIN!*

HIS NAME IS *BARAN.* CALLS HIMSELF A DOCTOR.

WHO ARE YOU?

FRIENDS OF THE MAYOR'S.

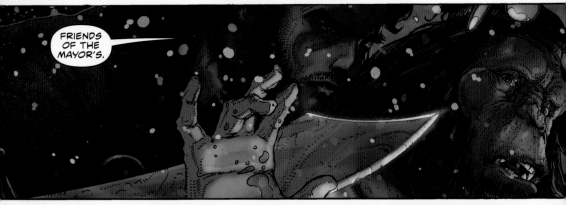

SHE LOST QUITE A BIT OF BLOOD, BUT I ASSURE YOU... ⧽COUGH⧽ SHE HAS BEEN WELL TAKEN CARE OF. ⧽COUGH⧽

RIGHT. AND YOU WERE LEAVING HER TO BURN.

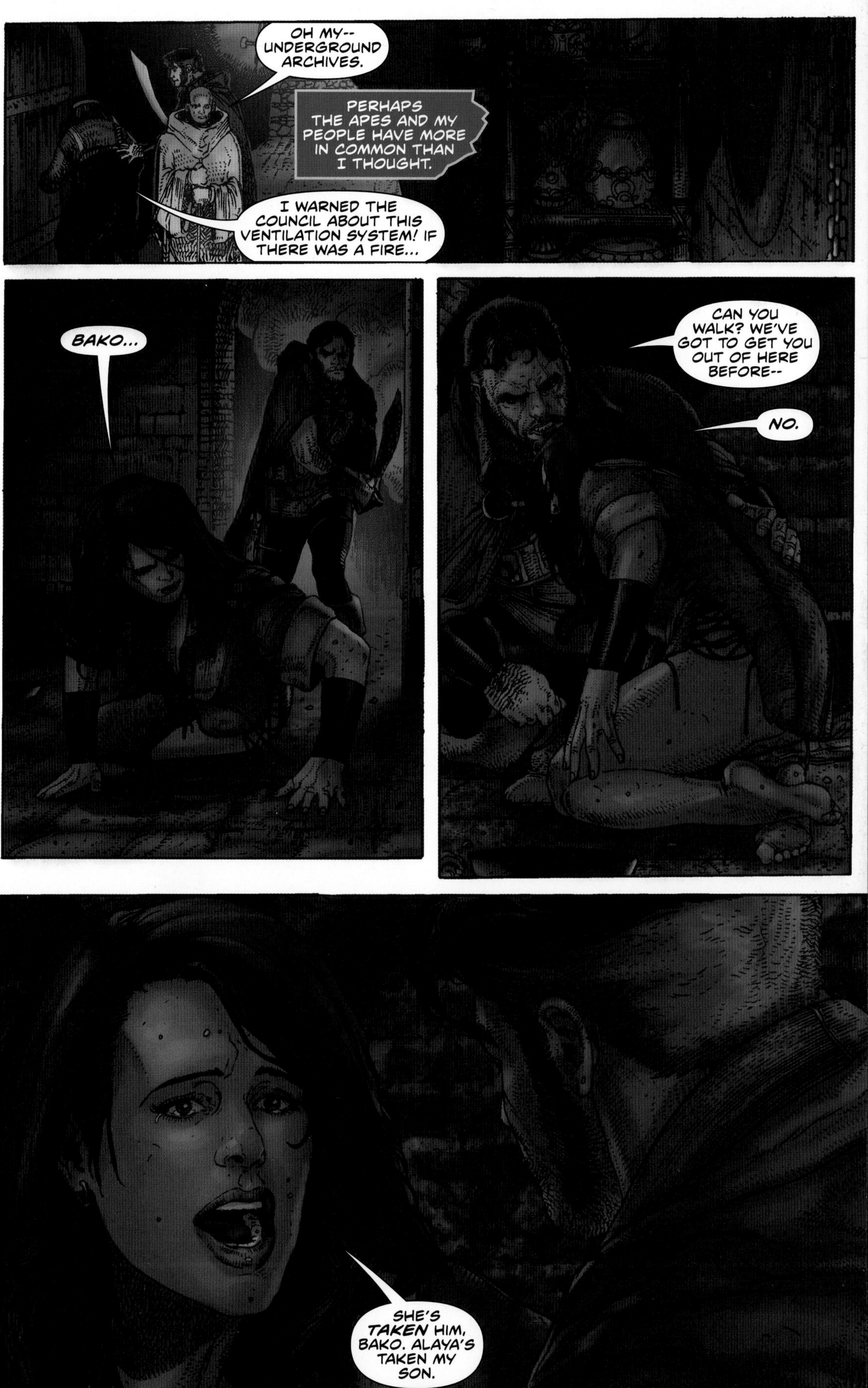
OH MY-- UNDERGROUND ARCHIVES.
PERHAPS THE APES AND MY PEOPLE HAVE MORE IN COMMON THAN I THOUGHT.
I WARNED THE COUNCIL ABOUT THIS VENTILATION SYSTEM! IF THERE WAS A FIRE...
BAKO...
CAN YOU WALK? WE'VE GOT TO GET YOU OUT OF HERE BEFORE--
NO.
SHE'S TAKEN HIM, BAKO. ALAYA'S TAKEN MY SON.

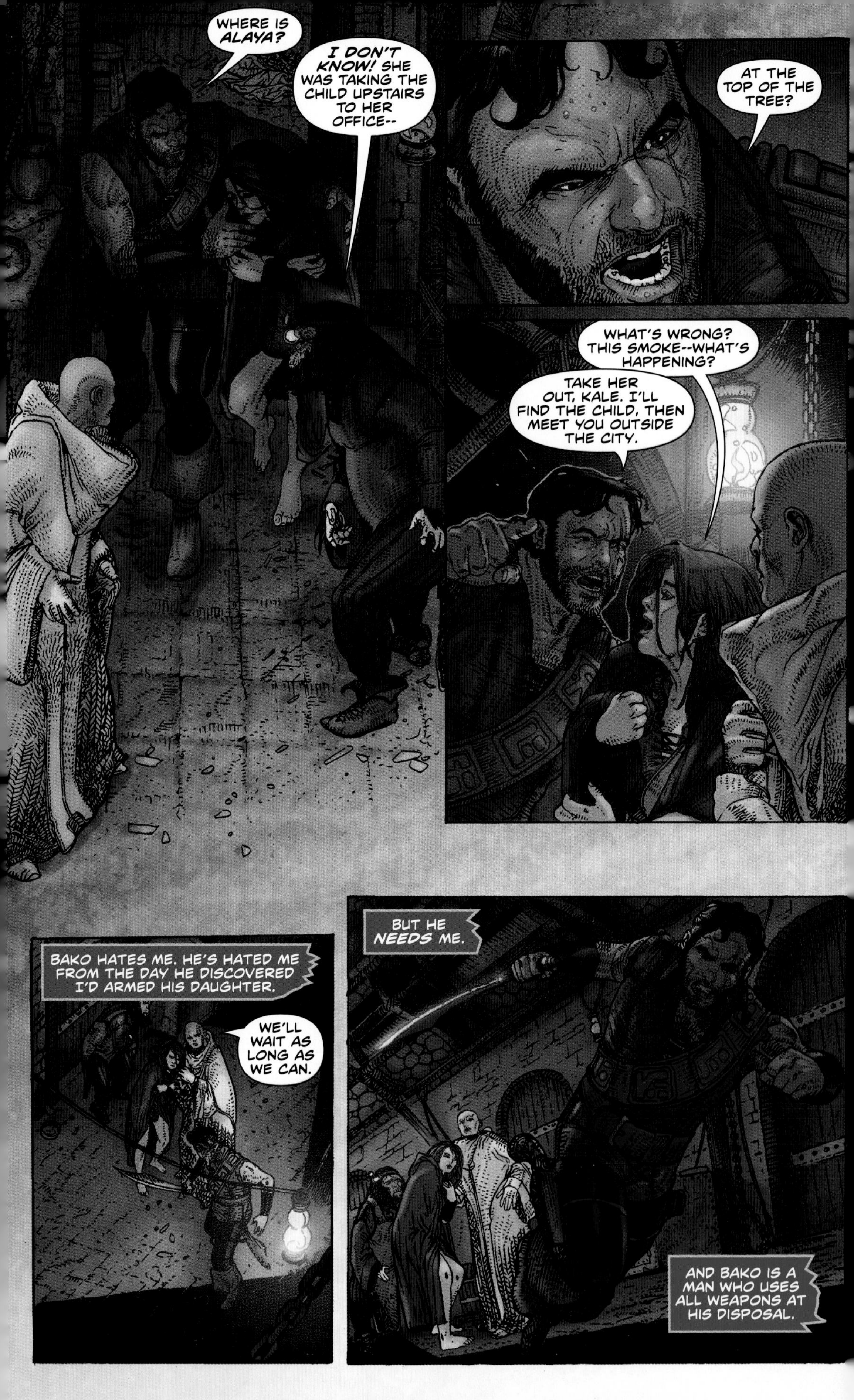
WHERE IS *ALAYA?*
I DON'T KNOW! SHE WAS TAKING THE CHILD UPSTAIRS TO HER OFFICE--
AT THE TOP OF THE TREE?
WHAT'S WRONG? THIS SMOKE--WHAT'S HAPPENING?
TAKE HER OUT, KALE. I'LL FIND THE CHILD, THEN MEET YOU OUTSIDE THE CITY.
BAKO HATES ME. HE'S HATED ME FROM THE DAY HE DISCOVERED I'D ARMED HIS DAUGHTER.
WE'LL WAIT AS LONG AS WE CAN.
BUT HE *NEEDS* ME.
AND BAKO IS A MAN WHO USES ALL WEAPONS AT HIS DISPOSAL.

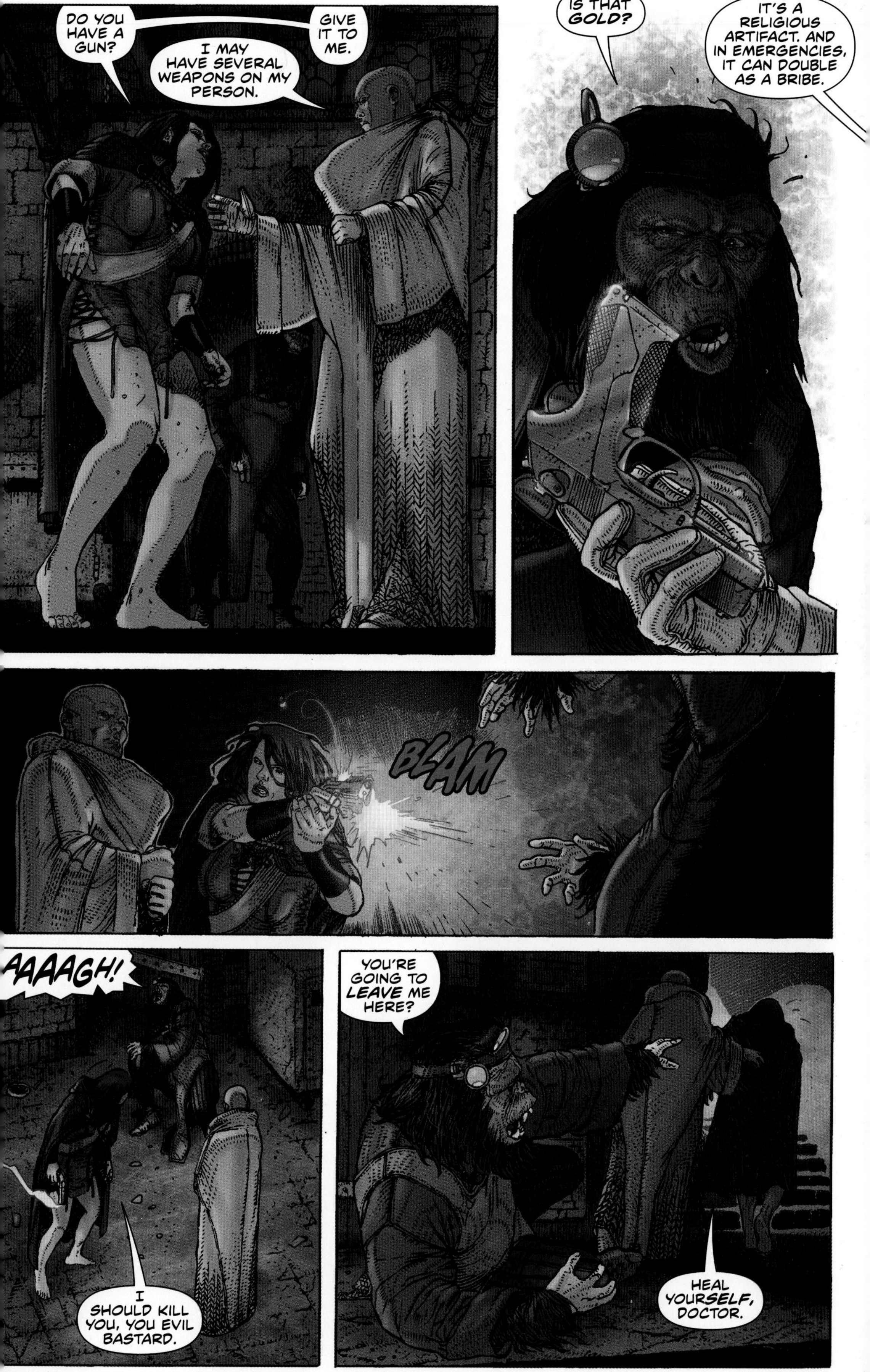
DO YOU HAVE A GUN?
I MAY HAVE SEVERAL WEAPONS ON MY PERSON.
GIVE IT TO ME.
IS THAT GOLD?
IT'S A RELIGIOUS ARTIFACT. AND IN EMERGENCIES, IT CAN DOUBLE AS A BRIBE.
BLAM
AAAAGH!
I SHOULD KILL YOU, YOU EVIL BASTARD.
YOU'RE GOING TO LEAVE ME HERE?
HEAL YOURSELF, DOCTOR.

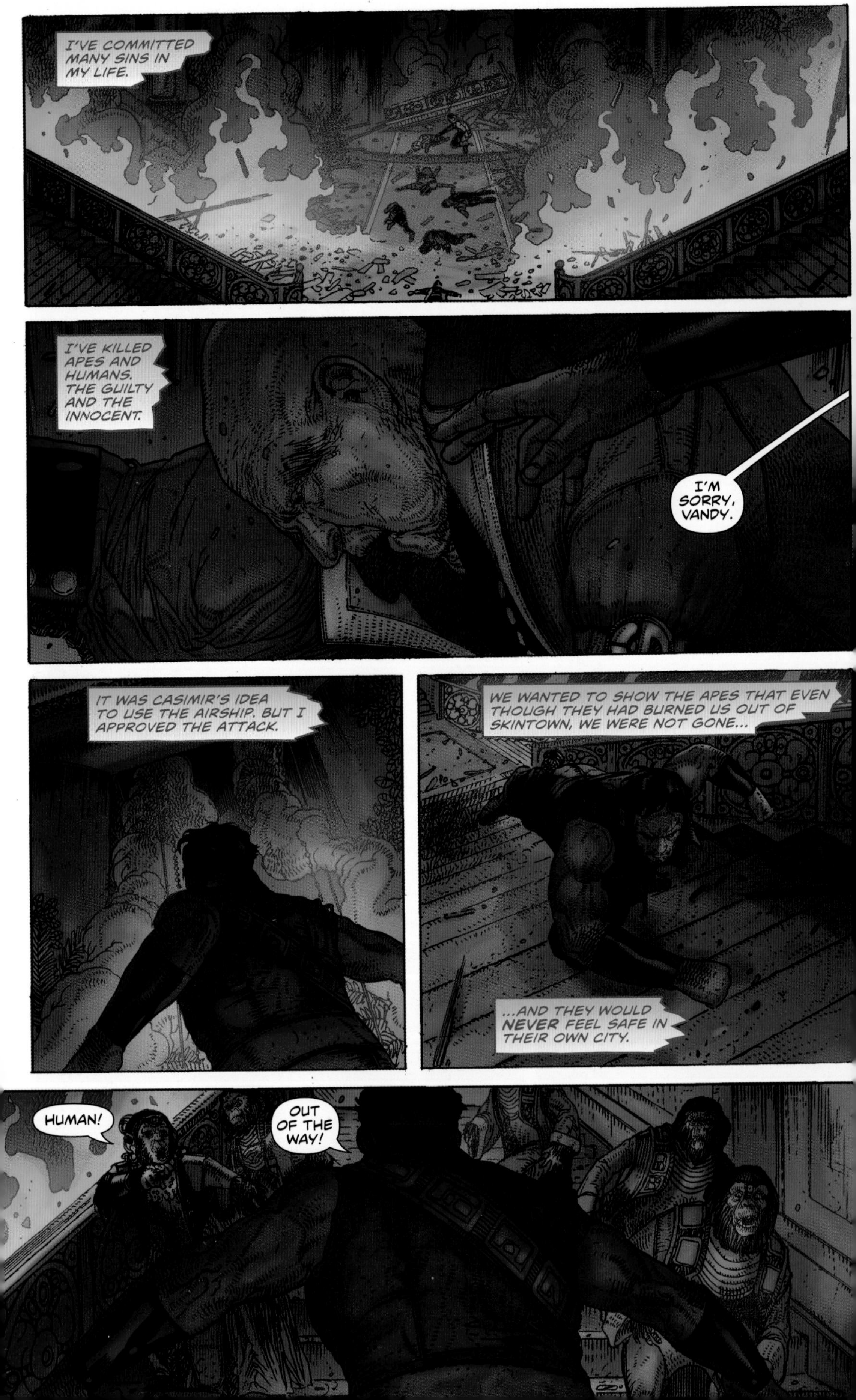

I'VE COMMITTED MANY SINS IN MY LIFE.
I'VE KILLED APES AND HUMANS. THE GUILTY AND THE INNOCENT.
I'M SORRY, VANDY.
IT WAS CASIMIR'S IDEA TO USE THE AIRSHIP. BUT I APPROVED THE ATTACK.
WE WANTED TO SHOW THE APES THAT EVEN THOUGH THEY HAD BURNED US OUT OF SKINTOWN, WE WERE NOT GONE...
...AND THEY WOULD NEVER FEEL SAFE IN THEIR OWN CITY.
HUMAN!
OUT OF THE WAY!

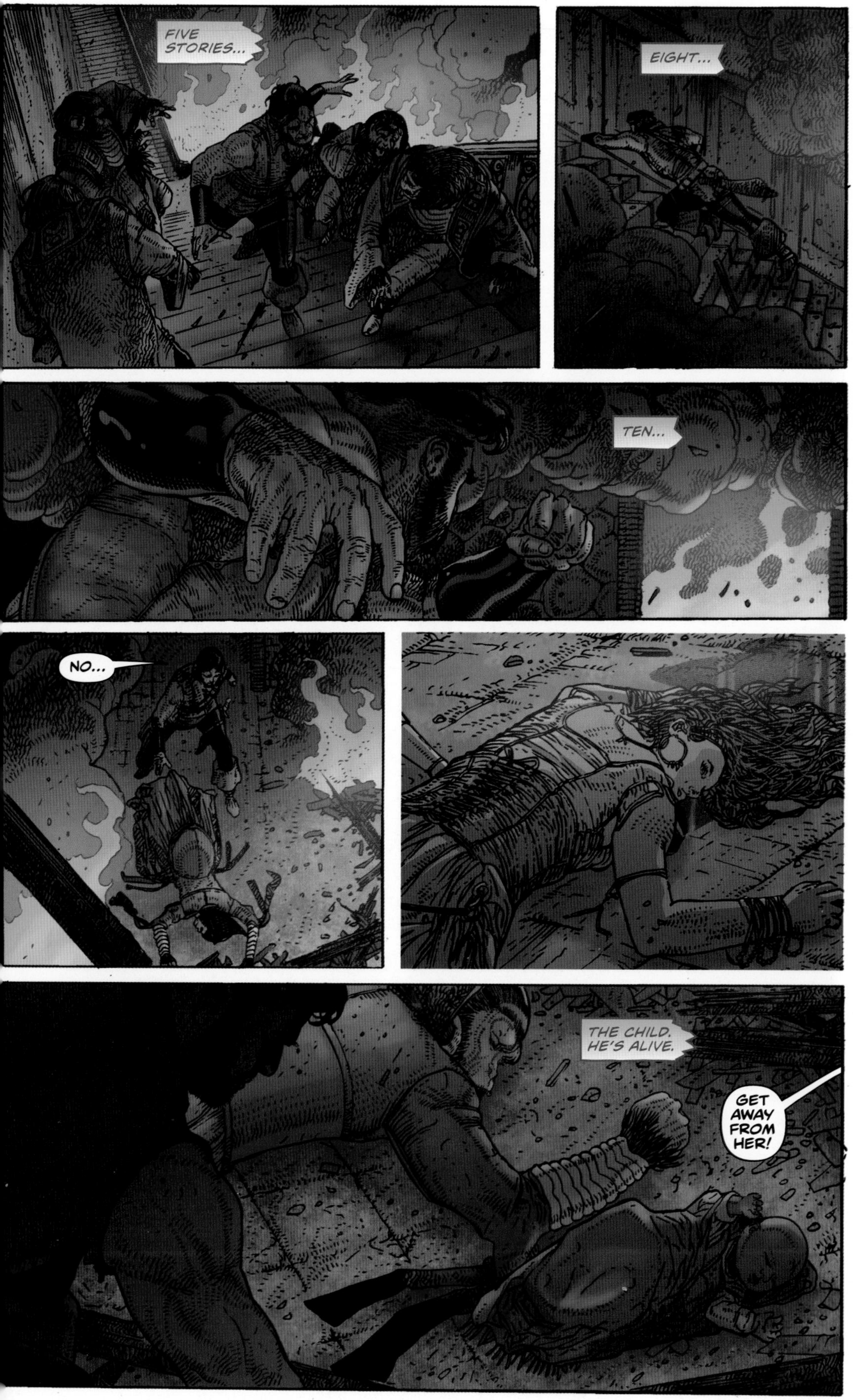
FIVE STORIES...
EIGHT...
TEN...
NO...
THE CHILD. HE'S ALIVE.
GET AWAY FROM HER!

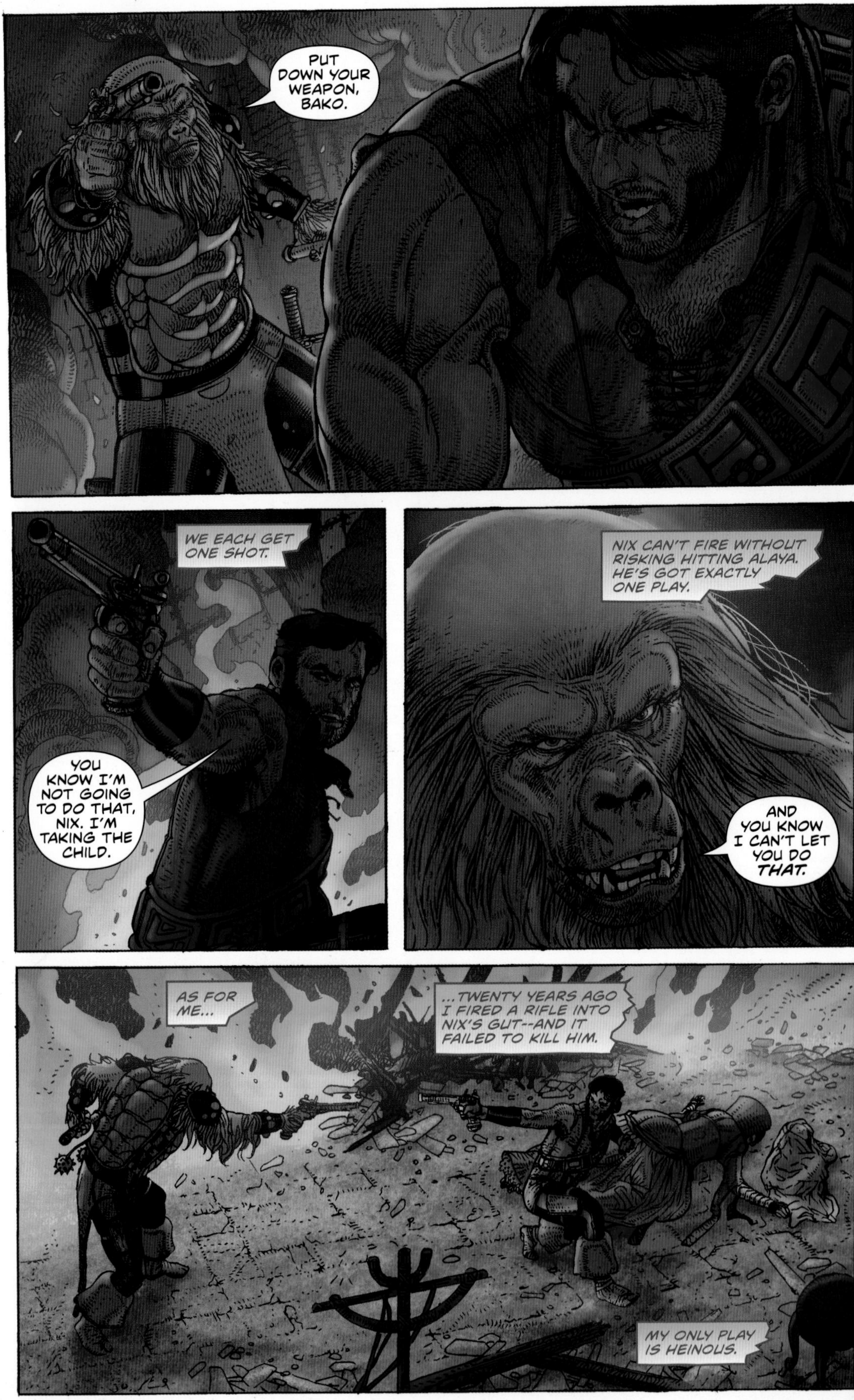
PUT DOWN YOUR WEAPON, BAKO.
WE EACH GET ONE SHOT.
YOU KNOW I'M NOT GOING TO DO THAT, NIX. I'M TAKING THE CHILD.
NIX CAN'T FIRE WITHOUT RISKING HITTING ALAYA. HE'S GOT EXACTLY ONE PLAY.
AND YOU KNOW I CAN'T LET YOU DO *THAT.*
AS FOR ME...
...TWENTY YEARS AGO I FIRED A RIFLE INTO NIX'S GUT--AND IT FAILED TO KILL HIM.
MY ONLY PLAY IS HEINOUS.

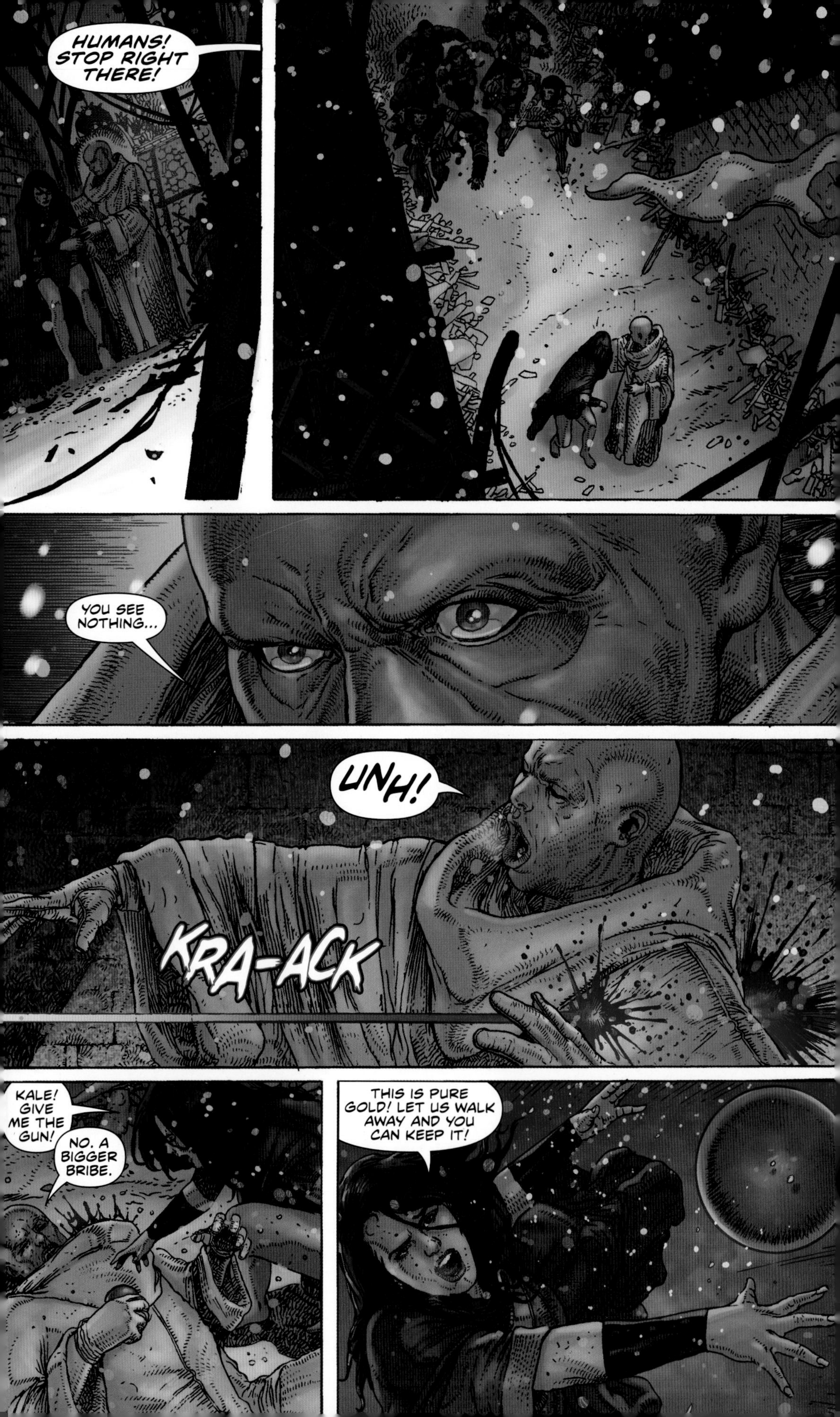
HUMANS! STOP RIGHT THERE!
YOU SEE NOTHING...
UNH!
KRA-ACK
KALE! GIVE ME THE GUN!
NO. A BIGGER BRIBE.
THIS IS PURE GOLD! LET US WALK AWAY AND YOU CAN KEEP IT!

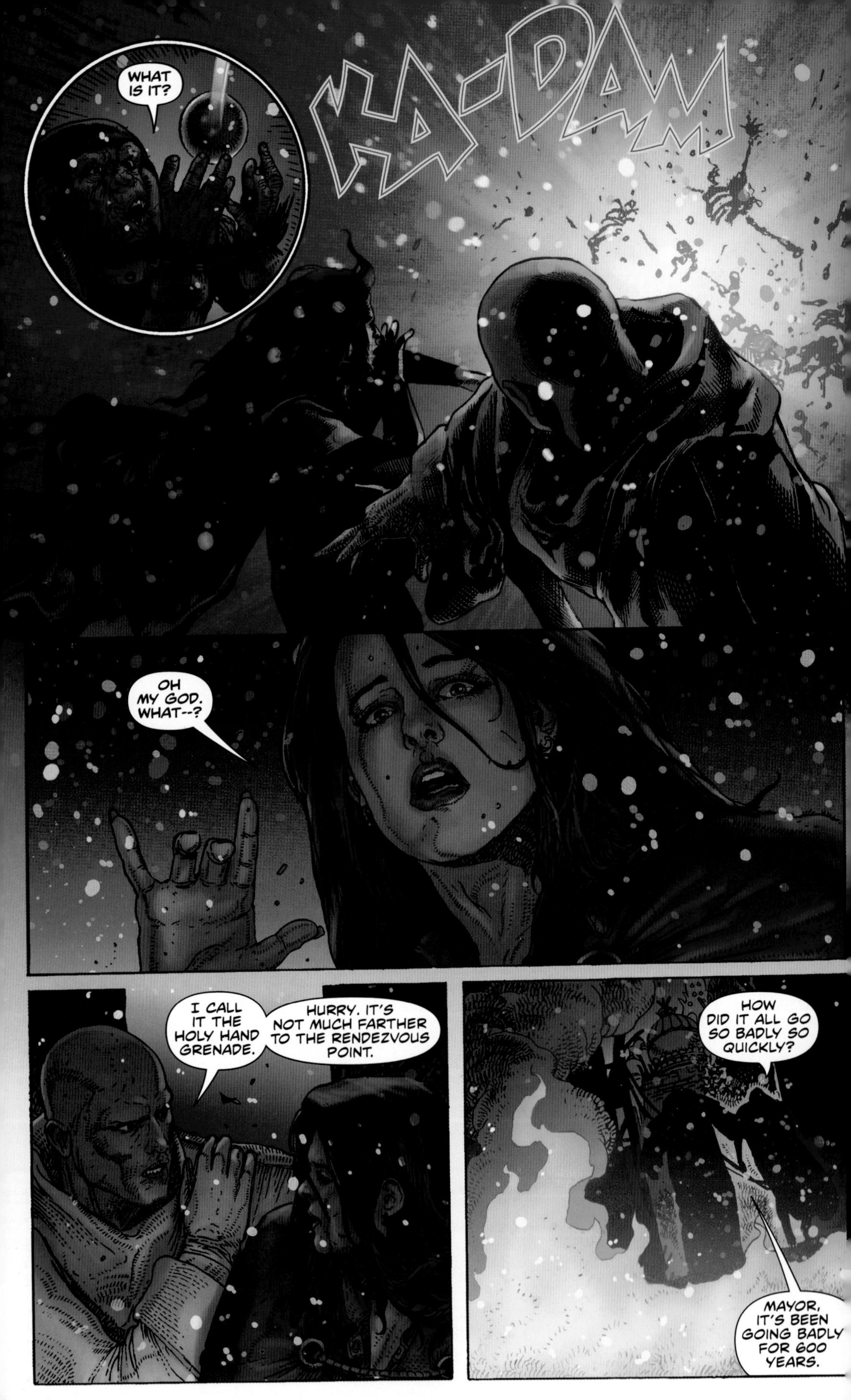
WHAT IS IT?
KA-DAM
OH MY GOD. WHAT--?
I CALL IT THE HOLY HAND GRENADE.
HURRY. IT'S NOT MUCH FARTHER TO THE RENDEZVOUS POINT.
HOW DID IT ALL GO SO BADLY SO QUICKLY?
MAYOR, IT'S BEEN GOING BADLY FOR 600 YEARS.

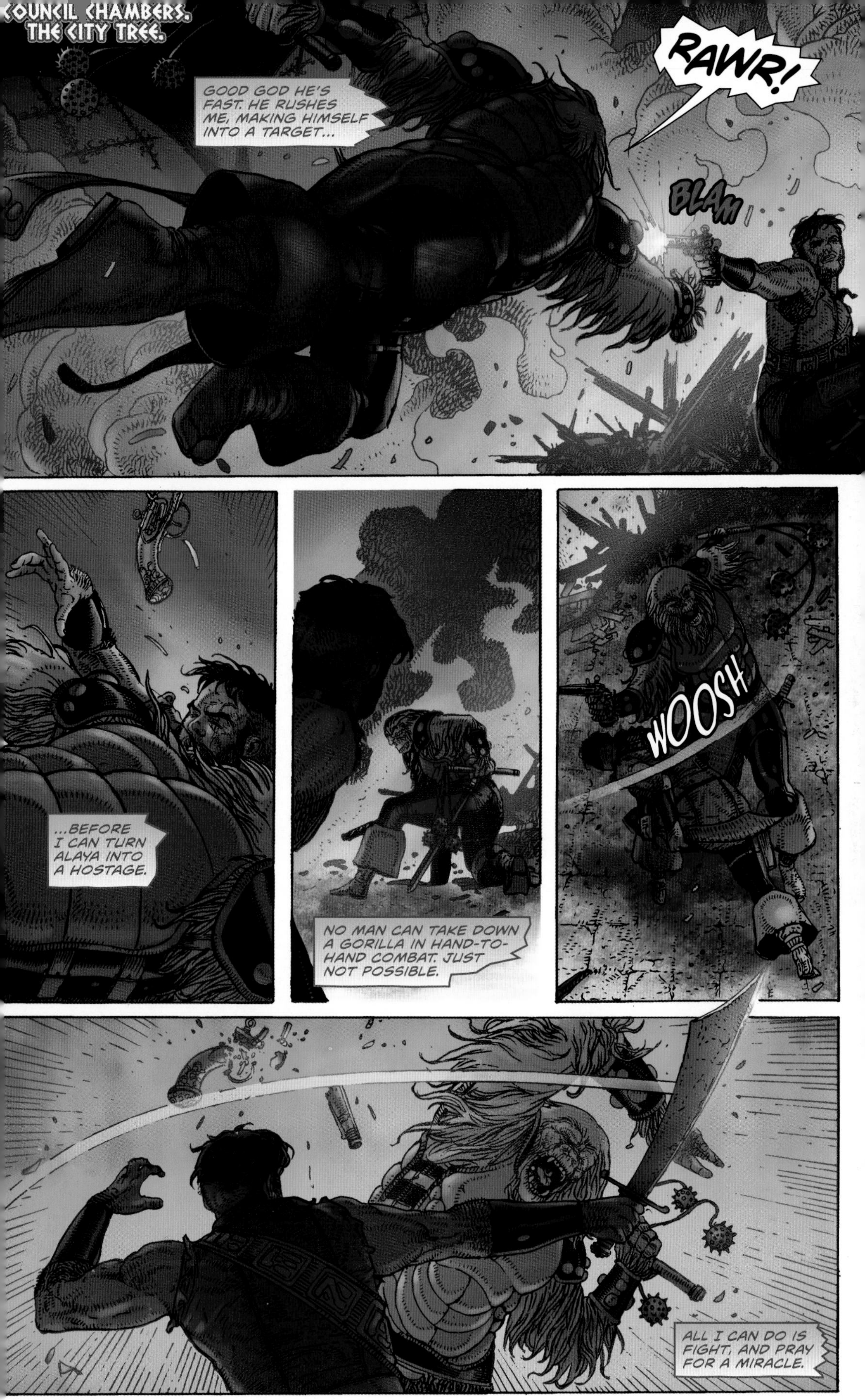
COUNCIL CHAMBERS. THE CITY TREE.
GOOD GOD HE'S FAST. HE RUSHES ME, MAKING HIMSELF INTO A TARGET...
RAWR!
BLAM
...BEFORE I CAN TURN ALAYA INTO A HOSTAGE.
NO MAN CAN TAKE DOWN A GORILLA IN HAND-TO-HAND COMBAT. JUST NOT POSSIBLE.
WOOSH
ALL I CAN DO IS FIGHT, AND PRAY FOR A MIRACLE.

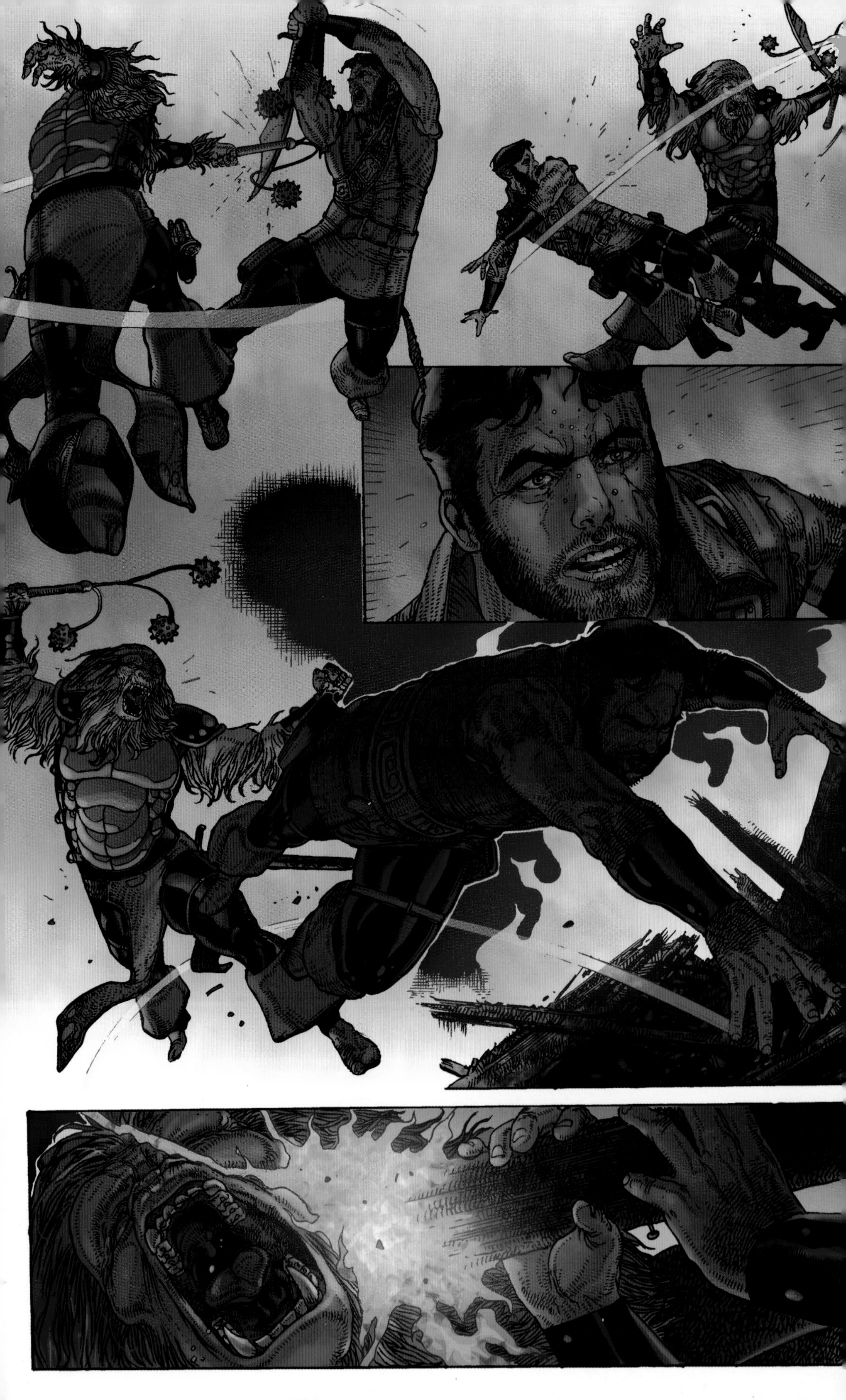

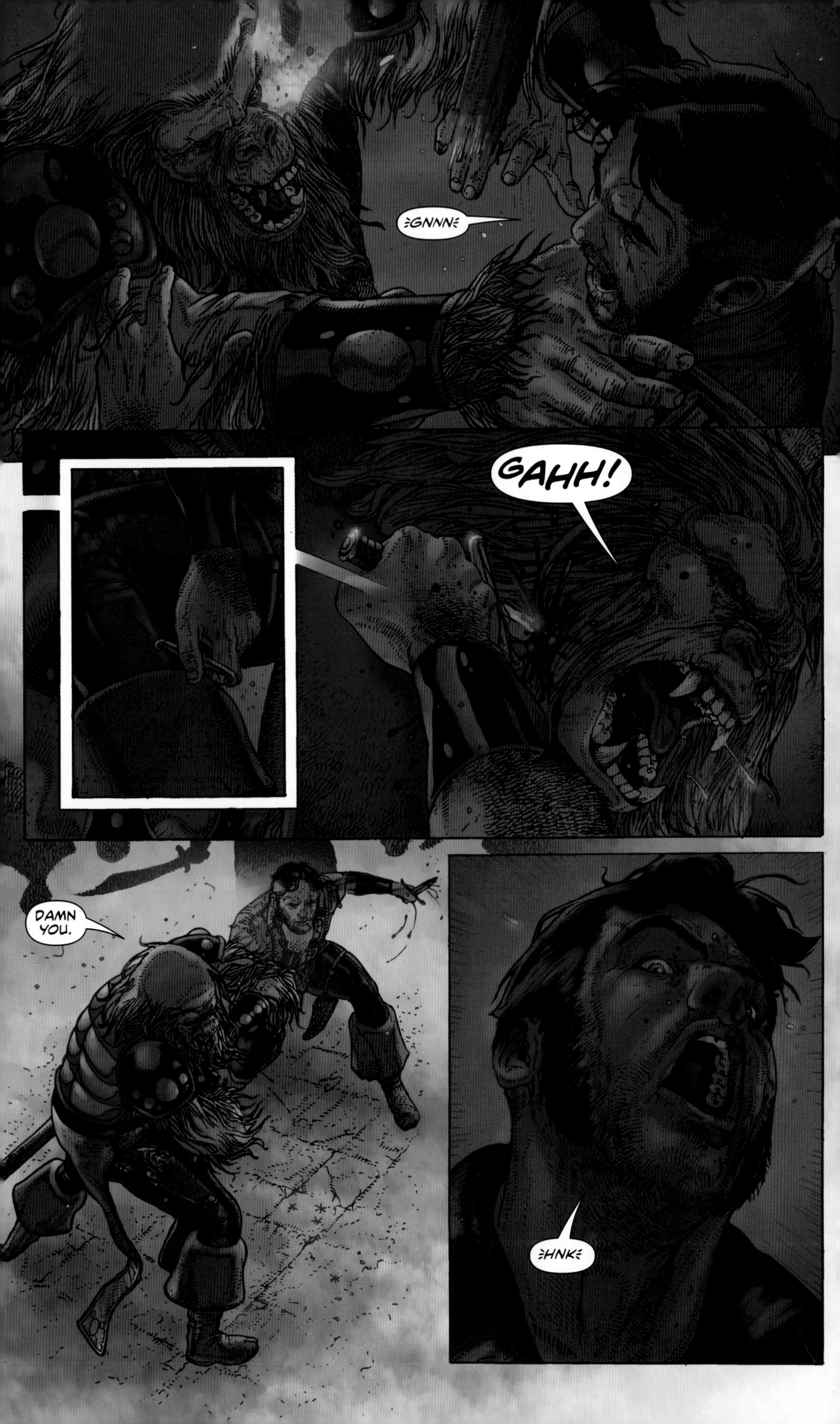
GNNN
GAHH!
DAMN YOU.
HNK

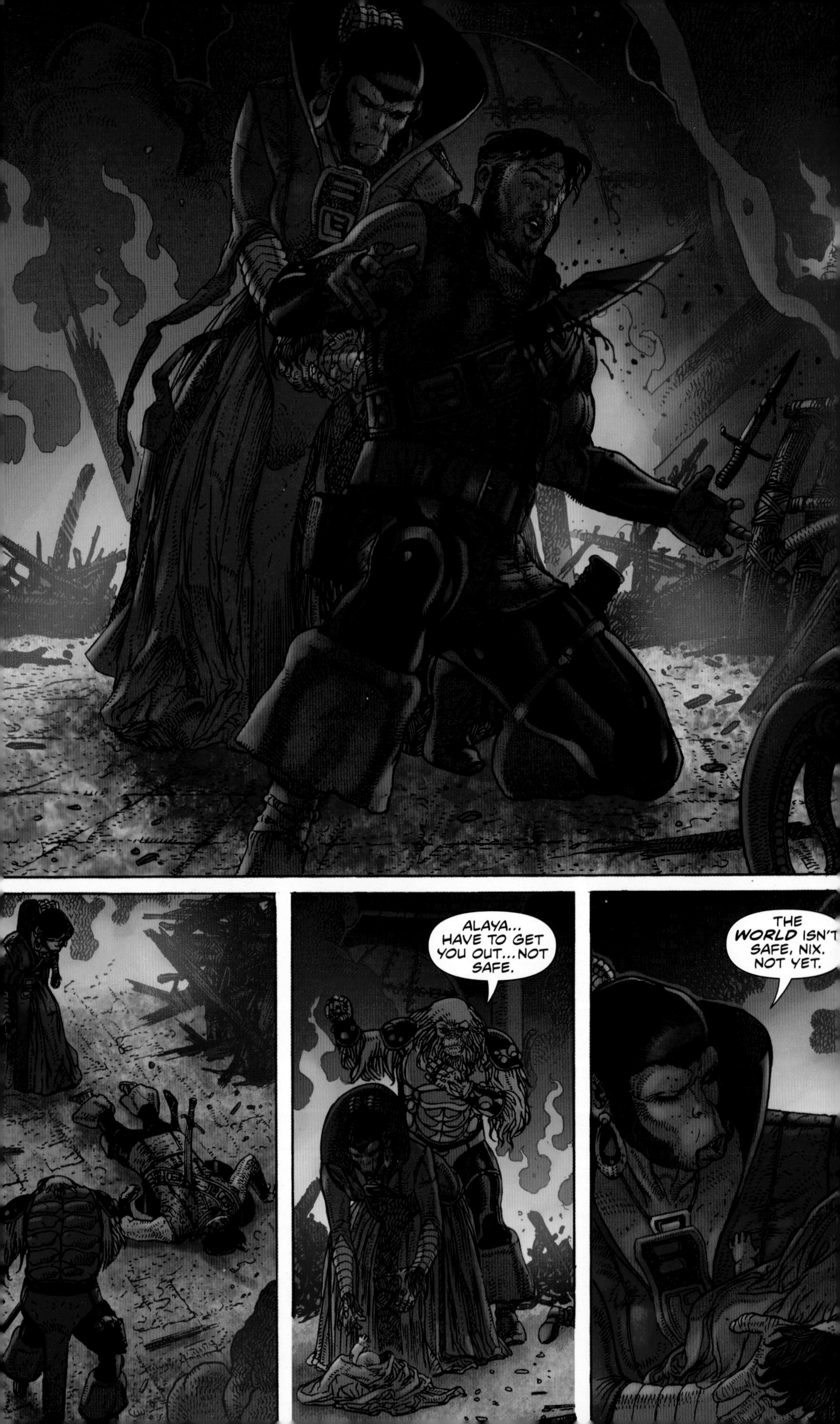
ALAYA... HAVE TO GET YOU OUT...NOT SAFE.
THE WORLD ISN'T SAFE, NIX. NOT YET.

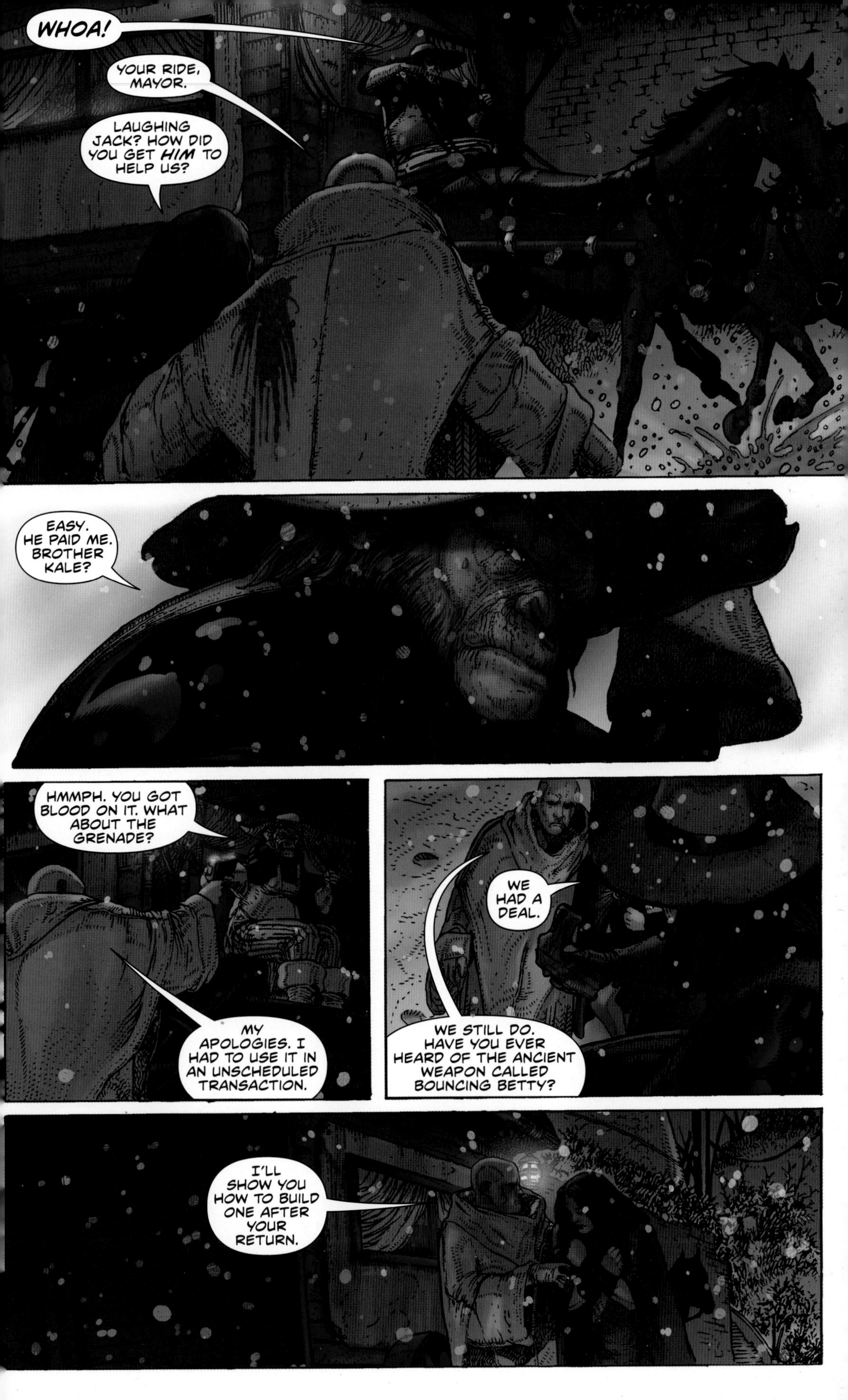
WHOA!
YOUR RIDE, MAYOR.
LAUGHING JACK? HOW DID YOU GET *HIM* TO HELP US?
EASY. HE PAID ME. BROTHER KALE?
HMMPH. YOU GOT BLOOD ON IT. WHAT ABOUT THE GRENADE?
MY APOLOGIES. I HAD TO USE IT IN AN UNSCHEDULED TRANSACTION.
WE HAD A DEAL.
WE STILL DO. HAVE YOU EVER HEARD OF THE ANCIENT WEAPON CALLED BOUNCING BETTY?
I'LL SHOW YOU HOW TO BUILD ONE AFTER YOUR RETURN.

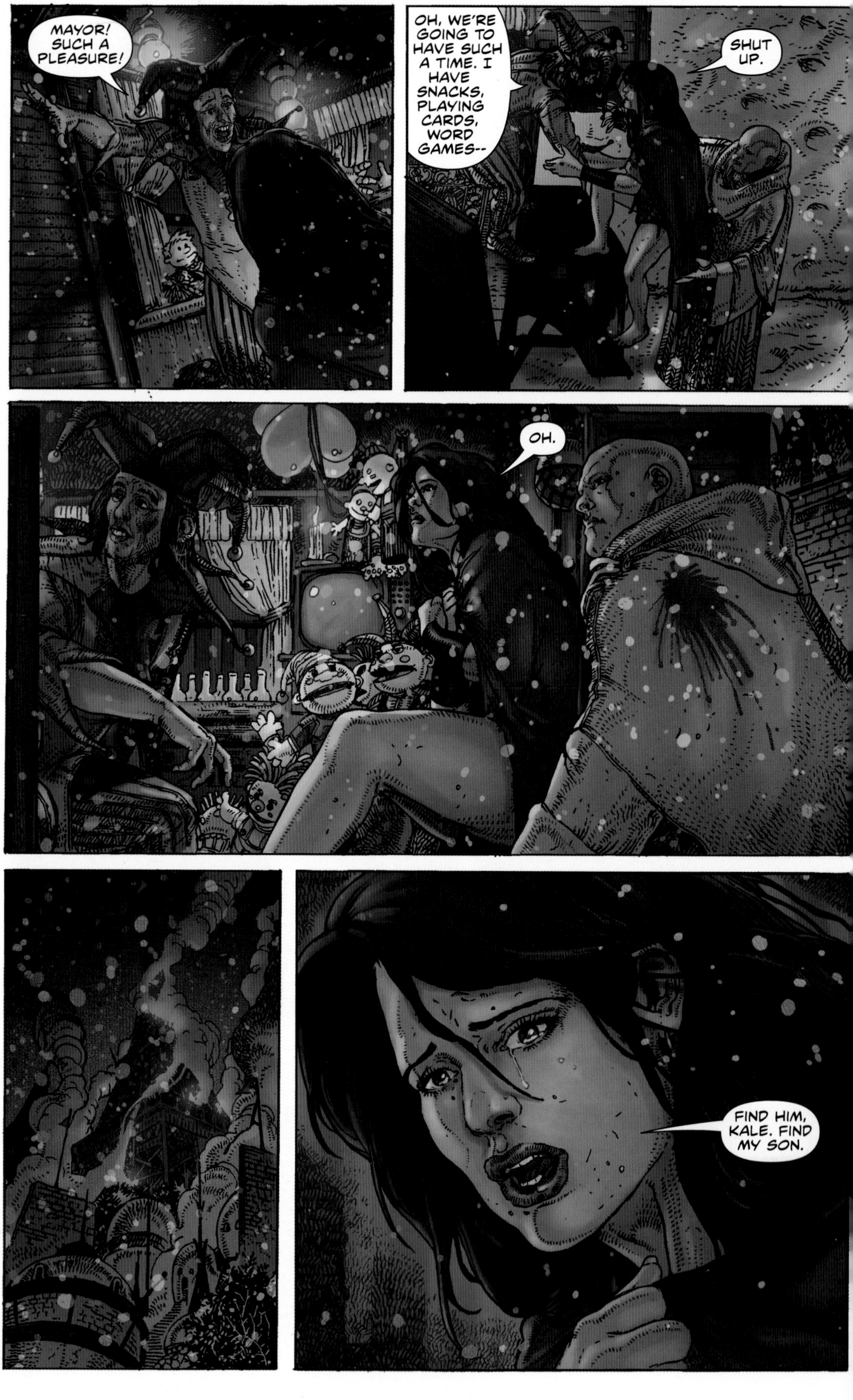
MAYOR! SUCH A PLEASURE!
OH, WE'RE GOING TO HAVE SUCH A TIME. I HAVE SNACKS, PLAYING CARDS, WORD GAMES--
SHUT UP.
OH.
FIND HIM, KALE. FIND MY SON.

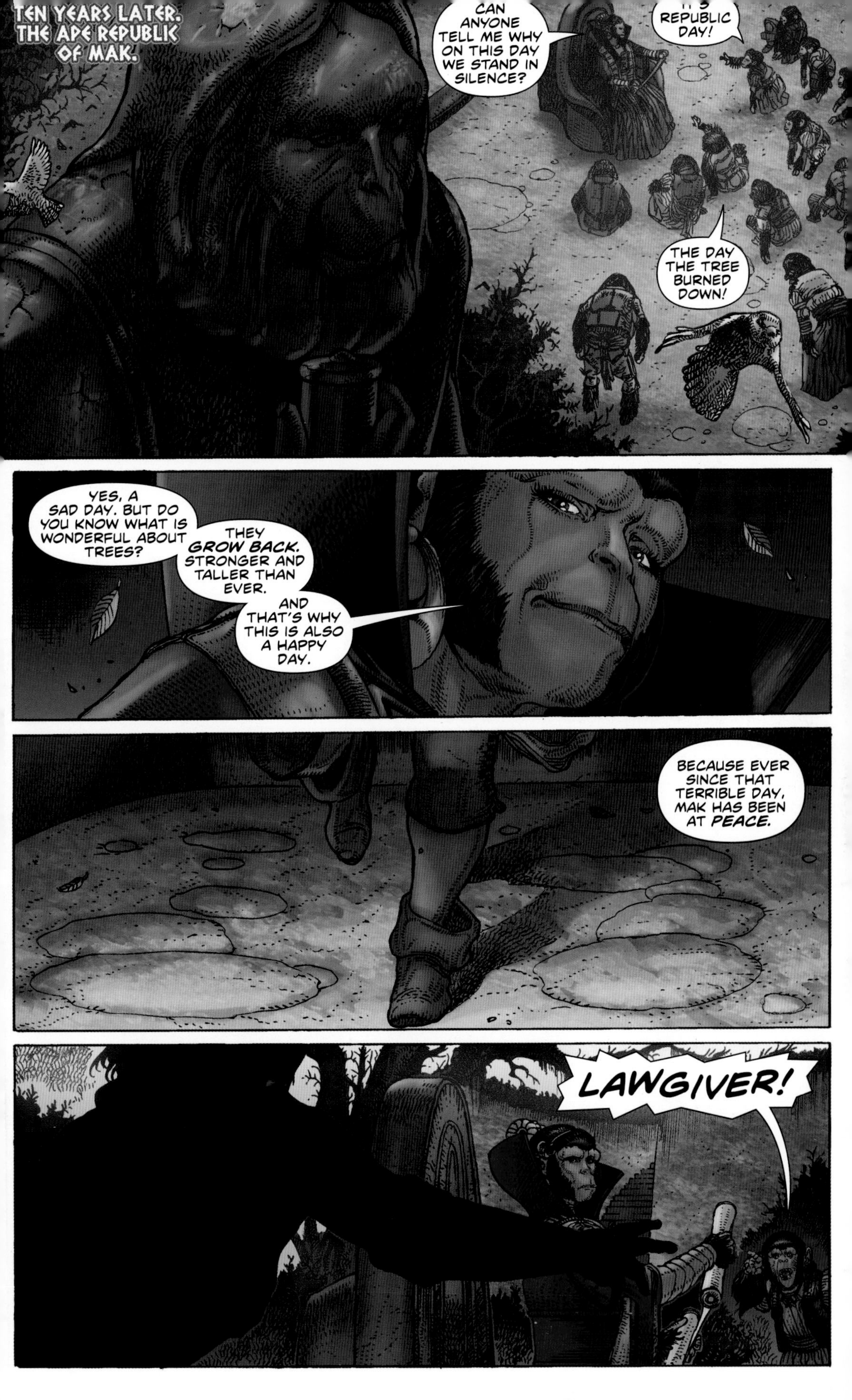
TEN YEARS LATER. THE APE REPUBLIC OF MAK.
CAN ANYONE TELL ME WHY ON THIS DAY WE STAND IN SILENCE?
REPUBLIC DAY!
THE DAY THE TREE BURNED DOWN!
YES, A SAD DAY. BUT DO YOU KNOW WHAT IS WONDERFUL ABOUT TREES?
THEY GROW BACK. STRONGER AND TALLER THAN EVER.
AND THAT'S WHY THIS IS ALSO A HAPPY DAY.
BECAUSE EVER SINCE THAT TERRIBLE DAY, MAK HAS BEEN AT PEACE.
LAWGIVER!

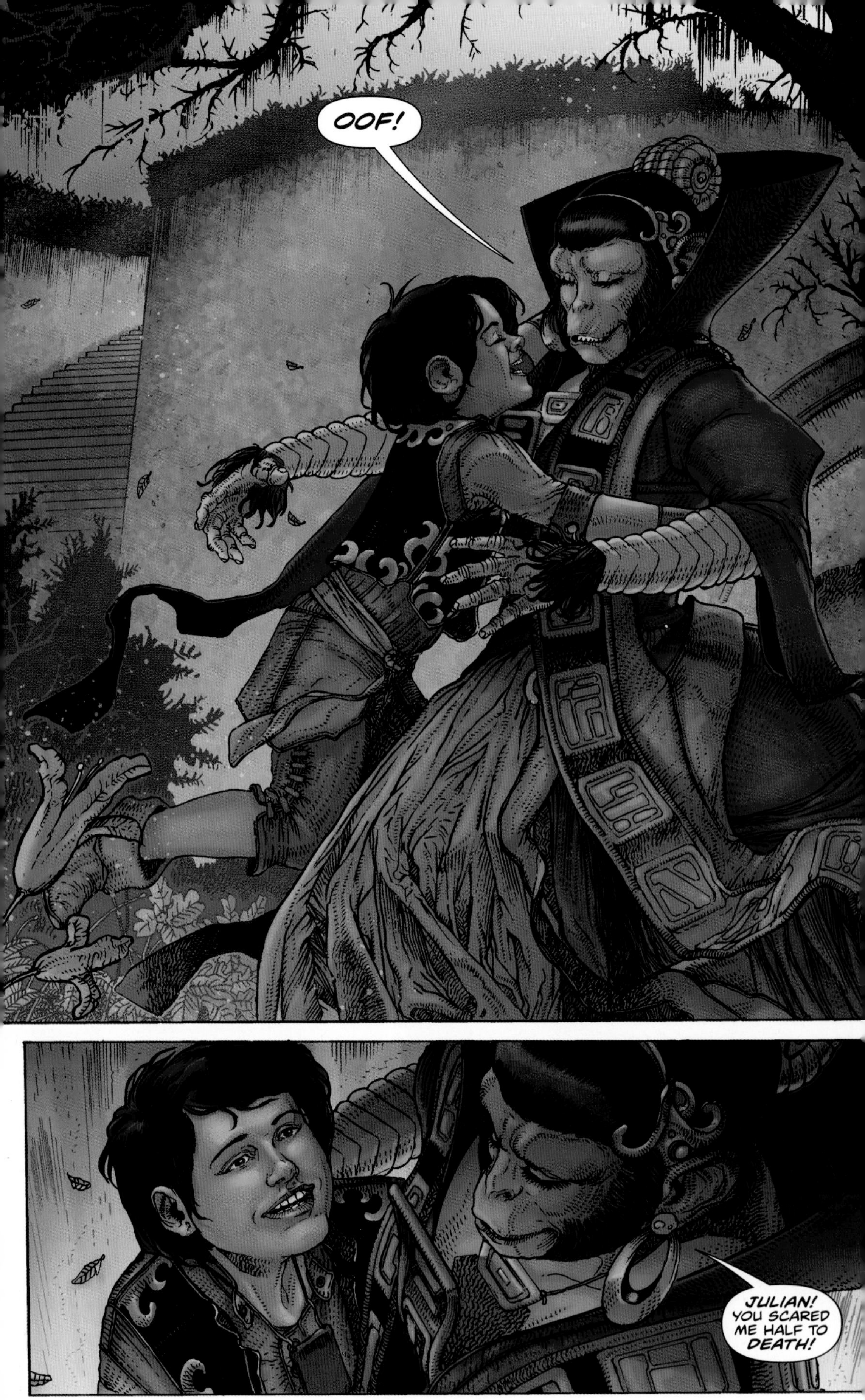
OOF!
JULIAN! YOU SCARED ME HALF TO DEATH!

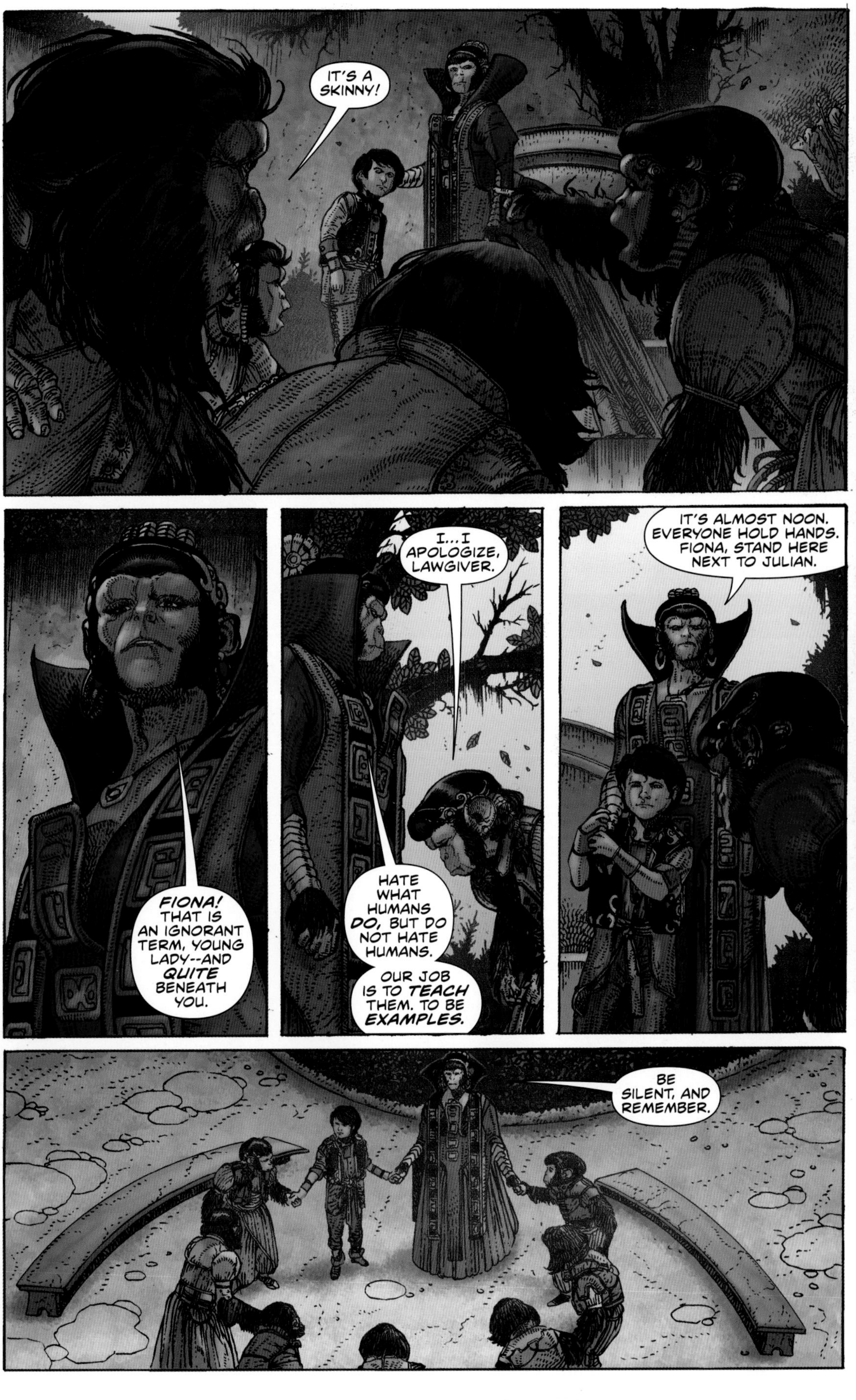
IT'S A SKINNY!
FIONA! THAT IS AN IGNORANT TERM, YOUNG LADY--AND QUITE BENEATH YOU.
I... I APOLOGIZE, LAWGIVER.
HATE WHAT HUMANS DO, BUT DO NOT HATE HUMANS.
OUR JOB IS TO TEACH THEM. TO BE EXAMPLES.
IT'S ALMOST NOON. EVERYONE HOLD HANDS. FIONA, STAND HERE NEXT TO JULIAN.
BE SILENT, AND REMEMBER.

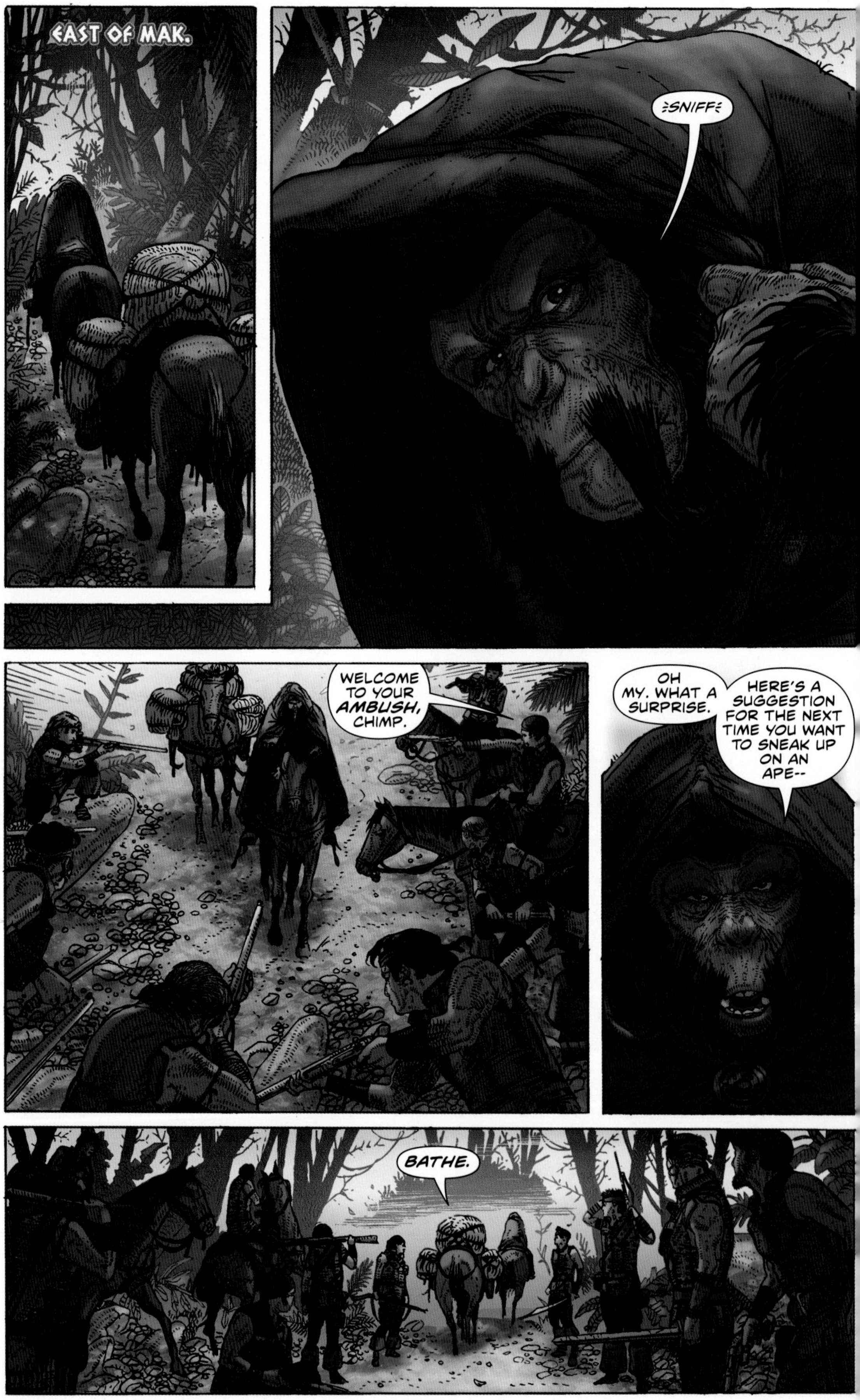
EAST OF MAK.
SNIFF
WELCOME TO YOUR AMBUSH, CHIMP.
OH MY. WHAT A SURPRISE.
HERE'S A SUGGESTION FOR THE NEXT TIME YOU WANT TO SNEAK UP ON AN APE--
BATHE.

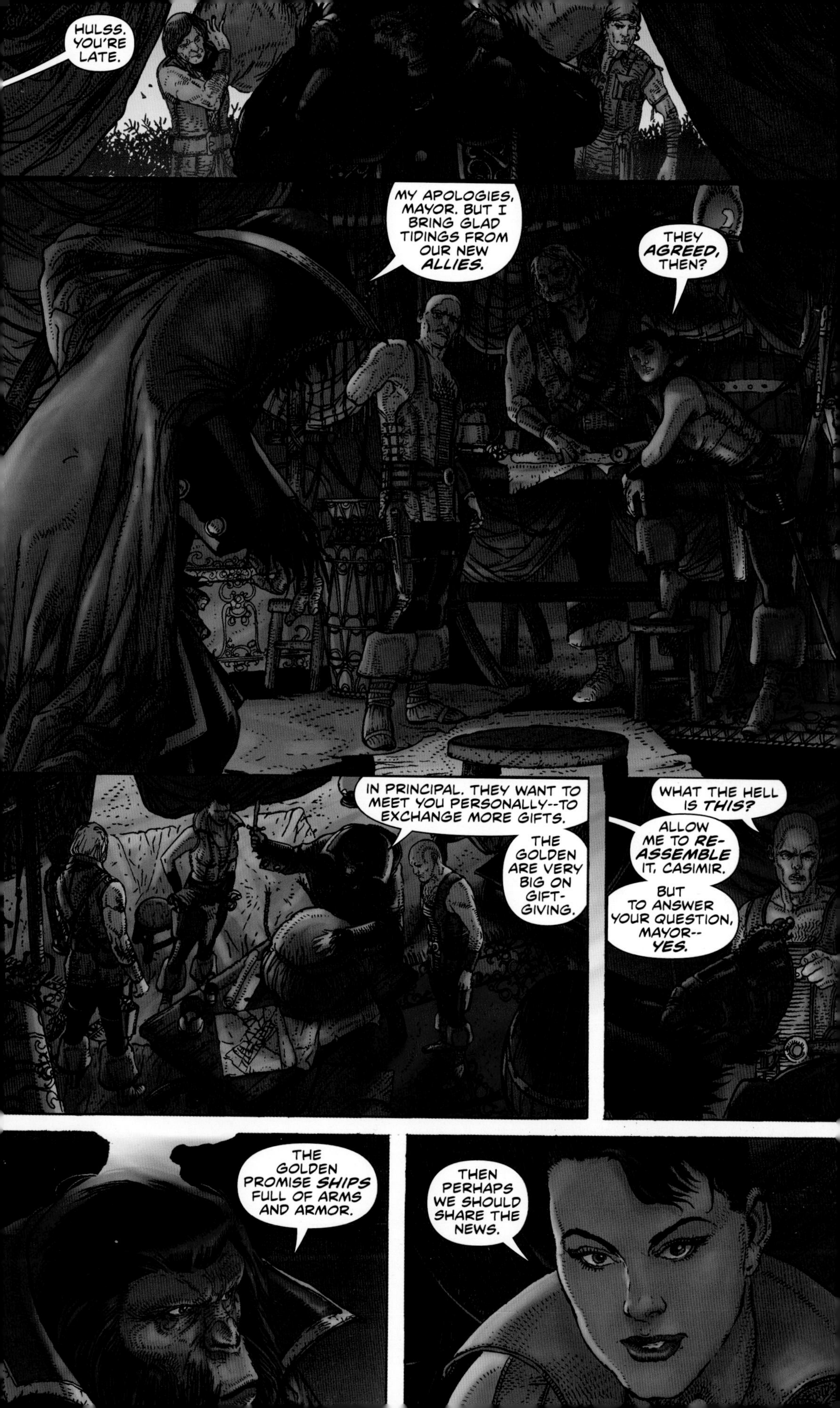
HULSS. YOU'RE LATE.
MY APOLOGIES, MAYOR. BUT I BRING GLAD TIDINGS FROM OUR NEW ALLIES.
THEY AGREED, THEN?
IN PRINCIPAL. THEY WANT TO MEET YOU PERSONALLY--TO EXCHANGE MORE GIFTS.
THE GOLDEN ARE VERY BIG ON GIFT-GIVING.
WHAT THE HELL IS THIS?
ALLOW ME TO RE-ASSEMBLE IT, CASIMIR.
BUT TO ANSWER YOUR QUESTION, MAYOR--YES.
THE GOLDEN PROMISE SHIPS FULL OF ARMS AND ARMOR.
THEN PERHAPS WE SHOULD SHARE THE NEWS.

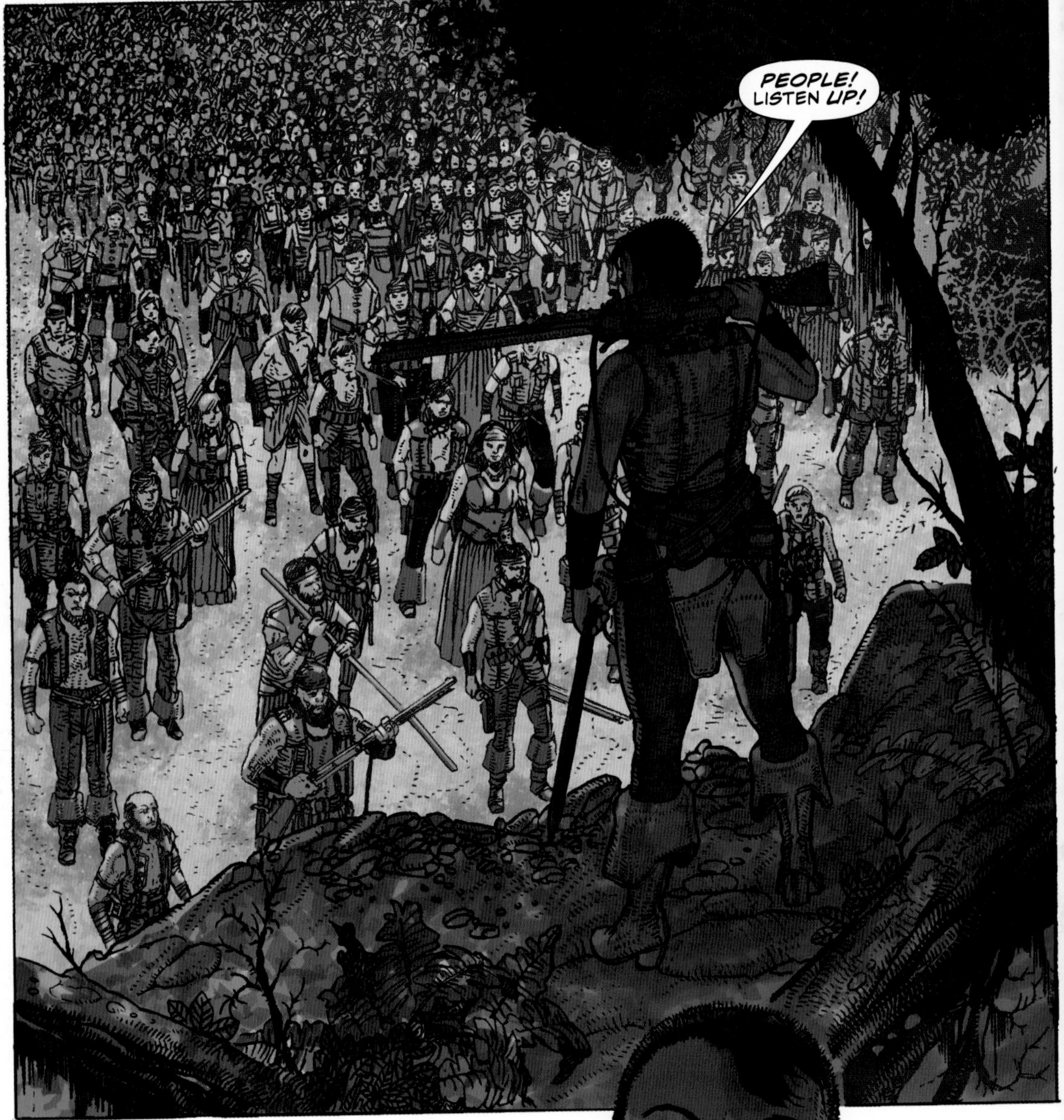
PEOPLE! LISTEN UP!

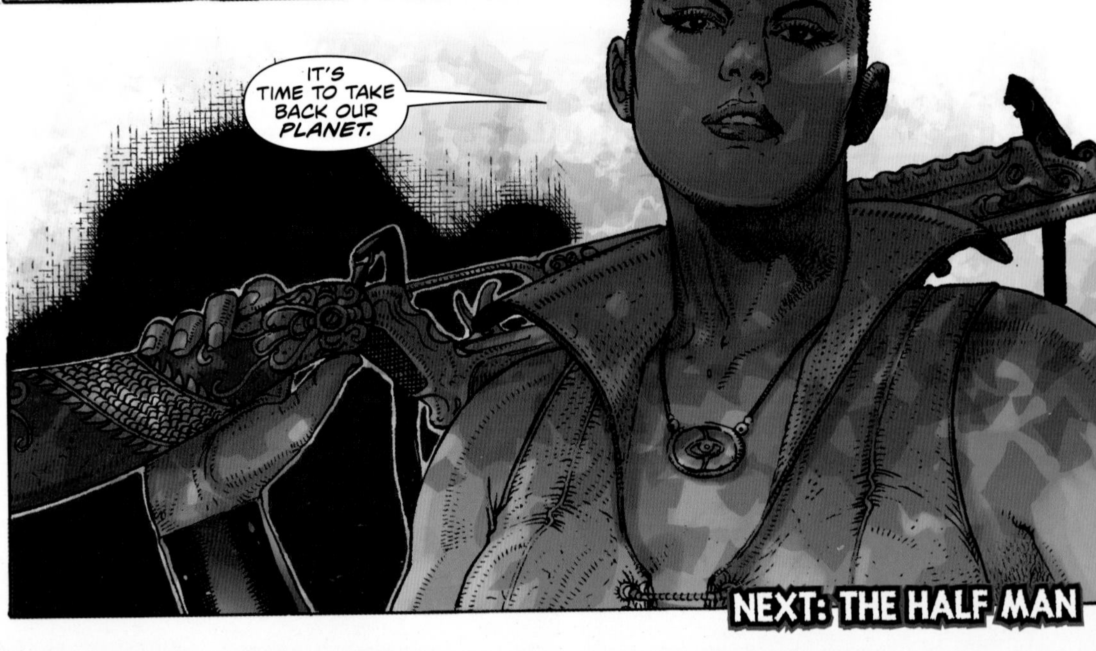
IT'S TIME TO TAKE BACK OUR PLANET.
NEXT: THE HALF MAN

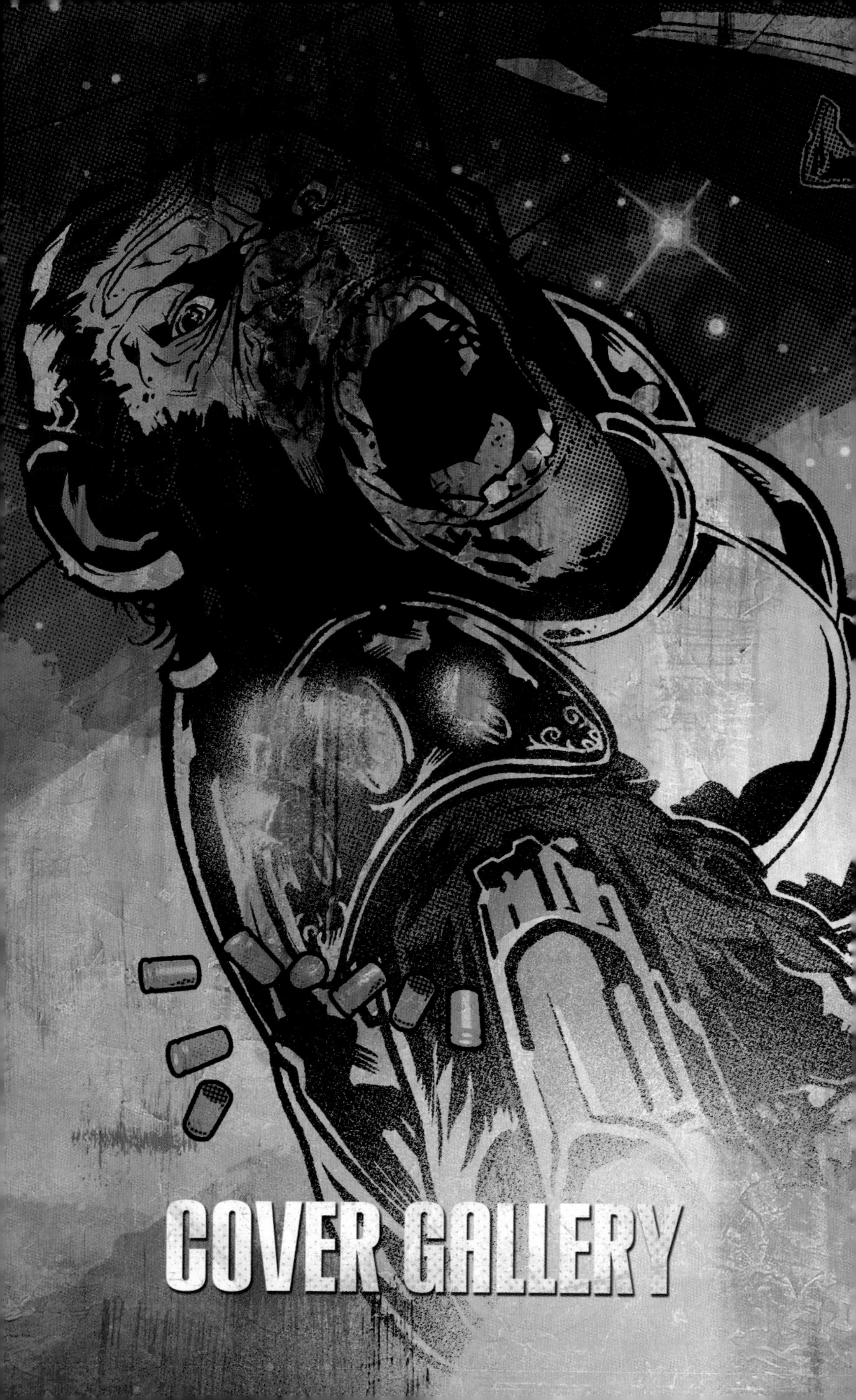

COVER GALLERY

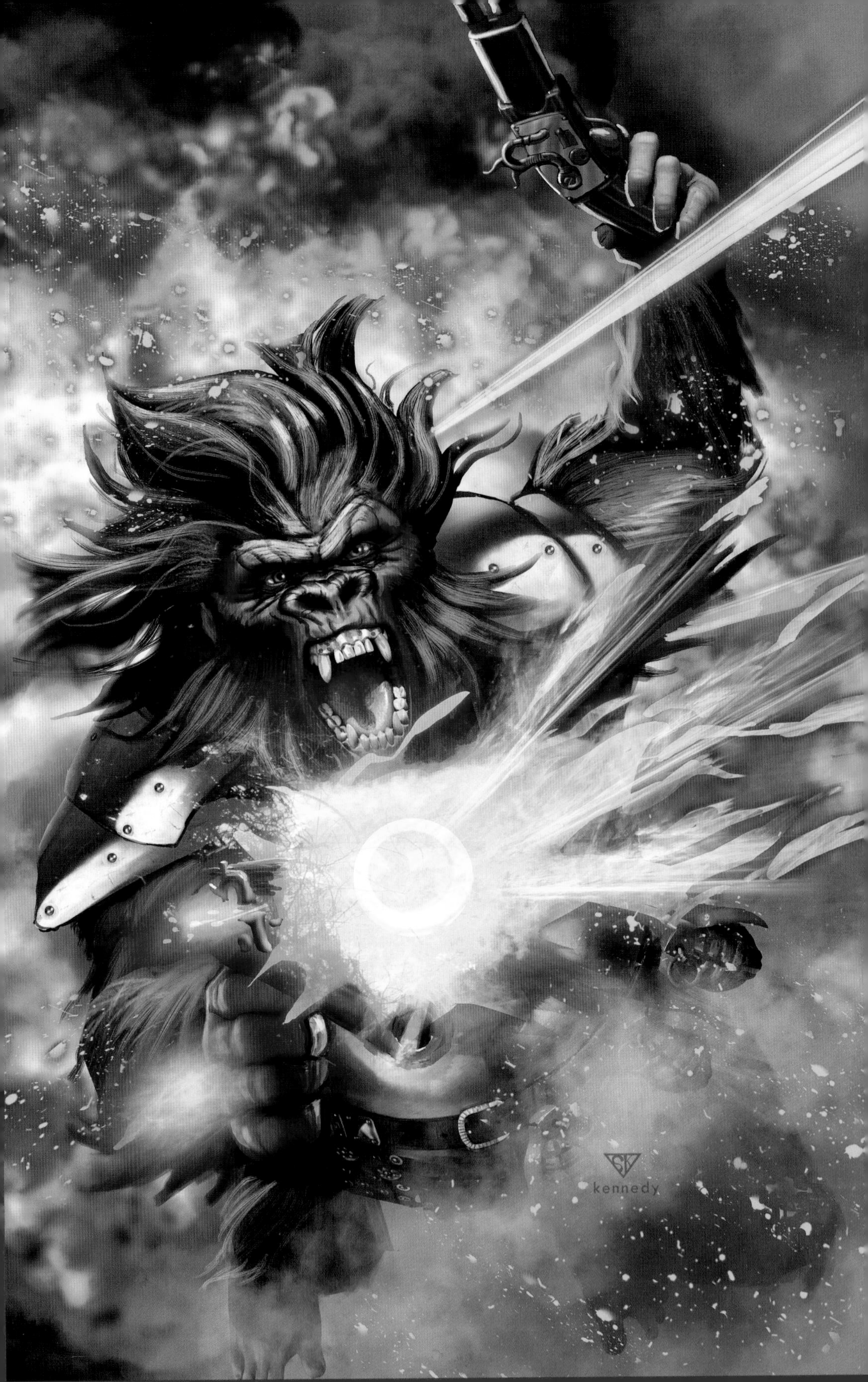
kennedy

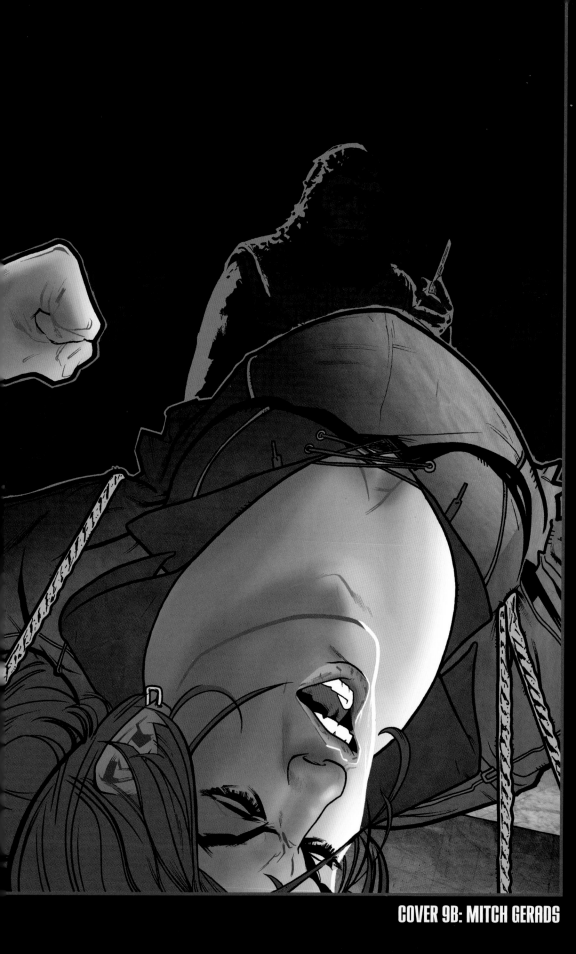

COVER 9B: MITCH GERADS

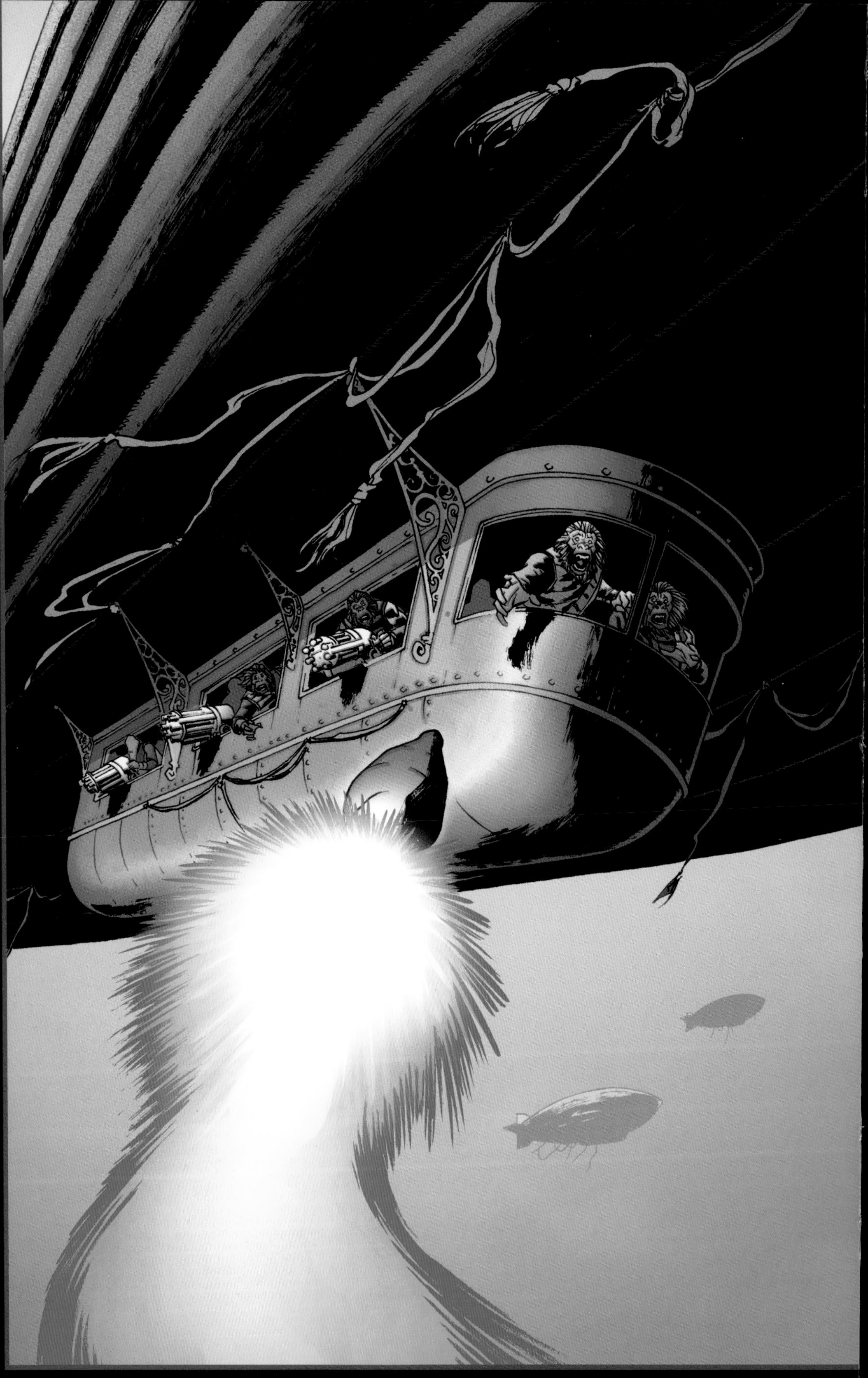

COVER 9C: DAMIAN COUCEIRO

WITH NOLAN WOODARD

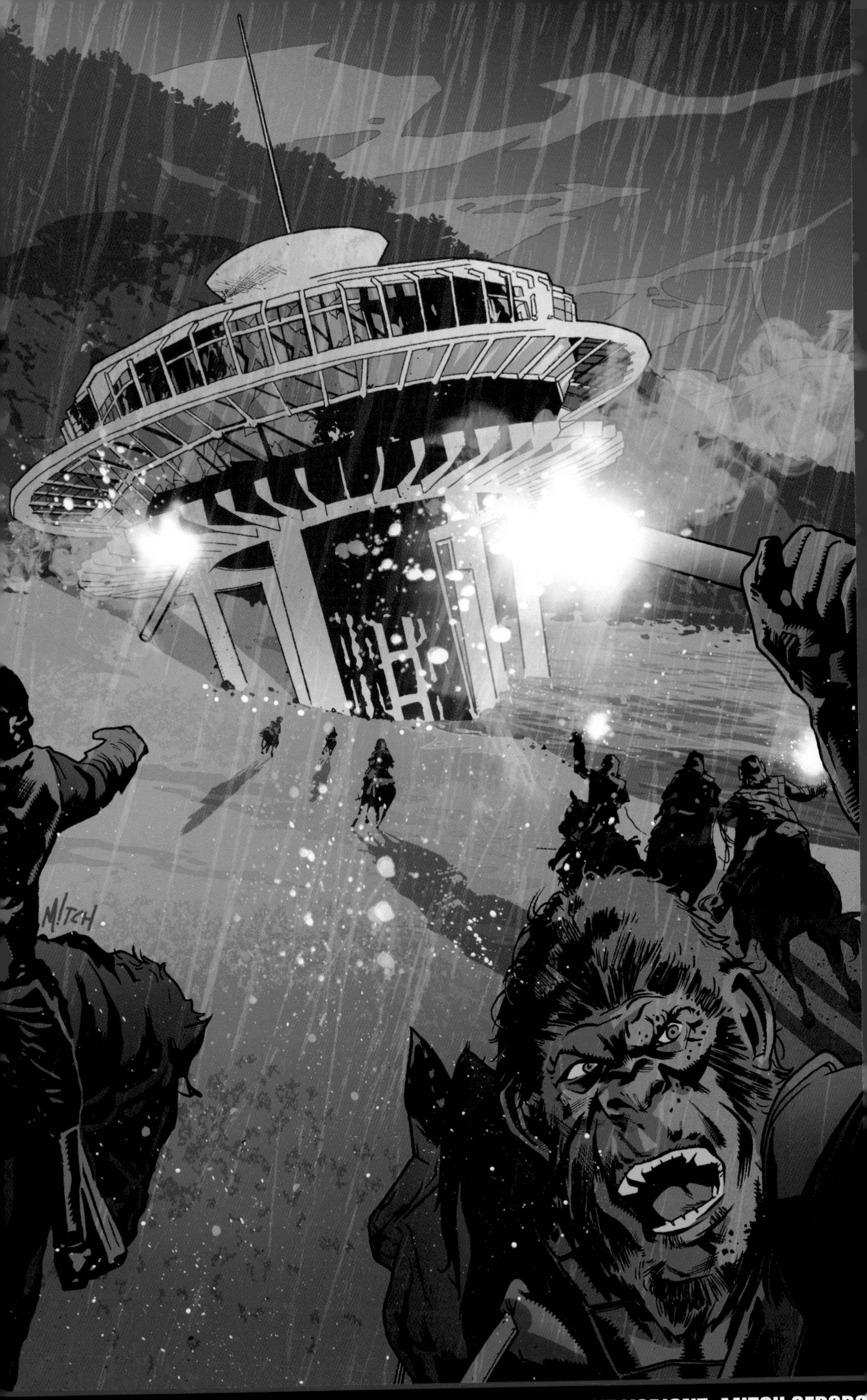
M!TCH

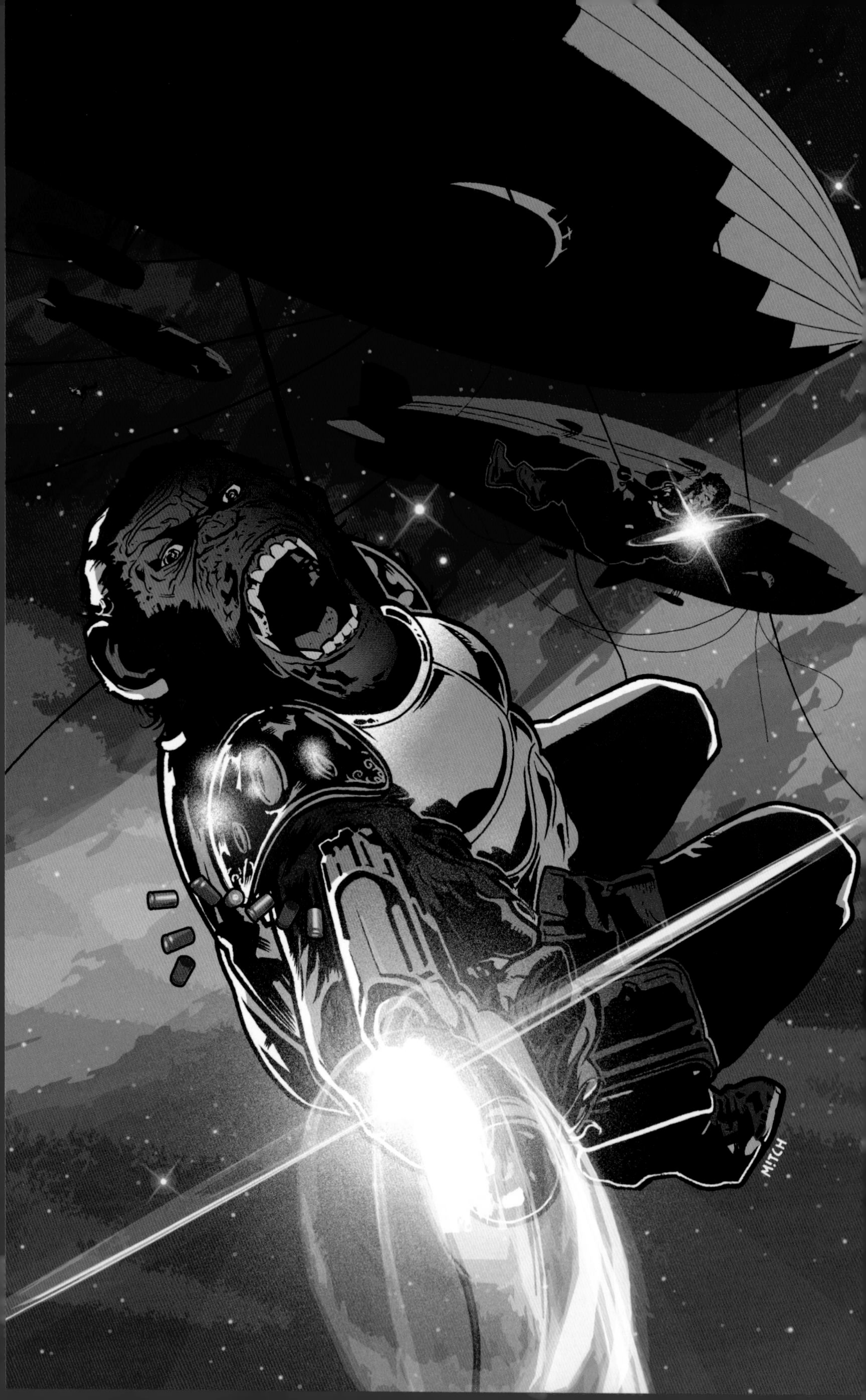
MITCH

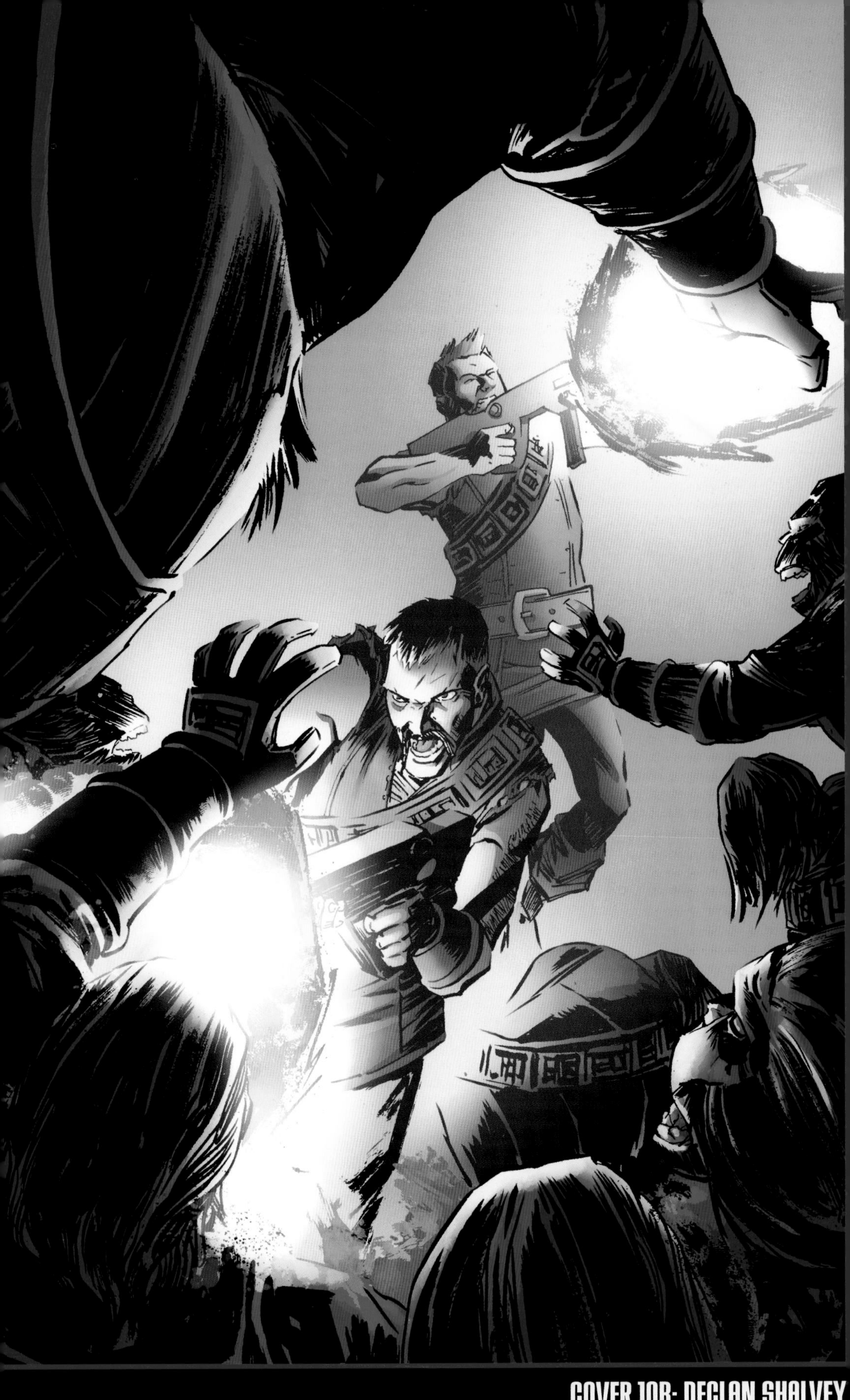

COVER 10B: DECLAN SHALVEY

WITH NOLAN WOODARD

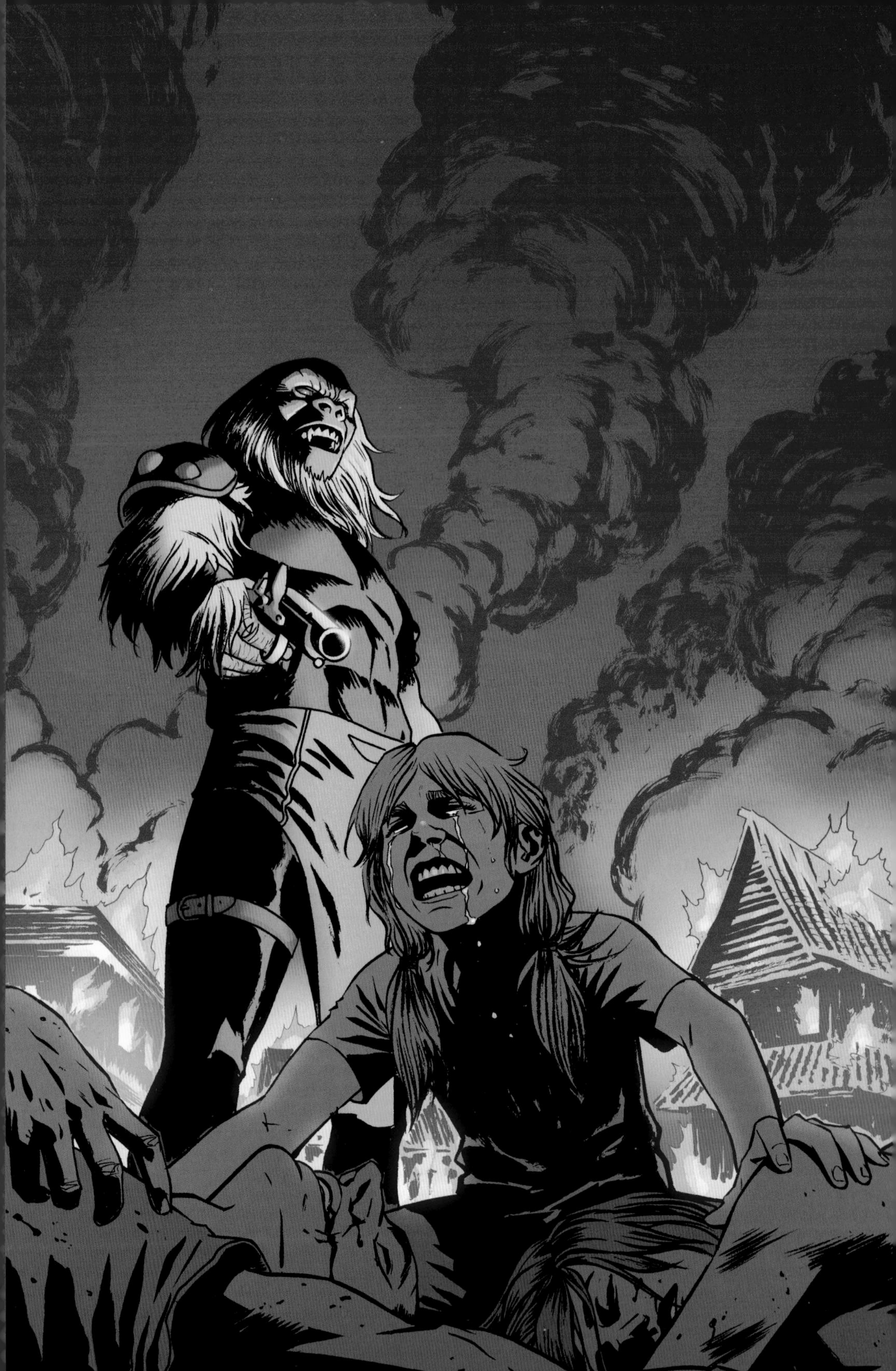

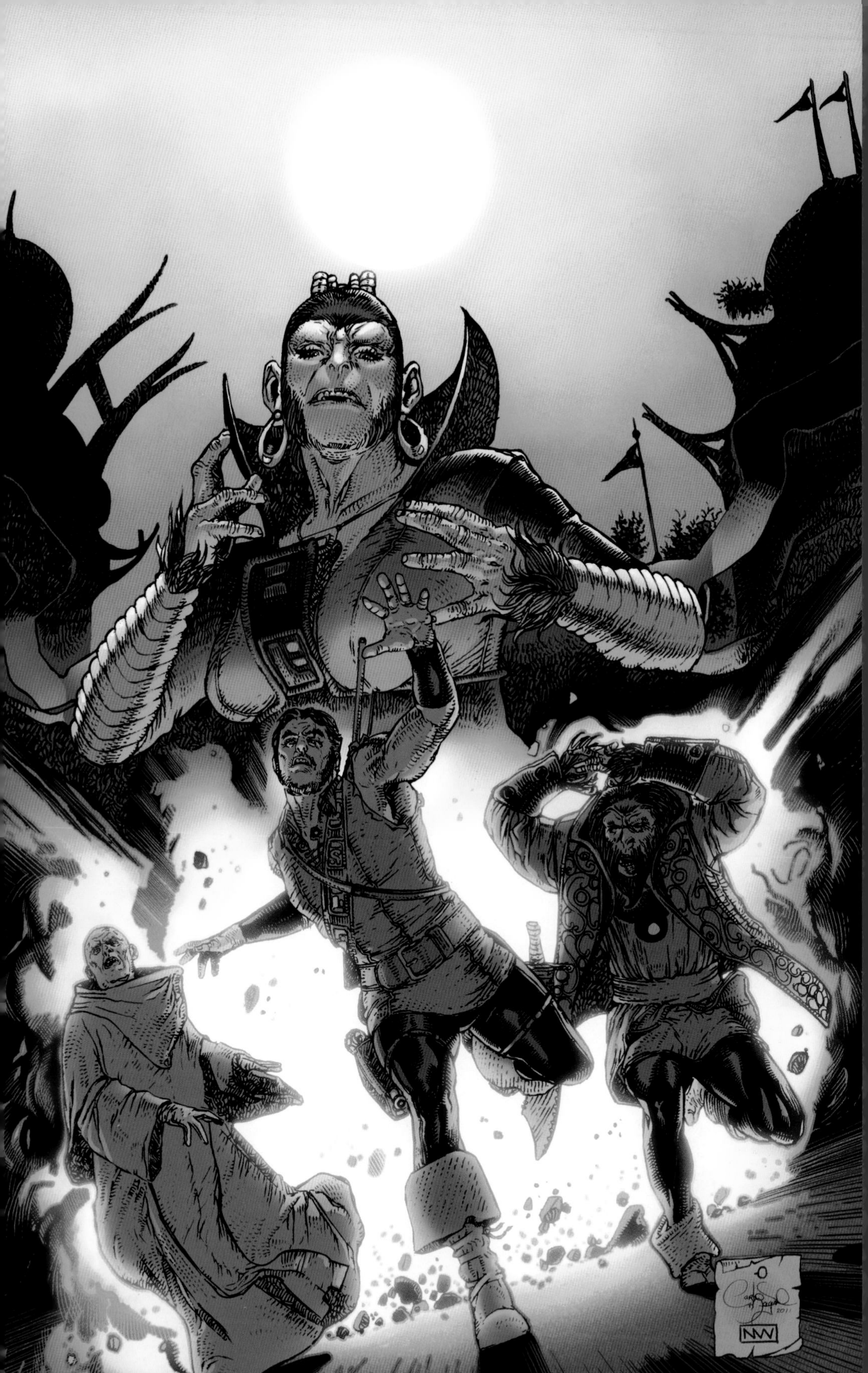

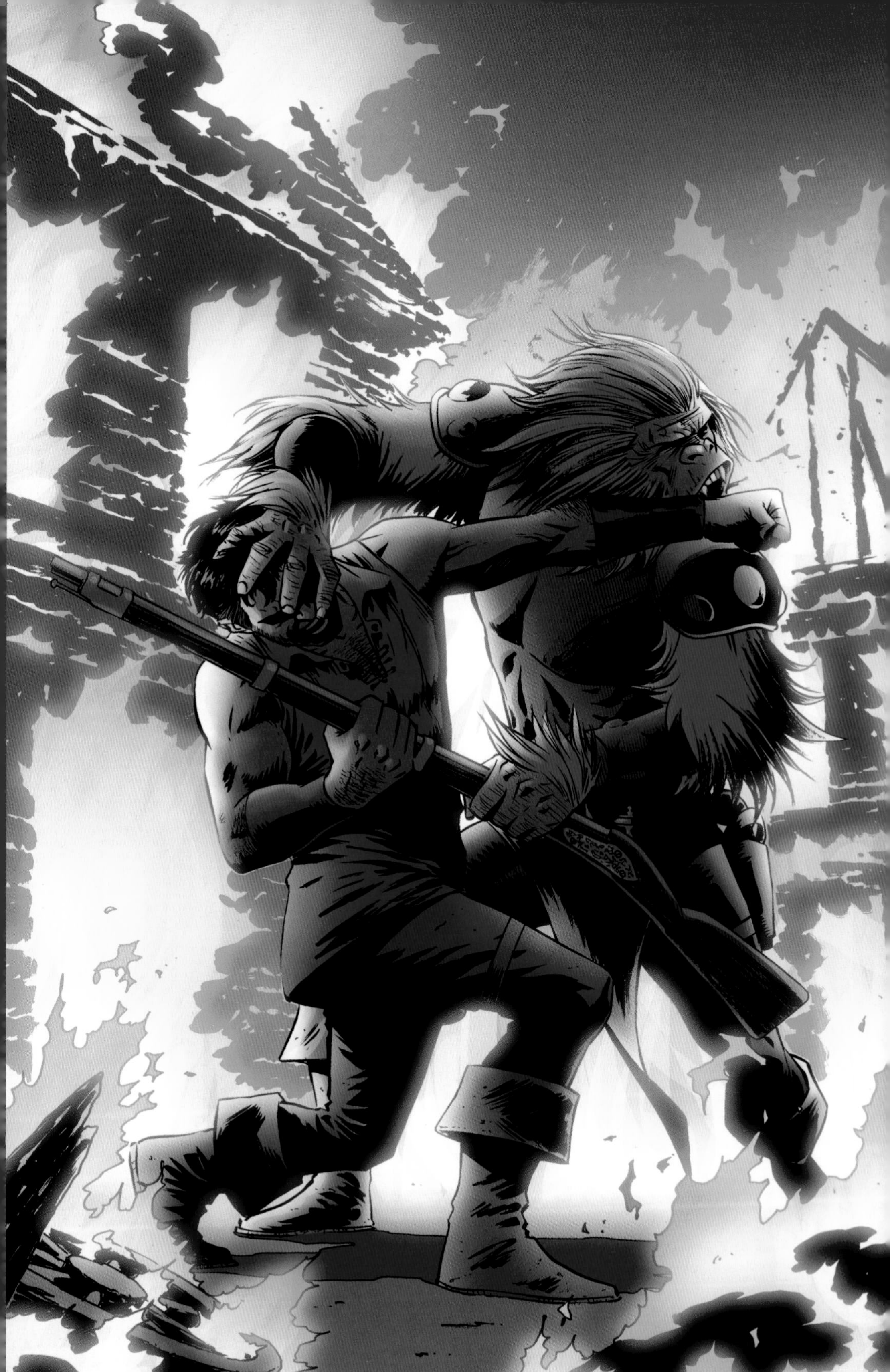

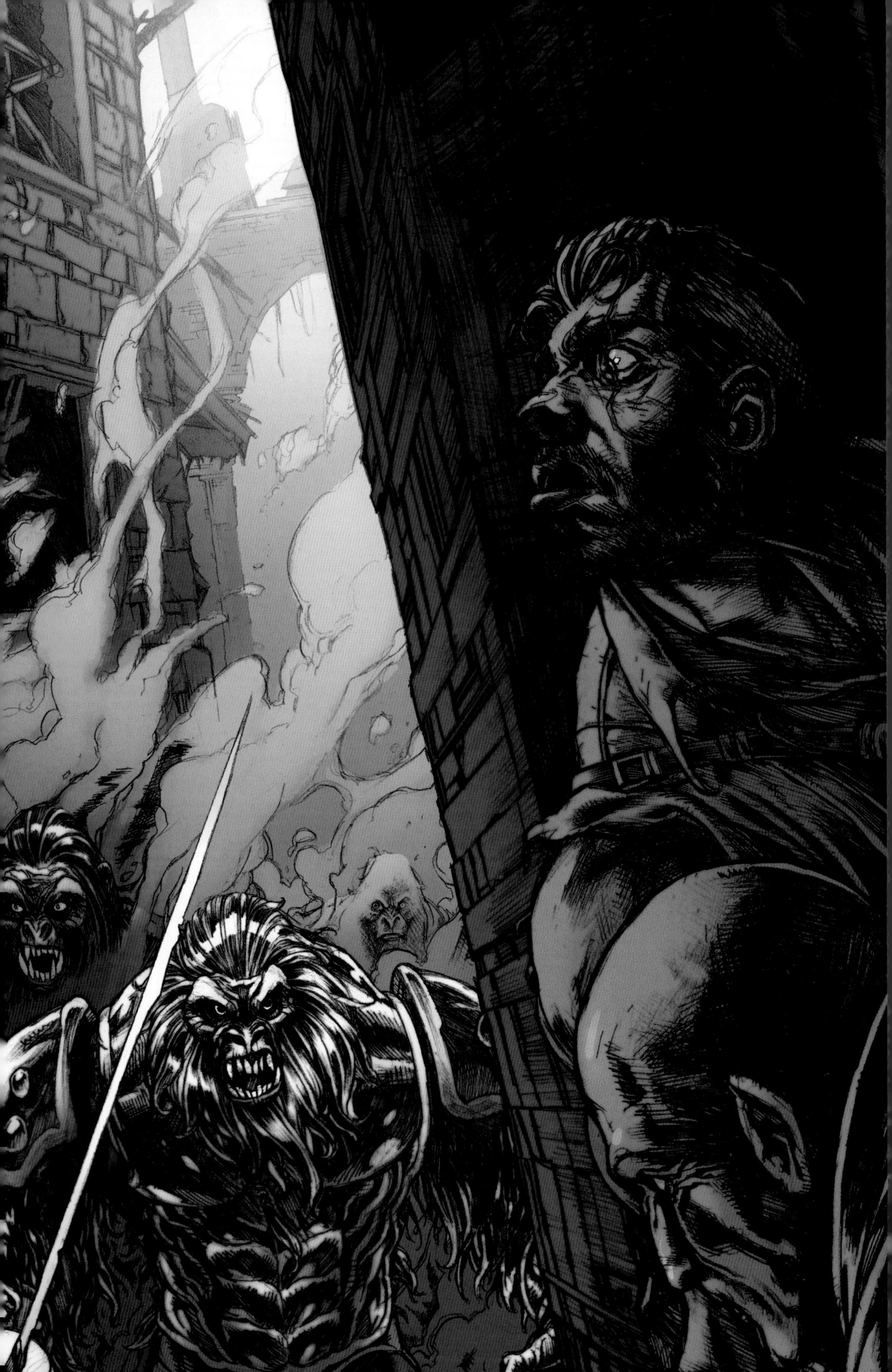

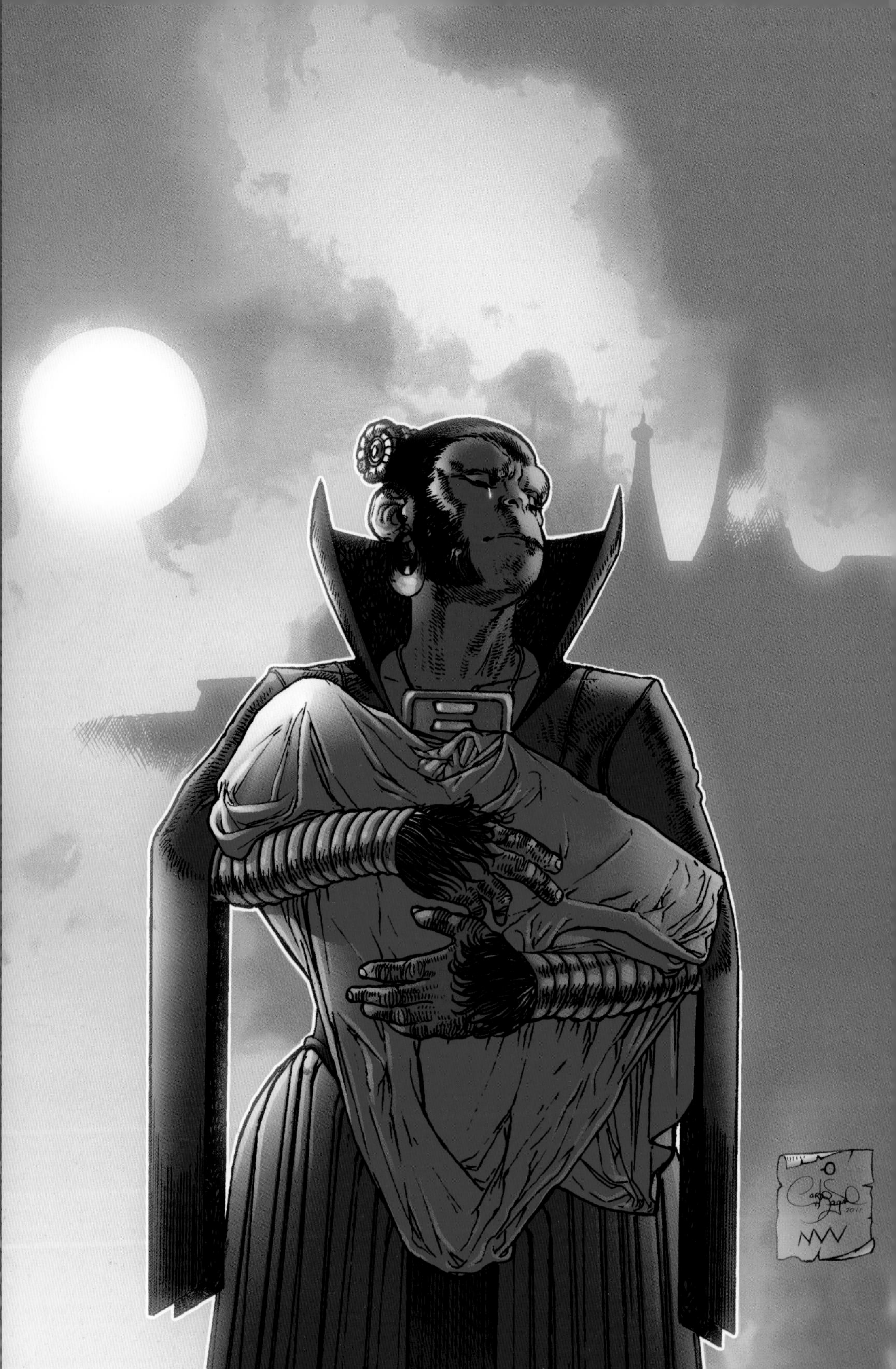

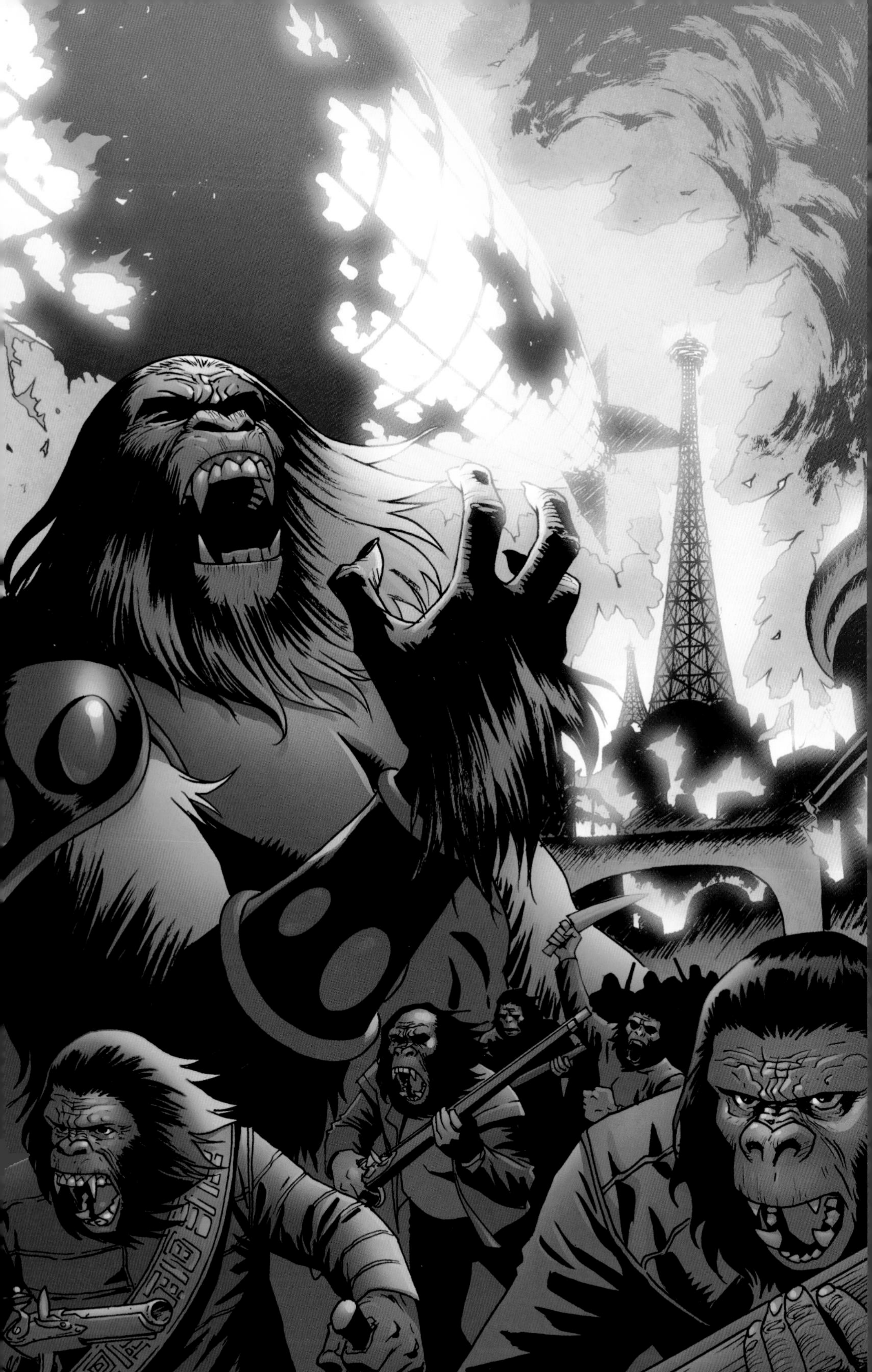

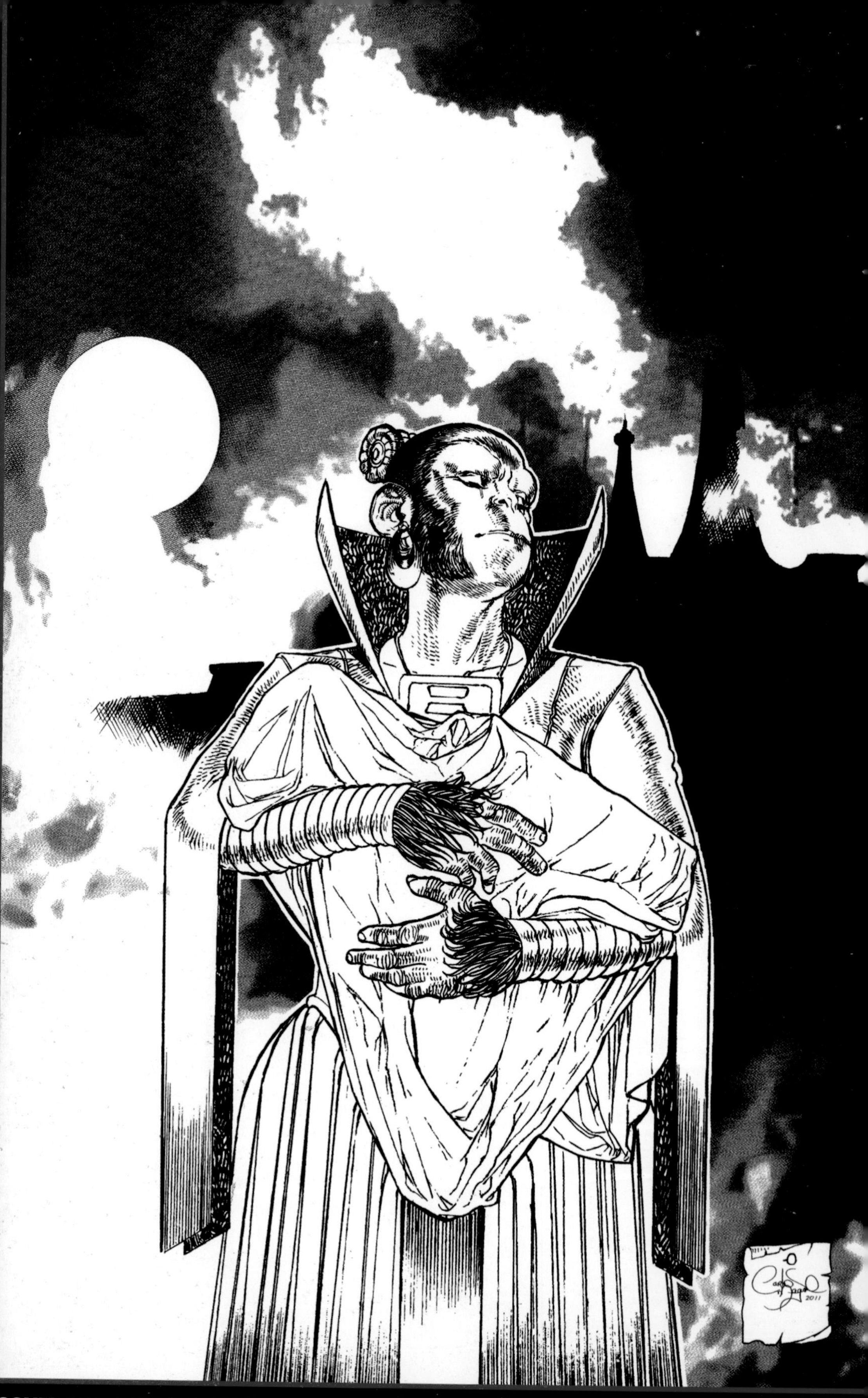

COVER 12C- CARLOS MAGNO